We are entering a new world of marketing. (reality, cloud, and artificial intelligence. And by getting us to think differently

Robert Scoble, Former Technology Evangelist at Microsoft and Editor of Scobleizer

Do you know what *Seamless* is? Of course not, you don't have time for that. You are more worried about your brand's irrelevance in the near future. A future with robots, AI, and everything connected. But, while it worries you that everything has changed, *Seamless* will take you on a quest to find the things that will never do. Don't worry about the robots, worry about the humans.

Ricardo Zamora, Director of Communications, Google Mexico

Seamless is an inspiring guide to the entertainment and media landscape of tomorrow. Tomorrow's brands are those that seamlessly take their clients on a transformational journey into the future and who seamlessly weave together the digital and analogue channels, and futurist Anders has given a visionary foresight into that magical future.

Mattias Behrer, CEO, Dentsu Aegis Network Sweden

Anders Sörman-Nilsson is the real deal. He's able to catapult us into the future, causing us to imagine possibilities and adding colour to a picture we might not yet have drawn. His teachings about the business landscape of tomorrow are not to be ignored: the companies that will win are those that prioritise seamless customer journeys and maximise the technologies available to them. Heed his advice and venture forth bravely!

Emma Isaacs, Founder/Global CEO, Business Chicks

Anders Sörman-Nilsson unpacks in his usual sophisticated and linguistically compelling way the massive opportunity available to innovative thinkers and businesses who can evolve towards our inevitable digital futures. Through case-study, historical perspective, and future-focused insight the reader is taken on a journey into the possibilities of our rapidly changing worlds.

Peter Sheahan, author, Founder and CEO of Karrikins Group

Seamless helps the reader approach the future. It uses vivid storytelling to get you to reflect deeply on the context of where we are at today, how we got here and unblocking the paths to allow us to see where we can go in the future. A very enjoyable read!

Peter Williams, Chief Edge Officer, Centre for the Edge at Deloitte Australia

Whilst we all quietly ponder the future of work and society, Anders takes that one step further by seeking answers to 'what if' and 'why' by linking past, immediate and future business and market case studies. In his inimitable style he weaves us into his context by sharing experiences and journeys, giving us a deeply personal and amusing view of what considerations can be made to plan for the future. I have no doubt that *Seamless* will leave you wanting to meet with Anders and seek more answers.

Professor Petrina Conventry, Industry Professor, University of Adelaide

In *Seamless*, Anders transports you effortlessly, in a fantastic journey, from a total analogue past to a present where a new digital universe expands a seemingly bounded reality to limitless new possibilities.

Mario De Agüero, CEO and Managing Director, GS1 Mexico

Having worked with Anders I can truly say he's onto a very interesting thread connecting familiar 'analogue' truths with our current online life. His previous book *Digilogue* was a true inspiration to us, and now with *Seamless*, he connects directly with the bigger purpose of the Internet – to carry the big ideas of tomorrow. You can't predict the future, but you can be ready. Reading Seamless is definitely a good start.

Rickard Bäcklin, Marketing Director, Telia Sonera International Carrier

Seamless is a unique read as it unravels the story of a futurist who takes off his consultant mantle, rolls up his sleeves, and embarks on an intimate journey to turnaround a business failing to keep up in a digitised world. Through a combination of business insight and personal vulnerability, Anders has created a timely guide for leaders and organisations who desire to transform their brands from the ordinary to the extraordinary.

Richard Ruth, Director – HR – Employee relations, Eli Lilly and Company

Making customer journeys seamless and digitally transforming the real estate industry is the future for the brands of tomorrow. Futurist Anders Sörman-Nilsson in *Seamless* provides impactful foresight and directions for navigating tomorrow!

Mike Green, Managing Director, Harcourts International

The analogue and the digital worlds are quickly becoming intertwined. If you work in branding or marketing, it's time to get dressed for the occasion. Because going into the future without a proper seamless outfit may soon mean you're out in the cold.

Niklas Alvarsson, Brand Designer at Spotify Business

The world of marketing and communications is undergoing a paradigm shift. At Dashing, we believe in evolving 'what's possible' for our clients, and in *Seamless*, futurist ASN sets out a compelling call to adventure for those who are willing to digitally transform their business, and embrace the extraordinary retail landscape of tomorrow. We believe the foresights contained in these pages are required reading for our clients, and for anyone seeking transformational business results!

Mike Palmer, CEO, Dashing

You think you're reading a crystal ball look into the future, but Anders Sörman-Nilsson quickly and powerfully demonstrates that the future is already here. A disruptive book that changes how you see business on the global stage.

**Jay Baer, President of Convince & Convert and
Author of *Hug Your Haters***

Anders has a unique ability to draw parallels and lessons from multiple fields and apply them to business. He jumps from horology to music to textiles to wine and back to deep research and then onto real world pragmatic solutions both effortlessly and well ... seamlessly. The way he has wrapped his insights about the future in this book around Joseph Campbell's The Hero's Journey is another great example of that. Always interesting and thought provoking, Anders is a gifted speaker, writer and influencer.

Richard Hirst, Director, International CEO Forum

Anders weaves together real-world examples and insight using his own unique style of storytelling to deliver a compelling view of the future.

Richard Cooper, Vice President, Director of Marketing Strategy, FIS

In the era of digital anxiety, futurists are more relevant than ever to inspire and to challenge our traditional way of thinking. Anders Sörman-Nilsson is currently one of the more inspiring future thinkers. With his family retail business as the starting point, Anders takes us on a personal journey among clothes, textiles and seamless thinking. All aimed at making us understand more about what is to come.

Magnus Gudehn, CEO, HiQ

A must read for any business leader driving for digital transformation in an age where one's imagination can be met. *Seamless* takes the reader on a journey of possibilities through great storytelling and is as much a relevant business insights book as it is a philosophical journey into what has influenced human interactions!

Mathias Kjessler, Senior Sales Director
Retail Sales + Marketing EMEA, Microsoft

Digital disruption and how we adapt to it is critical to the success of any business. Anders has an amazing ability to link the human effect and digital transformation together. His work consistently challenges my thinking on change management and keeping tradition alive while embracing the new disruptive digital world to create a seamless environment of change.

Dave Rosenberg, VP and Managing Director, ANZ, Westcon-Comstor

Anders engagingly narrates a future where the most successful leaders and brands will embrace many of the characteristics of his real hero's in embarking on the journey from an ordinary analogue to an extraordinary, and perhaps as yet unknown, digital future. *Seamless* is his aspiration for the ultimate destination and it is a rich exploration of what it takes to achieve transformational change at a time of digital disruption and why putting your customers first will be essential for success.

Danielle Bond, Marketing and Communications Leader, Aurecon

In his third book, *Seamless*, Anders takes the reader on a global adventure from the shopping districts of Stockholm and Tokyo to the wine regions of France, as he weaves together his story of seamless transformation in a world of digital disruption. Whether we can design transitions (between the analogue and digital worlds) that are seamless, effortless and frictionless is a decisive factor for the future of technology and the success of business leaders and is one of the key question our futurist author asks of us. If you are a business leader, this book will help you prepare for the journey and transition your business into a world of change ahead.

Don Sillar, Head of Sales, ANZ Wealth

Seamless is the ultimate hero's guide to the entertainment, content and media landscape of tomorrow. Tomorrow's brands are those that seamlessly merge the digital and analogue channels to transform the user experience, powering brand preference and sentiment. A masterful Anders takes us on a visionary journey into this magical future.

Mitchell Bowen, Managing Director, Aristocrat (Australia and New Zealand)

In a world that feels increasingly full of both exponential disruption and opportunity, *Seamless* is a timely and thought provoking book. Anders has a unique ability to help us make more sense of the future and *Seamless* has that ability to sharpen our focus and make a difference to what we can influence.

Matt Tapper, Managing Director, Global Markets, LION

Anders, yet again, weaves a wonderful series of stories and images together to caste his futurist gaze over the complex landscape of digital challenges. Digital technologies provide us with the opportunity to re-imagine the customer experience in new and exciting ways. Seamless is a timeless 'must read' for every leader trying to navigate this uncharted territory.

Dr. Kristine Dery, Research Scientist, MIT Center for Information Systems Research

In a provocative and clever style, Anders perfectly combines the art and science of looking into the future of brands, organisations and entire ecosystems. His unique, data-driven and complex perspectives challenge us to connect past, present and future in completely different ways than we are used to. As a reader you will gain insights that will challenge your traditional way of thinking about the marketplace and the future of products and services. This is a must read for out-of-the-box thinkers and leaders who are interested in a smart, informative and fun book.

Ana Dutra, CEO, The Executives' Club of Chicago and best-selling author of *Lessons in LeadershiT: detoxing the workplace*

As a futurist, you need not only look forward, but also backwards. Anders Sörman-Nilsson understands this well, and also points it out in his new, astonishing book on the balance between tradition and disruption, between analogue and digital, between staying at your core and reinventing yourself. Knowing and being a customer at George Sörman, I can luckily see that the transition to the future also for a family business is possible, if you dare to leave the comfort zone of today and travel to places far and frightening. No doubt much thanks to Anders' future understanding, based on great wisdom of the past and present.

Ulf Boman, Future Strategist and partner of Kairos Future, Stockholm

Sörman-Nilson provides a deeply personal and engaging, yet highly practical, case for pursuing the quest for seamless intimacy. With insightful examples tailored from a rich fabric of global business and social experience, this book shows us in great depth how we can weave the traditional analogue with the emergent digital to generate new products, services, markets, and even businesses for a more sustainable and enriching future.

Richard Hall, Deputy Dean, Leadership and Executive Education, Monash Business School

At LoyaltyOne we see how impactful digital disruption has been for brands and customer behaviour. We partner with thought leaders like futurist Anders Sörman-Nilsson to provide us with critical foresights into what customer transformation and loyalty looks like beyond the horizon. In his visionary quest to drive change, Anders shows us that tomorrow will be exponentially better than yesterday – for those that are willing to embrace the call to adventure.

Bryan Pearson, President, LoyaltyOne, Alliance Data

Anders' book is the thread between our safe, comfortable known world and the world of massive disruption. He has an elegant and educated approach to guiding us to glimpse a future of massive possibility. Change is one of those certainties in life. Anders' words provide a timeless, guiding pathway to the future.

Shane Kempton, CEO, Professionals Real Estate Group

In his new book, *Seamless*, Anders Sörman-Nilsson underlines why he is one of the leading contemporary thinkers about digital transformation. In this book he expertly weaves together a deeply personal account of his family business with sharp and insightful observations from across a wide range of leading firms and sectors to produce an expertly tailored guide to how individuals, brands and communities can leverage the power of digital. The core concept of seamlessness – combining empathetic human design with the new affordances of technology – is a powerful contribution to the debate.

Nick Wailes, Associate Dean (Digital and Innovation),
UNSW Business School

Tradition and technology need to stand side-by-side in the future. In *Seamless*, futurist Anders Sörman-Nilsson vividly illustrates what can happen when technology and tradition collide, and illustrates how heritage brands and start-ups can successfully embark on a an adventurous future odyssey. A must-read!

Erik Wilkinson, Global Sales Director, Eton of Sweden

Innovation would lose its sense if there weren't smart minds being able to translate the ever changing and advancing technology to impacts on business and not least humans. Anders is one of those smart minds. *Seamless* will again be a masterpiece of exploring a new era by helping us understand it better through taking us on his journey, sharing his wealth of personal experiences and providing profound knowledge and great relevant examples.

Steffen Lange, Director Customer Engagement & Commerce, SAP

I believe in organisations being deeply committed to providing seamless customer journeys and personal transformation. I believe that both the successful brands and organisations of tomorrow are those that can truly partner with their clients and customers as a guide into a more meaningful and healthier future. Futurist Anders Sörman-Nilsson in this book provides the foresight and practical insight that transformational brands need in order to go on this quest.

Matt Bennett, Head of Global Customer
Management, Beiersdorf

We must look to the future and focus on our client requirements, competitive pressures and solution design for what our clients will want and need tomorrow. The pace of change is relentless and the rate of digital transformation continues to accelerate. Anders challenges us to imagine this future and its implications and consequences for our clients, industry and our business and we need to listen and understand that we need one foot in the future and one in the present to win in this market.

Andrew Briggs, Group Executive of Sales, Dimension Data Group

Anders Sörman-Nilsson analyses historical patterns to provide an insightful interpretation of the future. Underlying his message is the importance of good old fashioned storytelling to engage customers and connect them to your brand. *Seamless* is a very thought-provoking read.

Matt Lucas, Head of Content and Social Media, Australia Post

Retail payments are undergoing massive transformation as we embrace contactless, mobile NFC, tokenisation and in-app payments in both the offline and online worlds. This will re-shape customer interaction with retailers, removing friction from the experience, creating seamless journeys and rendering payments invisible. As the customer navigates between the ordinary, analogue world and the extraordinary digital world, we need contributions from futurists like Anders Sörman-Nilsson to help us plot our paths in to the future.

Bruce Mansfield, Managing Director, Eftpos

Anders Sorman-Nilsson has provided a compelling narrative, which provides readers with both the context and framework to adapt and transform themselves and their organisations. It's an essential guide to navigating the disruption we are all experiencing in our personal and professional lives.

Martin Perelmuter, President, Speakers' Spotlight

Seamless is an excellent guide to how we can navigate and stay relevant in the digital age. Anders Sorman-Nilsson helps us realise why digitalisation is not just a risk, but an opportunity to enhance our unique qualities.

Rasmus Ankersen, Chairman, FC Midtjylland A/S

seamless

seamless

A hero's journey of digital disruption,
adaptation and human transformation.

anders sörman-nilsson

with research from Anton Järild and the foresights team at Thinque

WILEY

First published in 2017 by John Wiley & Sons Australia, Ltd
42 McDougall St, Milton Qld 4064
Office also in Melbourne
Typeset in 10/13 pt Cabin Regular
© Thinque Pty. Ltd 2017
The moral rights of the author have been asserted
National Library of Australia Cataloguing-in-Publication data:

Creator:	Sörman-Nilsson, Anders, author.
Title:	Seamless: a hero's journey of digital disruption, adaptation and human transformation / Anders Sörman-Nilsson.
ISBN:	9780730332886 (hbk.)
	9780730332855 (pbk.)
	9780730332862 (ebook)
Notes:	Includes index.
Subjects:	Technological innovations.
	Business communication.
	Customer services.
	Success in business.
Dewey Number:	658.4063

Cover design by Hema Patel
Internal figures by Clementine D'Arco
Cover image (paperback): © Marthu

Figure 1.4 and 1.5: Photographs by Greve Kalling
Figure 1.6: Photograph(s) taken by Relmi Damiano
Figure 2.2: Photograph by Philip Bäckman
Figure 4.1: Photograph by Gustav Arnetz
Figure 5.2: © picturelibrary / Alamy Stock Photo
Figure 5.3: © Gordon Shoosmith / Alamy Stock Photo
Figure 12.2: Photograph by Anton Järild
Figure 12.3: Photograph by Birgitta Sörman-Nilsson

Printed in Singapore by C.O.S. Printers Pte Ltd

10 9 8 7 6 5 4 3 2 1

Disclaimer
The material in this publication is of the nature of general comment only, and does not represent professional advice. It is not intended to provide specific guidance for particular circumstances and it should not be relied on as the basis for any decision to take action or not take action on any matter which it covers. Readers should obtain professional advice where appropriate, before making any such decision. To the maximum extent permitted by law, the author and publisher disclaim all responsibility and liability to any person, arising directly or indirectly from any person taking or not taking action based on the information in this publication.

CONTENTS

ABOUT THE AUTHOR

Anders Sörman-Nilsson
Avant-garde ideas that expand minds and inspire a change of heart

Anders Sörman-Nilsson (LLB / EMBA) is a global futurist and innovation strategist who helps leaders decode trends, decipher what's next and turn provocative questions into proactive strategies. With an average of 240 international travel days a year, Anders' view is that the future and the now are converging in a city or village near you, giving the curious, the creative and the courageous a competitive and sustainable edge. At the same time, that same future contains fearsome forecasts for futurephobes.

This Swedish-Australian futurist has shared stage with Hillary Clinton, Nobel Laureates, and Portuguese, Swedish and Australian heads of state. He is an active member of TEDGlobal, has keynoted at TEDx in the United States and Australia, was nominated to the World Economic Forum's Young Global Leaders in 2015, and was the keynote speaker at the G20's Y20 Summit in Sydney. His thought leadership has been featured in international media like *Monocle, Business Insider, Sky News Business, Chicago Tribune, Financial Review,*

CIO Magazine and *Boss*. In addition to *Seamless*, he is also the author of the books *Digilogue: how to win the digital minds and analogue hearts of tomorrow's customers* (2013) and T*hinque Funky: Upgrade Your Thinking* (2009).

As a futurist and strategist, his foresights are meticulously researched, deeply impactful and always fascinating with futures tailored to his clients, which is why brands like Apple, Cisco, Mercedes Benz, Hilton, SAP, Gartner and Macquarie Bank have turned to Anders over the years to help them turn research into foresight and business impact.

When he is not globetrotting, he enjoys feeling deeply connected with his partner, Nicole, enjoys lazy long weekends in Pittwater on Sydney's northern beaches, morning swims, and hanging out with his family and friends – from Elvina Bay to Färingsö, Stockholm.

ACKNOWLEDGEMENTS

George Orwell once said that an 'autobiography is only to be trusted when it reveals something disgraceful'. While this book is by no means an autobiography, the story behind it has taken me to both depths of despair and elated excitement, from furious frustration to zen sensations. It certainly is revelatory, vulnerable, and hopefully you will find it authentic, illuminating and impactful. We have gone to places we hope you don't need to go, so that you may learn from our mistakes, successes, and failures.

There are a few people to mention for whose support I am deeply grateful.

Nicole, for being the love of my life and for choosing to reconnect with me. You were 'the one that got away', and now we have refound each other in the midst of the turmoil that is the story behind the book. Without you, none of this would have been possible. Thanks for always hearing me out, your support, calm, wisdom, connectedness, love and warmth. I cannot wait to be futurephiles together.

To mum and dad. Thanks for accepting the challenge of facing the future together. If you decide to read this book, remember that it is written from a place of deep love and appreciation for everything you have done for me and my brother. Sometimes the best love is tough love, and yes, this love letter is a bit tough. I hope something good will come of it, and either way, I am looking forward to our social, family futures together. They are destined to be even more positively exciting soon.

To the team at Thinque. Specifically... thank you to Emma for your loyalty, support, excitement, flexibility, patience, warmth, and forward focus. You have been through thick and thin with me, and have always been a joy to tackle challenges with. To Anton and Clem–thanks for your great work on the book, from research, travel, and design, to emotional support–and being intimately involved on the hero's journey.

To my brother Gustaf. I admire your ability to remain above the issues that can create inertia, and your cool in the face of family drama. You will always be my brother, and I treasure our bond and our philosophical discussions and debates. We haven't agreed on how best to help mum and dad, but I am already enjoying the next chapter of our lives together, and not discussing family affairs any longer is a healthy upgrade. I hope. I look forward to spending even more time together with you and your family now that we are all back in Sydney.

To Hem. Your design skills, thinking and encapsulating of strategy in visualisation and brand identity are world class. Thanks for lending a helping hand in shaping yet another book that should equally be judged by its cover.

To the team at Wiley. Charlotte–you are the guru of editing and I love working with you. You take what is half-baked and you make it sophisticated and polished. Chris–thanks for your patience, and chasing me for permissions, chapters, forms, designs, and content. Kristen–thanks for finding me and for being a great collaborator–we did *Digilogue* together, and I am eternally grateful for the relationship with Wiley that has ensued. Lucy–you have taken over the baton really nicely, and again thanks for your patience and flexibility. *Seamless* has been a long time coming, but we got there, and I am thankful for your belief in the project and its merits.

To my speakers management agency–Ode Management. Leanne, Heidi, Tanja, Jay, Julie, Tanya, Becs, Michelle, Amanda, Teri, Mike, Sam, Simla–thanks for pushing and challenging me to curate this book, and to share my vulnerability and authentic voice. It's been a fun 7 years together and I look forward to continuing to make a big splash and inspiring futurephilia and seamless futures around the world.

To Georg Sörman. Thank you for starting the movement and creating the brand that lives on 100 years later, and which has provided so much analysis, soul searching, sartorialism, and neon elegance, and somehow managed to make your idea virus live on from generation to generation–a Georg Sörman meme indeed. Let us see if the 4th and 5th generations will continue your legacy.

■ PROLOGUE

Start preparing for the future today, because it is where you will spend the rest of your life.

Failing to succeed — a futurist's confessions

These lines were written to the soundtrack of Coldplay, perhaps fitting, given my long-time love affair with the band. Whether I am newly in love, deeply connected with a partner or undergoing the tempest of a break-up, Coldplay seems to have composed a song that is in tune with my emotional vibrations. One of these songs that captured my heart was 'The Scientist' in 2003. Yes, I can obsess nostalgically about a song for a long time. I was living in Vienna, Austria, when I first became obsessed, and completing my specialisation in International Law at the University of Vienna. The album had come into my hands during a train trip with my good friend, Mark, when we travelled from Stockholm via St Petersburg, Moscow, through Belarus, to Warsaw in Poland and Berlin in Germany, all the way down back to Vienna, after spending a few summer weeks in my native Sweden. I bought the album, I remember, from a street vendor in St Petersburg, and judging by the fact that I picked up about fifteen CDs from him, I don't believe I paid the normal retail price. However, the CDs were really good quality for pirated copies, and *A Rush of Blood to the Head* became the soundtrack during a challenging six-month period in my life.

Whenever a song really resonates with me, as my brother will attest, the song will be on repeat, usually because my ego tells me the song was penned just for me. This was the case with 'The Scientist', which just so happened to be in the same register as my emotional state – influenced as it was by the break-up, reunion, long-distance relationship, near-infidelity and eventual long-term commitment with my girlfriend at the time, Hema. But let us go back to the start. Let us explore 'The Scientist' for a moment. In the interest of the convergence between digital and analogue worlds, if you want to listen to the song while reading these next few lines you can do so legally and digitally by using this link on Spotify: ow.ly/WvTqb. It will literally take you back to the start.

Anyone who has ever experienced the turmoil of a tumultuous relationship and important life decision can relate, I am sure, to the lyrics in the song and the feeling of wanting to go back to the beginning of a relationship and start it all over again. Beyond the lyrics, there was also something magical about this idea of returning to a point in the past, especially when it became the inspiration for the song's video clip (which you can watch on YouTube at ow.ly/WvTOT and which won multiple MTV Video Music Awards for Best Group Video, Best Direction and Breakthrough Video in 2003). The video is so powerful because it employs an innovative *reverse narrative* that begins at the end and goes back to the beginning, taking us back to the start, using a reverse video technique. This technique meant Chris Martin, the band's lead singer, had to spend one month learning to sing 'The Scientist' in reverse, so that when you view the video, his lip movements perfectly sync up with your auditory input of the song, while he is walking backwards in reverse from the end of the scene to the beginning.

As a futurist, and sometimes described as a reverse historian, this creative warping of time and going back to the source is something I want to curate for you now. Let me take you back to the start of a futurist's confession. Because my journey as the futurist mentor in one of my life's most dearest relationships didn't go to plan, was by no means 'seamless', was filled with friction, and failed to achieve success(ion) in the short term. So this movement between friction and seamlessness plays out within this book. However, in set-backs lie the green shoots of future success, so please indulge me in sharing my futurist's confessions as we embark on a hero's journey of digital disruption, adaptation and transformation. Let me take you back to the start.

■ INTRODUCTION

The future really belongs to those brands that are able to weave together the past, the present and the future into a seamless and inspirational hero's journey.

The modern metaphor of seamless

The mathematics of metaphor are fairly simple: $x = y$. For example, in Shakespearean terms, 'Juliet is the sun'. Now, we all know that she is not literally the sun, but that she has the sun's characteristics; attributes such as 'warm', 'glowing', 'bright' and 'beautiful' are bestowed upon Juliet by virtue of the metaphor. But while this mathematics may seem simple, our use of metaphor has a powerful influence on how we think about our lives. And, as I expand on later in this book, text (ideas) and textiles (fabrics) have always been closely linked, both literally and metaphorically.

For example, interestingly in the English language, we can both weave stories and tell lies by reference to textiles. As noted by the English Language and Usage website (in their analysis of the metaphor 'Thought is a thread, and the raconteur is a spinner of yarns'), expressions like 'loom of language', 'weave a story/spell', 'thread of discourse' and 'warp and woof' indicate textile–story associations, while 'fabricate evidence', 'spin a yarn', 'tissue of lies', 'pull the wool over your eyes', and 'out of whole cloth' indicate that textile metaphors are morally neutral and can be used for authentic tales as well as the invention of false anecdotes to serve the interests of the raconteur. Metaphors can be a useful mental shortcut, by explaining x in reference to y, and, given our age-old connection to textiles – their production, their constituent parts, their art and science, and characteristics – the traditions of textiles are still highly relevant in a modern context, in the expression of ideas about the future, and in gaining buy-in to something as intangible and abstract as strategy.

Even a word such as 'context', used in storytelling, news, debates, dialogue and therapy, is an example of the intermeshing of text and textiles. Context comes from the Latin root of 'con' (together) + 'texere', thus denoting 'together to weave', meaning the circumstances that form the setting for an event, statement or idea, and in terms of which it can be fully understood. 'Pretext' is another such intermeshing. This again comes from a Latin root – 'prae' (before) + texere, indicating 'before to weave' and meaning a reason given in justification of a course of action that is not the real reason. 'Subtext' is a third example, and means an underlying and often distinct theme in a piece of writing or conversation. And the idea of 'subtle' nuances in a conversation comes from the 'sub-tela', from Latin 'subtilis' (thin, fine, precise) or a 'thread passing under the warp'.

These links between text and textiles lead us to the topic for this book (everything is connected). While the idea of 'seamless' has both a literal and a metaphorical meaning, its origins, of course, lie in textiles. According to Merriam-Webster, the literal meaning of the word seamless is 'having no seams'; its metaphorical meaning is 'having no awkward transitions, interruptions, or indications of disparity'. More simply, Merriam-Webster defines seamless as 'moving from one thing to another easily and without any interruptions or problems' and as 'perfect and having no flaws or errors'.

Again according to Merriam-Webster, its synonyms include: absolute, faultless, flawless, ideal, immaculate, impeccable, indefectible, irreproachable, letter-perfect, picture-book, picture-perfect, perfect, unblemished. Its antonyms include: amiss, bad, censurable, defective, faulty, flawed, imperfect and reproachable.

Let's expand on this idea of seamlessness, and why I believe it to be the elixir of our business and personal futures.

The mythical origins of seamlessness

While we will ultimately investigate seamlessness for its modern application, the profundity of the term takes us back in history, and is relevant to its future application as the 'Holy Grail' of design. The idea of seamlessness in textiles, in fact, does hold religious and spiritual connotations. The 'Seamless Robe of Jesus' (or Holy Robe) is the garment said to have been worn by Jesus during or shortly before his crucifixion. According to the Gospel of John, the soldiers who crucified Jesus cast lots when deciding who would keep the garment, rather than dividing it, precisely because it was woven in one piece, without seams, providing a mythical association to the technique of circular knitting that may have made Jesus' garment and imbues it with a supernatural quality. (See John 19:23-24 for the full details.) According to Wikipedia, and depending on which brand of Christianity you choose to listen to, the robe can today be found preserved in Trier (Germany), Argenteuil (France), or Sankt Petersburg and Moscow (Russia). The idea of the 'seamless garment' has since been mythically and morally adopted by Christians in the 'seamless garment philosophy', which holds that issues such as abortion, capital punishment, militarism, euthanasia, social injustice and economic injustice all require a consistent line of moral reasoning which value the sacredness of human life. The Roman Catholic pacifist Eileen Eagan, for example, said that 'the protection of life is a seamless garment. You can't protect some life and not others.' Seamlessness in other words, runs deep.

Its literal, textile roots come from the technique of circular knitting. This is a form of knitting that creates a seamless tube and so ensures less friction on the body (which the seams may otherwise have caused on our delicate skin – I, for one, moisturise often). Seamless items are imbued with a sense of high quality, and deep empathy with their wearers. While this can certainly be done by hand-knitting, the process of circular, seamless production can also be done by machine. Let me illustrate this with an example from a business trip to Tokyo, Japan, in 2014.

I was in Tokyo to work with our long-time client, Fuji Xerox, at their flagship event for their Premier Partners in Asia Pacific. Beyond the opportunity of working with the Fuji Xerox Chairman, Tadahito Yamamoto, I was also looking forward to exploring Tokyo by foot, and in particular I had my sartorial eye set on the Loopwheeler store in Sendagaya. The irony of this attraction is that as a futurist, I am well versed in the idea that change, adaptation and agility are key to brands' survival in a fast-evolving landscape. However, it's exactly the extreme reluctance of Loopwheeler to adapt and modernise (along with Merz b. Schwanen in the Swabian Alps of Germany, it is one of the only two remaining factories producing authentic loopwheel terry cloth) which makes the brand so sustainable.

Originally, I had come across this brand in *Monocle* magazine's 52nd edition. While reading the 2012 article 'Reinvent the Wheel – Wakayama' by Kenji Hall, I fell in love with the collaboration between man and machine that results in the supercomfy Loopwheeler sweatshirts. Loopwheeling equipment is always based on a tubular knit (or tube body) construction, which means that the resulting garment (usually a t-shirt or a sweatshirt) is made of a single piece of seamless fabric. In other words, the fabric is knitted around a tube and comes out without side seams, as one tubular shape. Loopwheeler takes this approach a step further – trust the Japanese to positively geek out about the process – and takes their customer empathy to the next level.

The vintage machines used by Loopwheeler are from a bygone era of industrialisation. But this doesn't render them irrelevant. On the contrary. While Hall points out in his article that 'the machines are a throwback to an analogue era, almost driven to extinction by technological progress', the evident inefficiency of the 1920s machinery (they produce just one metre of cloth an hour, or enough for eight sweatshirts a day) is counterbalanced by founder Satoshi Suzuki's 'focus on craftsmanship and quality', which has 'won Loopwheeler a small, cult-like following that spans the globe' – evidenced by my pilgrimage to Suzuki's Sendagaya shopfront.

Suzuki became interested in manufacturing techniques, and how they impact on durability and softness in garments, while at university. During his visits to factories, he learned that loopwheeling machines don't stretch the textile threads taut like modern manufacturing equipment, which means that the resulting fabric can better withstand wear and tear. The machines (which according to Hall resemble large caterpillars) spin twenty-four times a minute – slower than vinyl on a record player – and, rather than the fabric being pulled down by a machine, gravity is the only force that pulls the circular tube of fabric gently down the loopwheeling machine. And as the proud owner of two Loopwheeler garments – a cardigan and a t-shirt, bought on two separate business visits to Tokyo in 2014 and 2015 – I can attest to their comfort, quality and fit. As a tangent, given the tales of cotton dust in their factory, I must also linguistically alert you that the metaphor of 'cottoning on to an idea' has textile roots and, according to some linguists, describes the attachment of cotton to machinery, while others say it describes the comfortable attachment to its wearer. Either way, the comfortable intimacy between customer and garment is something that has become part and parcel of the cultural weave at Loopwheeler. And the quest for this seamless intimacy is what this book is all about.

The idea that I described in my last book, *Digilogue: How to win the digital minds and analogue hearts of tomorrow's customer* – of the coming together of the different worlds of the analogue and the digital – evolves in the transformational context of *Seamless*. Today, and into the foreseeable future, heroes, hero brands, and mentors must nudge, guide and move themselves and their clients between an ordinary world – often the analogue – and an extraordinary, magical world, the digital. Whether we can design transitions that are seamless, effortless and frictionless is a decisive factor for the future of technology and the success of business leaders. And as the British science fiction author Arthur C Clarke pointed out in his third law: 'Any sufficiently advanced technology is indistinguishable from magic'. That seamless fusion – that Holy Grail of magical indistinguishability – is what this book is about.

Australian brand Telstra seem to have cottoned on to this idea of seamlessness. In their 2016 magical brand ad, they refer to Clarke's aforesaid technology law, in positioning how technology can bring people together in a magical, extraordinary world, across the tyranny of distance and the ordinary world, via virtual reality headsets, drones and videoconferencing bedtime stories. Challenged to wander in the magic of wonder, the viewer is asked to suspend belief for a moment, and enter the magical world of Telstra-enabled connectivity, where the walls between science fiction and fact have broken down. Whether Telstra is that enabler remains to be seen, but suffice to say that we are now standing on the precipice of technological magic, and we are being challenged by history and philosophy as to whether we are prepared to take a leap of faith.

We stand at the gates of another technology revolution, shaped by artificial intelligence, machine-to-machine communications, the Internet of Things, predictive customer service, learning machines, and the fusion of biology with technology, automation and roboticisation. These advanced technologies will either wreak havoc on the world as we used to know it, or enable us to transform and evolve at much greater speeds than ever known to humans. The lines between science fiction and reality are blurring thanks to augmented and virtual realities. These technologies, in their inherent magical advancement, can enable and empower heroes in a futuristic fashion on their journeys into tomorrow. And when the art of empathetic human design converges seamlessly with the science of technology, we may be able to guide, inspire and lead our partners, clients and loved ones between ordinary, analogue worlds and special, extraordinary, digital worlds. This seamless interplay between two worlds is the magical elixir for great brands and leaders of tomorrow. And this is the quest that lies behind this book.

Embracing the frictive hero's journey

After setting out on what has become a three-year quest to explore the idea of seamlessness, and in my sense-making efforts and reflections on the trials and tribulations of guiding digital adaptation and human transformation in an age of digital disruption, I began to see certain patterns. Phases began to emerge. Shapes started taking *shape*. And structures started to surface.

My journey started to echo the adventures, space odysseys and myths that I had grown up with. In my odyssey as a futurephile to expand minds and inspire a change of heart, I could see analogues with the mythical greats of my childhood. I saw how the heroes and mentors of my youth - Luke Skywalker, Yoda, Han Solo, Frodo, Gandalf, Willow, Madmartigan, Raziel – had all set out on similar adventures into the future. And the phases of my journey started looking eerily similar.

As early as the 1940s, Joseph Campbell codified the structure – the monomyth – of some of the great tales of human imagination, religion and myth. Later on this structure became known as Joseph Campbell's 'hero's journey'. *The Wizard of Oz*, *Frozen*, *Cinderella*, *Finding Nemo*, *Harry Potter*, *Moby Dick*, and *Catcher in the Rye* are all tales that follow this structure of the hero's journey – that is, of adaptation and transformation, moving between the ordinary worlds of status quo and special, or extraordinary, worlds of future possibilities.

The twelve steps identified by Campbell that form the hero's journey consist of inner journeys and outer journeys (which lead to character transformation), and switches between ordinary worlds and extraordinary worlds. As laid out by website Movie Outline (in the article 'The Hero's Journey – Mythic Structure of Joseph Campbell's Monomyth' the twelve steps of the inner and outer journeys are as follows:

1. *Inner:* ordinary world, status quo; *outer:* limited awareness of a problem.
2. *Inner:* call to adventure; *outer:* increased awareness.
3. *Inner:* refusal of the call; *outer:* reluctance to change.
4. *Inner:* meeting with the mentor; *outer:* overcoming reluctance.
5. *Inner:* crossing the threshold; *outer:* committing to change.
6. *Inner:* tests, allies and enemies; *outer:* experimenting with first change.
7. *Inner:* approach the inmost cave; *outer:* preparing for a big change.
8. *Inner:* ordeal; *outer:* attempting a big change.
9. *Inner:* reward (seizing sword); *outer:* consequences of the attempt (improvements and setbacks).
10. *Inner:* road back; *outer:* rededication to change.
11. *Inner:* resurrection; *outer:* final attempt at big change.
12. *Inner:* return with the elixir; *outer:* final mastery of the problem.

This cycle is also shown in figure I.1.

Figure I.1: the Hero's journey is a 12-step continuing cycle

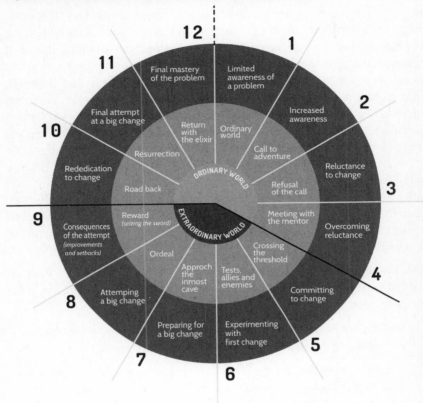

Now, while I haven't literally had to fight off Death Stars, partner up with Wookies and slay garbage snakes in my quest for seamlessness, I have witnessed how change, transformation and adaptation follow similar patterns, challenges and rhythms, exhibiting similar cadences to the hero's journeys I was glued to as a child. Again, I realised the quest I was on, and the quest I was hoping to inspire others to embark on, was the seamless journey between the ordinary – in this case, analogue – world and special, extraordinary – digital – worlds. Just please don't assume that I was the hero in the story that you are about to immerse yourself in. (More on this later.)

As a futurist and strategist, I get to invite people into something that isn't yet; to ask the question, 'What if?', and to imagine distant adventures and metamorphosis. 'What is' gets contrasted with 'what could be'. And

I encourage the people I meet to embark on their own hero's journeys and odysseys into the unknown, just like I have been doing over the last few years. Perhaps not surprisingly, given *Digilogue* was partly inspired by the enduring human love for analogue watches and horology, this book maps the structure of the hero's journey onto an analogue clock face, using the twelve steps to explore the journey to the destination of the planet of 'Seamlessness', moving from 1 o'clock to midnight (at which stage I hope this book doesn't turn into a Cinderellan pumpkin). We will also see, however, that digital adaptation and human transformation cannot be truncated quite as neatly as a two-hour Hollywood epic, and that moments of friction can derail adventures, even for some of my biggest heroes. And we will explore the uncertainties of what might happen in situations where the journey takes you off-path and where 'good' doesn't necessarily destroy 'evil'. The inherent tension and friction of making each paradigm shift will also be discussed and highlighted, with the ambition that you will be able to curate your own hero's journey away from this friction and toward seamlessness – that magical place where successful leaders and brands of the future reside.

To concretise this methodology of the hero's journey, let's take an executive summary look at how it played out for Frodo in the *Lord of the Rings* movies:

1. *Ordinary world:* Frodo and his best friend, Sam, and his two cousins Merry and Pippin live happily in a small village in the Shire.

2. *Call to adventure:* Gandalf calls upon Frodo to set out on a quest to destroy 'the one ring to rule them all'.

3. *Refusal of the call:* Frodo is initially reluctant to leave his cosy life in the Shire, but changes his mind when he realises that his and his friends' lives will always be at risk as long as the ring exists.

4. *Meeting with the mentor:* Frodo meets again with Gandalf and then with the rest of the Fellowship, a group of trusted allies of Gandalf's who have sworn to help Frodo in his odyssey to destroy the ring. The Fellowship consists of Frodo's hobbit companions; two men, Aragorn and Boromir; Gandalf; the dwarf Gimli; and the elf Legolas.

5. *Crossing the threshold:* With the aid of the Fellowship, Frodo begins his quest – his long journey to the volcano Mount Doom, the only place where the ring can be destroyed.

6. *Tests, allies and enemies:* Frodo encounters many obstacles, allies and enemies on his odyssey. He journeys over the mountain pass, barely escapes the wrath of Balrog, becomes allies with the elves, is almost captured by the forces of Saruman, is attacked by Gollum and nearly eaten by a carnivorous spider (Shelob).

7. *Approach the inmost cave:* As he moves through stage 6, Frodo also has to separate from the Fellowship, alone with Sam, to continue his long journey to the fires of Mount Doom. The Fellowship meanwhile cannot continue with Frodo, because they must help defeat the forces of Sauron that are growing more powerful with each passing day. Frodo and Sam use Gollum as a guide to travel the secret back paths to reach the entrance of Mount Doom.

8. *Ordeal:* Frodo must achieve his goal of reaching Mount Doom to destroy the ring, while the Fellowship and its allies must defeat Sauron's forces contemporaneously.

9. *Reward (seizing the sword):* Frodo destroys the ring in Mount Doom, while the Fellowship and its allies overcome the forces of Sauron.

10. *The road back:* Frodo falls unconscious from exhaustion and Sam and Frodo are rescued by Gandalf and his eagles.

11. *Resurrection:* Several weeks after losing consciousness Frodo awakens in time to witness Aragon's marriage to his long-time love Arwen, and Aragon's ascent to the throne. Simultaneously all the members of the Fellowship (with exception of Gandalf) are knighted by Aragon.

12. *Return with the elixir:* Frodo returns to the Shire enervated by his epic journey and the Fellowship of the Ring (and eventually, Frodo journeys to the Undying Lands to live peacefully for the rest of eternity).

Sorry if I ruined the ending for you. However, even if you now know the structure behind this epic, and feel like you have just seen the process behind the magician JRR Tolkien's tricks, these tricks are hardly his alone. This type of mythical structure is deeply embedded and in rapport with our subconscious souls, and has always been part and parcel of that most fundamental of human skills – the art of storytelling. Indeed, throughout this book, I use the hero's journey contained within another epic – *Star Wars IV: A New Hope* – to more fully illustrate this type of narrative arc, and the similarities contained within the story arc of my own, closer to home, hero. Through this journey, you will learn how to design and guide your partners, clients and collaborators in quests that lead to true adaptation and transformation.

For as long as stories have been told, the most engaging and connected of human stories are those of transformation, change and adaptation – which is perhaps why I, as a futurist and science fiction geek, was so strongly drawn to support my hero on their transformational journey, so that they could one day return home with the elixir to their business problems. (And good story also holds something back. We'll get to this hero in chapter 1.)

The narrative arc that I have just described stands in stark contrast to the idea of seamlessness. If you think of Frodo's journey, for example, nothing about it was seamless. Rather, the whole experience was filled with seams, friction, obstacles and paradigm shifts. Moving from one stage to another was neither easy nor without interruptions or problems, and Frodo and his fellowship didn't perform perfectly and certainly not without any flaws or errors. Few of us do. However a dream, a destination, a vision, a strategy was always part of these epic journeys. And, at the end, there was a sense of relief, of calm, of a beautiful life, of peace, of perfection.

So I want to uphold 'seamless' as a kind of 'end of the rainbow' state – a utopia, Holy Grail, and paradisiacal, mythical place. It is a special world that we can all imagine. Because it is brands, leaders and organisations that are able to design journeys – customer journeys, talent quests, change projects and transformational odysseys – empathetically and in such a way as to guide their stakeholders from a status quo of living an ordinary, boring life in the Shire, through a special world of dragons, demons and disruptions, to return fully transformed, that will excel in our near-horizon future.

The hero's journey is one of both inner and outer transformation, and of movement between ordinary worlds and special worlds. And again, the transitions between inner and outer transformation, and between different worlds, can be either frictive or seamless (see figure I.2).

Figure 1.2: the journey between what is (the status quo) and what could be

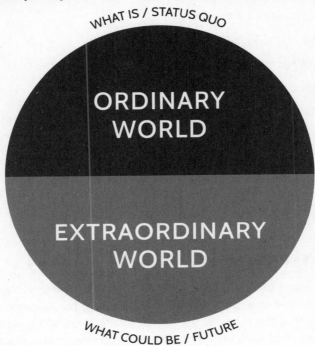

WHAT IS / STATUS QUO

ORDINARY WORLD

EXTRAORDINARY WORLD

WHAT COULD BE / FUTURE

And this moves us to the second of Arthur C Clarke's laws – that 'The only way of discovering the limits of the possible is to venture a little way past them into the impossible'. This book is designed to take you into the magical world that is the future – of current *im-possibilities*. Please let me co-design an extraordinary one with you. And as I say to my clients and friends, you better start preparing for the future today, because it is where you will spend the rest of your life.

With this in mind, fellow futurephile hero, join me on a space odyssey, signposted by the following twelve steps, equally the chapters in this book:

1. Ordinary world/status quo
2. Call to adventure

3. Refusal of the call

4. Meeting with the mentor

5. Crossing the threshold

6. Tests, allies and enemies

7. Approaching the inmost cave

8. Ordeal

9. Reward (seizing the sword)

10. Road back

11. Resurrection

12. Return with the elixir

Butterflies, bow ties and infinity

One more point before we get started: you may recognise in the cover of the book both the ancient symbol of infinity and the horizontal '8'. This symbolises that the hero's journey is, of course, a constant multi-cyclical one. You take this journey with any challenge you meet in business or in your personal life, complete it (hopefully), or get up and dust yourself off and go again. You'll also recognise this iconography of the horizontal 8 (infinity sign) hidden in the bow tie. The word for 'bow tie' in French is *papillon*, which is the same as the French word for 'butterfly' (and in fashionable Italy, *farfalla* has the same double meaning). In other words, 'butterfly' – the symbol of metamorphosis and transformation – transfers similar attributes to its distant shape-sharing wearable cousin the bow tie. Shape, models and iconography are central to this book and, as we all know from the great brands of the world, analogues, allegory and hidden meanings are all around us, playing with our subconscious minds.

The horizontal 8 symbol of infinity, in turn, comes from the mathematical infinity symbol (sometimes called the 'lemniscate') which is credited to John Wallis, who in turn was inspired by a variant of the Roman numeral for 1000 (originally 'CID', also 'CƆ'). In modern mysticism the infinity symbol has become fused with the variation of the 'ouroboros', an ancient image of a snake eating its own tail, representing life reborn. The infinity symbol can be drawn in one continuous movement, with the loops potentially signifying the balance of opposites – male and female, day and night, dark and light, and who knows? Maybe analogue and digital (see figure I.3). The convergent point may symbolise union and two things becoming one. With all these layers of meaning, the symbol stands for wholeness, integration and completion.

Figure I.3: the infinite movement between the ordinary, analogue, world and the extraordinary, digital, world

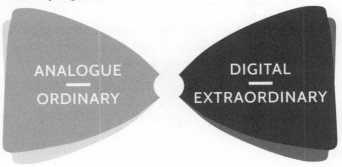

But we can draw out the connections between these symbols even further. The term 'lemniscate', used in algebraic geometry, comes from the Latin *lēmniscātus*, which means 'decorated with ribbons', which in turn may have originated on the ancient Greek island of Lemnos, where ribbons were worn as decorations, much as sartorial men (and, of course, some women) wear bow ties, another form of ribbons.

You see, even the etymological heritage of the infinity symbol and the meanings attached to butterflies and bow ties are mythically intertwined, seamlessly and infinitely. Who knows? Maybe there is only one story, a monomyth behind this. And the seamless symbol of the hero's journey is aptly the infinity sign, endless, enduring and transformative as it, as well as the butterfly and the bow tie. And within this, the convergent point – the point where the infinity symbol crosses itself, where the 'wings' of the butterfly and the bow tie come together (see figure I.4, overleaf) – becomes the seamless interplay between ordinary and extraordinary worlds, and in our case the dynamics between the analogue and the digital in the context of digital adaptation and human transformation.

Figure 1.4: the seamless interplay between ordinary and extraordinary worlds

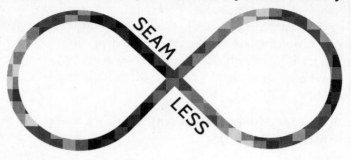

So, with this talk of hero's journeys, seamlessness, infinity signs, butterflies and bow ties, I invite you to move from your ordinary world, the status quo, and to enter an extraordinary place – your future.

STEP 1
HERO'S JOURNEY WHEEL FOR MAMMA SÖRMAN-NILSSON

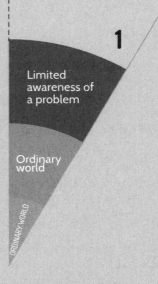

1

Limited awareness of a problem

Ordinary world

ORDINARY WORLD

Digital disruption sweeps the world of retail.
Our heroine dreams of making her retail brand (Georg Sörman) strong and profitable again, but feels her hard work is taking her nowhere.

Status quo

This is the place where the hero or heroine hangs out before his or her journey begins. She is happily oblivious of the adventure that is just around the corner, and where she lives is pretty cushy. We learn intricate details of this everyday life, along with the heroine's characteristics and outlook on life. This cements the heroine as a fellow (wo)man, helping us identify with them, and helping us empathise with their challenges through the upcoming journey.

Here's how the ordinary world looked at the start of *Star Wars: Episode IV*:

- *Inner journey:* The evil Empire oppresses the galaxy.

- *Outer journey:* Limited awareness of the problem; Luke dreams of joining the academy and he feels he is going nowhere on his uncle's desolate farm, but doesn't see any way out.

And here's how the ordinary world looked like for a more personal hero of mine (you might recognise some of the characteristics):

- *Inner journey:* Digital disruption sweeps the world of retail.

- *Outer journey:* Limited awareness of the problem; our heroine dreams of making her retail brand (Georg Sörman) strong and profitable again, but feels her hard work is taking her nowhere.

1: Status quo

Change doesn't care whether you like it or not.
It happens without your permission.

The love letter to my superhero

In December 2012 I sat down to write a love letter to my first pure love, my first hero. For years I had tried to influence the recipient. To help her realise her potential. To unleash the latent potential she was possessing. To help her let go of the legacy, the misplaced expectations, the unhelpful remnants passed down to her from her parents (particularly her father, the patriarch) so she could step into her own and release her own unique creativity. From a distance, I had watched the recipient, whom I love, suffer in silence. Now was the time to write all my thoughts and strategies down. The indicators strengthened my belief that the recipient would be finally ready to read, reflect, and act upon my letter.

The recipient, the first woman I ever truly loved, was my mother Birgitta. She is an energetic and elegant woman. She is full of life and exudes strength and determination. As one of my friends says, when she enters the room, her presence transforms the atmosphere to the point of near-intimidation. Mostly positively. Since 2003, she had been struggling, more or less overtly, but retained a proud veneer. She remained a woman who stoically believed in the Lutheran ethic of hard work, and that rewards follow that hard work, but she was starting to notice something odd. That logic no longer held true. The harder she worked, the more elusive the results became. And the harder she worked at following in the footsteps of her father, and his father before him, the more invested she became in her identity as a struggling, but hard-working woman.

My love letter to my mother first took the form of my Global Executive MBA thesis, and its main focus was whether the fortunes of a then cash-leaking bricks-and-mortar shop and mispositioned brand could be turned around and elevated – and, if so, how? But my work on this love letter began long before I sat down to write it. In May 2012, on a walk together with her springer spaniel Cicero, in a pine forest forty-five minutes outside of Stockholm, I asked my mother whether she wanted to become partners in the future. Whether she wanted my help to turn things around.

I wanted to help my mum leave a legacy and be able to retire with pride. Mum had taken on significant personal and financial risk when she bought out her two sisters between 2006 and 2007, after reporting to them as board members and shareholders between 2003 and 2006. In the family, we call Mum 'Cinderella', because she is the youngest sibling, and is the only sibling to have worked professionally in the family business. And she has reaped no free lunches from it. Other than time spent in the US as an exchange student in the late 1960s, and when she met my dad in Stockholm in the late 1970s – her Prince Lars-Olof Charming – and three years spent in Australia, my mother's life has reflected typical family business stuff.

My mum spent three years absent from the business between 1997 and 2000 while we lived in Canberra, Australia, and my father completed his post as Swedish defence attaché to Canberra. During this time, my cousin Lucie covered for Mum in the business. From 2000, Mum slowly took over the reins of the business as the health of her father, Per, deteriorated until his passing away in 2003. From 2003 to 2006, my mum and her two sisters owned an equal number of shares in the company, with my grandmother, Ingrid, the majority shareholder after her inheritance from her husband, Per. During this time my mother was the managing director, and reported on the increasingly poor figures to her sisters and her mother. When my grandma Ingrid, bless her soul, passed away in 2006, the tone between the three sisters gradually deteriorated, and Mum bought out her two sisters in a process that was begun in around 2006 and completed by 2008 (see figure 1.1 for more more detail). The buy-out included Georg Sörman (Georg Sörman Pty Ltd), which covered the retail business of two shops – one on the island of Kungsholmen and one in Gamla Stan (Old Town), Stockholm.

Figure 1.1: Georg Sörman family lineage and Cinderella's challenge

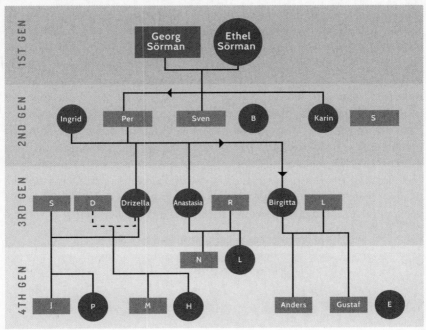

Since the buyout of her two sisters, an historical déjà vu of my grandfather Per's emotionally disastrous buyout of his two siblings in the late 1960s, Mum's relationship with her two sisters is virtually non-existent, and tense at best. So I also wanted to prevent a similar situation repeating itself for a third time, because I am very close to my brother, Gustaf, and want(ed) to keep it that way. And I wanted to reconnect with my parents and create something enduring together, while they still had the energy and health to do it.

So basically, I wanted to help Mum show up her sisters, who she felt cheated by, by reinventing the family business brand and rebuilding it successfully. To help her reinstate her sense of self-worth. And to stop the vicious cycle of Mum managing the business on artificial ventilation, without changing the fundamentals that were causing the bleeding.

And, on our walk in the woods outside Stockholm, this wonderful superwoman, the first woman I ever truly loved – my mum – said that she would be honoured if I put my mind to the reinvention of her third-generation family business, Georg Sörman – Stockholm's oldest menswear shop. My futurephile mind went to work. And it hasn't stopped since.

Text and textiles; ideas and fabrics

Mum's ordinary world is one of textiles, fabrics and provenance. Hard work is something physical, not philosophical, theoretical or text-based. Yet, curiously, text and textiles have a closely interweaved history – literally and metaphorically. Both originate from the same Latin root, *texere*, which means to weave together – not so incidentally it turns out. While text, like a book, can weave together narrative, story, concept, thoughts, musings, romance or even a strategic direction, so textiles and the fashioning of textiles weave together different strands of thought. As you are reading this you can probably already see the intermeshing that is going on in this text. That text and textiles, in mystical ways, belong together. And that metaphors of textiles are found like a thread spun through the fabrics of life. (As in the last sentence, and as in the jumper shown in figure 1.2.)

Figure 1.2: Inis Meáin jumper from Georg Sörman, Stockholm

This is perhaps why a research project at the University of Glasgow is focused on creating a big data visualisation of thirteen centuries of startling cognitive connections between metaphors and different strands of thinking. Metaphor, it turns out, governs how we think about our lives – the past, the present and the future. The first online Metaphor Map from the University of Glasgow showcases more than 14 000 metaphorical connections, based on four million lexical data points, going back to AD 700, based on a mapping of the Historical Thesaurus of English, which spans thirteen centuries. According to Dr Wendy Anderson, the findings of the project include that 'metaphor is pervasive in language and is also a major mechanism of meaning-change'. The ensuing map also revealed the strong connection between textiles and text, such as the description of social networks in textile terms like 'weaving and spinning'; another example is something being defined as 'tweedy' if it is rustic, or 'chintzy' if petit-bourgeois. In a modern context, it is perhaps not surprising then that textiles are ever-present, and that textiles are a foundation for our conceptual ability to craft complicated structures and systems – like binary digital technology, for example, which sprung out of the punch card for the Jacquard loom. The idea of a 'thread' is often used to indicate the following of a plan, moving in a particular direction, or embracing a vision for the future.

Text and textiles, of course, also coincide in that fundamental human activity of story-telling. Consider this old proverb in the context of storytelling, for example: 'Thought is a thread, and the raconteur is a spinner of yarns'. In this example, a thought is bestowed with the characteristics of a single thread, and the raconteur (storyteller) is bestowed with the characteristics of a professional spinner of yarns, who spins together disparate threads to make a whole. In other words, a storyteller is someone who takes individual thoughts and combines them into a comprehensive story. In this instance, the inherent idea is of storytelling as weaving, and of thoughts as the story's constituent parts. It's so hard to avoid these linguistic patterns. Please bear with me. It is textiles that have created the 'ordinary world' my mother was so used to; they represent the 'status quo' she has been working so hard to maintain. But textiles and their textures run deep for all of us.

Let us consider for a while why that is the case. Textiles are filled with meaning. We have already seen in the Introduction the religious connotations of the 'Seamless Robe of Jesus'. As it turns out, textiles and fibres run through our human consciousness on several levels. In fact, if we view textiles through the lens of Maslow's needs hierarchy (as Beverly Gordon from the University of Wisconsin does in her 2010 article 'The fiber of our lives: A conceptual framework for looking at textiles' meanings', published by the Textile Society of America), textiles play a role with regard to each of the steps on his hierarchy: self-actualisation, esteem, love/belonging, safety and physiological. (Figure 1.3, overleaf, shows Maslow's hierarchy of needs.) We understand our reality in reference to textiles – we may speak, for example, of the 'fabric of our lives', 'life hanging on by a thread', 'strands of DNA', and 'moral fibre'. We have already explored how central textiles are to the fundamental human tradition of storytelling, and threads are often used to denote a pathway forward – think of the linkage between Theseus finding his way out of the labyrinth and today's WhatsApp threads. Textiles also feature through life's journeys and milestones, and are thus imbued with considerable meaning cross-culturally.

Figure 1.3: Maslow's hierarchy of needs

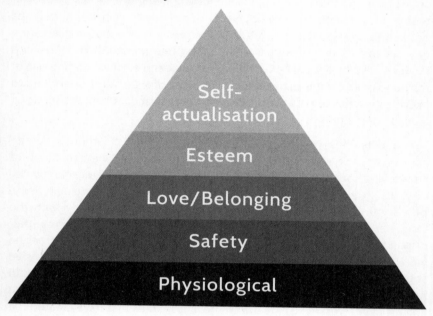

The following sections look at the ways textiles fulfil and work within Maslow's needs hierarchy, and how they have become so central to my mum's identity.

Physiological

Textiles play a key role in providing shelter, and ensuring our survival. Growing up in Sweden – so short summers with long winters – in a textile family I soon learnt the common adage that 'there is no such thing as bad weather, only bad clothes' (which sounds even better in Swedish: *det finns inget dåligt väder, bara dåliga kläder*). In other words, make sure you cover up to withstand the elements, boy. See figures 1.4 and 1.5 for some clear indications of the ways my family have always used textiles to withstand the elements – in this case, while hunting (sartorially, of course).

Figure 1.4: a Sörman hunting trip; my grandfather Per (second from left) and great-grandfather Georg (centre)

Figure 1.5: sartorial textiles to withstand the elements (and help capture food)

Textiles have been traditionally used to capture food (nets), to build tents, and to carry food and water, and they continue to be used in this way to the present day. Natural and more modern, technical fibres (like those used by my favourite ski clothes brand Norrøna) have enabled native and non-native Swedes to navigate temperatures of up to negative 50°C, and to sail the cold Baltic sea in their search for food.

Safety

When I fractured my shinbone on the French Mediterranean coast during the summer of 2015, the immediate treatment was elevation, cooling, and bandages made out of textiles. Police and military wear bulletproof vests. Doctors and nurses wear sanitary 'scrubs' in operating theatres, and sew us up with thread post-surgery. When I went parasailing in Queenstown in 2014, the parasail got me down safely. We use safety nets literally in acrobatics, and metaphorically in welfare states. And indoors, textiles like carpets can be used to insulate and provide us with a feeling of safety. From the moment we are born, textiles and blankets are used to provide us with a sense of protection. And this continues throughout all life stages.

High-end Swedish bed manufacturer Hästens (The Horse's) is famous for providing its customers with not only great sleep since 1852 but also a feeling of safety by using horsehair as one of the component parts of their artisan approach to bed manufacturing. Hästens manufacture their beds and mattresses by hand, using natural materials like cotton, horsehair, wool and flax, and manage to appeal to our inherited need for safety in sleep through their seamless storytelling and craftsmanship. And given the success of companies like Hästens, we can also see how textile manufacturing has provided shelter and safety, through income, for entrepreneurs in the textiles space.

Love/belonging

As a long-time fan of Stockholm's football club Djurgårdens IF, I have been indoctrinated with the colours and symbolism of that brand since birth. Whenever I attend a game at our new home – Tele2 Arena in Stockholm – I and my fellow Djurgården fans are greeted by the Ultra's navy and blue textile flags, or their use of the symbolic blue, yellow and red emblem. This idea of showcasing a sense of belonging through textiles is not novel. For centuries militaries have employed colour and textiles to get people to 'rally behind the flag', and textile flags carry a lot of deep sentiment internationally – Americans, of course, pledge allegiance to their flag.

In late 2015 and early 2016, New Zealand held two referenda on changing its flag to break with its colonial British past, and to better differentiate it in a modern context (incidentally they chose to stick with the status quo). When I was awarded my Global Executive MBA from the University of Sydney, the ceremony took place in academic gowns, and the tassel on the headpiece was ceremoniously moved 180 degrees as we were awarded our new social and academic status.

Equally, the production of textiles can be a bonding process, so when in 2014 I commissioned a handmade carpet from Agra in India to provide 'the red carpet treatment' for my mum's haberdashery Georg Sörman, the vendor was adamant that only one of the local families could carry out this particular weave – together. And as an Anglophile brand, selling Scottish knits, the heritage of Scottish tartans is even part of Georg Sörman's visual identity, alluding to the sense of love and belonging inherent in the family tartans of Scotland. And, of course, I don't want to diminish the sexual and reproductive connotations of clothing, which modern brands like Agent Provocateur are utilising in their positioning.

Esteem

Textiles provide a sense of prestige and accomplishment – ordering a suit on Savile Row, for example, or having bespoke shirts made on Jermyn Street in London carries a lot of savoir faire. And while flipping the tassel on the graduate headpiece ensures belonging to a crew of cognoscenti alumni, equally my father 'earned his stripes' in the Swedish military – as he stepped through the ranks, his uniform indicated that he, like a good scout, was progressing in accomplishment. The present-day suit draws from military uniforms in design, and you could be forgiven for thinking that people in the financial district in NYC are actually wearing uniforms (given their similarities).

Choosing to wear brands, perhaps oversized polo horses, on our chests may indicate social status or that we lead a particular lifestyle (or desire to), and may provide some wearers with a sense of self-esteem. Others want to be more subtle in their choices, so that only the sartorial literati understand the subtle elegance of the wearer's choices. The same polo horse brand, for example, is also using textiles in innovative, communicative ways through its smart, sports-garment genre, which digitises data from your blood, sweat and tears so that you can boost your self-esteem by constantly monitoring yourself intimately. And intimates and lingerie are, of course a key traditional component of wedding ceremonies and attire around the world, helping to create certain connections and mindsets. Or so I am told.

Self-actualisation

Textiles can also be an enabler of achieving one's full potential, including in creative activities. If you are seamstress, a fashion designer, or pattern maker, this speaks for itself. If you are an artisan or craftsman or craftswoman who is passing on the family's unique skills to the next generation, the polishing and continuous improvement of those skills is part and parcel of achieving one's full potential. My girlfriend, Nicole, is a fashion designer with a background at Yves Saint Laurent in Paris and created a global swimwear label – Ephemera – a few years ago. I know from our conversations how much she enjoys the process of imagining, creating, testing and designing – giving life to her ideas through textiles – and at the same time helping her customers transform and self-actualise each summer. To the great pleasure of the women who wear the brand, and their admirers, male and female, of course.

Along with the design aspects, the generative process of creating textiles or weaving them together is an intrinsically rewarding process, which is said to have mental and spiritual benefits. As Beverly Gordon also points out in her article, 'engaging with the repetitive, rhythmic steps of sewing, knitting, weaving and similar techniques can create a sense of peace or calm' and 'cloth-making creates the "relaxation response", a measurable state where brain waves change and heart rate, muscle tension and blood pressure decrease and a feeling of serenity ensues'. I should be so lucky to have the delicate skills required to make textiles by hand. Kudos and respect to Nicole and seamstresses and weavers before her.

In some traditional weaving communities, song and textiles are intricately intermeshed. In fact, singing in unison is often a critical component of the act of creation. As Ruth Clifford points out in her Travels in Textiles blog, 'The loom acts as a sort of instrument, creating a rhythmic and repetitive accompaniment for the weaver to sing along to while involved in the repetitive, physical movement of weaving.' For example, before the advent of mass mechanical weaving in Scotland, Scottish women used to sing Gaelic songs in syncopation, improvised to the rhythm of the beat of 'waulking the tweed' (as highlighted in the documentary *Lomax the Songhunter*). And as Victoria Mitchell, author of the 1997 article 'Textiles, Text and Techne' illustrates, 'through the senses, touch and utterance share common origins in the neural system and in the pattern of synaptic, electro-chemical connections between neurons.'

In other parts of the world, the act of creation and bonding takes on a spiritual dimension, with Deepak Mehta in *Work, Ritual, Biography* showing the interconnectedness between prayer and textiles among Muslim Ansaris, who recite religious prayers while weaving. Within these religious prayers, or *du'as*, are answers to questions that Adam asked Jabrail, when the first loom was introduced from heaven. 'In uttering [the *du'as*] the weaver invokes the loom as memory … to weave is to pray, to pray is to weave'. Have I sold you on the idea of crafts as a cool way to self-actualise and live a spiritually connected life, yet?

However, textiles are also interweaved into the lives for those of us who are lucky enough to be spending time self-actualizing ourselves, and I hope to count myself as one of those lucky ones. I know textiles fill many of my own needs (as they did for the men in my family before me – as figures 1.3 and 1.4 show). As I look around myself writing these lines (an activity of self-actualisation or survival, depending on your viewpoint) I am leaning back into a cloth-covered wooden chair, two weaved sails are filtering the Bondi afternoon sun and wind, a patchwork carpet is giving the brushed cement on the outdoor balcony some contrasting warmth, a denim pillow is providing my lower back with some much-needed improvised ergonomic support, and four hand-bound design books are elevating the MacBook Air I'm working on. All while the day bed on the opposite end of the balcony is trying to seduce me into an afternoon siesta – which, as you can tell, I am resisting. Meanwhile, a pair of Tretorn canvas shoes are leaning on the redbrick wall toward the kitchen, while my feet are enjoying the suede straps of my Birkenstocks, and I am occasionally reminded of the mercerised cotton in my Derek Rose underwear; my legs and arms, clad in Imogene + Willie shorts from Nashville and a Maison Kitsune polo shirt, are meditating on these last days of the Indian summer in Sydney in 2016. Two Eton Shoreditch denim shirts are lazily fading in the sun, awaiting a visit to the downstairs laundry, and I am procrastinating on this seemingly less important duty. The book you are reading clearly takes precedence.

Textiles also enable me do what I do as a futurist. Ancient history, modern and futuristic application. With 240 international travel days on average for the past three years, I spend a lot of my time traversing the globe, hunting for the future in distant places. This 'hunter-gatherer' lifestyle has a timeless quality, in the sense that my foraging for the future is enabled by textiles (see figure 1.6). My olive-green Filson garment bag, which I spoke about at TEDxSanJuanIsland in 2015, keeps my suits and clothes in check, and helps to straighten them up after commuting between Stockholm and Seattle on British Airways. The textile interiors of my Rimowa carry-on luggage keep my pocket squares from Amanda Christensen in shape, so that my futurist personal brand of the 'guy who always wears a handkerchief' remains intact.

When I travel, urban and rural, business and pleasure intermesh. In other words, my wardrobe needs to consist of a mix of natural fibres and technical garments that enable me to switch modes in an agile fashion.

Figure 1.6: future-foraging travels enabled by textiles

My father – 'The Colonel' Lars-Olof, as our partners at Private White V.C. in England call this maestro at Georg Sörman – always told me to 'dress for the occasion', which means a savoir faire for the international subtleties of dress, and ensuring an air of elegance no matter where you turn up. This idea of personal brand and using textiles in our quest for self-actualisation is seemingly a timeless notion. My dad calls it etiquette, and it is as timely as it is timeless – particularly for a futurist foraging for food for thought. Excuse the alliteration.

So textiles are important, helping us to fulfil all levels on Maslow's needs hierarchy. They have also fulfilled my mother's needs for most of her life, helping to create a world she loves and is hesitant to leave behind. My mum's world is one of physical fabrics, and it has deeply shaped her identity. She is a traditional men's haberdasher through and through. Textiles saturate her ordinary world. Moving beyond this ordinary, analogue world, into a world of extraordinary, digital possibilities, digital demons and dragons and threats, has always seemed anathema and unnecessary to her. However, the evil empire of digital disruption doesn't care about those mental boundaries – just as it didn't care for the mental boundaries set up by some of France's most established wine producers.

Reinvention and transformation is friction

Set among the rolling hills of Languedoc-Roussillon, my friends and colleagues Matt, Pete, Mark, and I toast each other at the Chateau Les Carrasses with a glass of rosé on another gorgeous May spring day overlooking the chateau's grounds, on which we are staying for a long weekend. The salty Mediterranean air is slowly warming up the terroir in the Sud de France region, where we are on the last leg of our immersive Global EMBA. My girlfriend, Nicole, jovially describes this final module of the University of Sydney Global Executive MBA near Perpignan as the 'wine-tasting course'. And, yes, it does take some effort to convince her, as I imagine it will take to convince you, of the business merits of spending time in the sloping hills of the local vineyards consulting with the owners on turning around their heritage businesses. It's just a happy coincidence that they happen to be in the business of viniculture. And convenient if, like me, you enjoy the outputs of French viniculture. À ta santé!

Before we move on, indulge me by letting me give more depth on a cultural and contextual term which is of great significance to this chapter – the idea of 'terroir'. Perhaps you've heard of it, particularly in its association with wine. According to the Oxford Dictionaries, terroir refers to the complete natural environment in which a particular wine is produced, including factors such as the soil, topography and climate. But terroir is more than this. The term also captures all the environmental factors that affect the growth and flavour of a crop, and how these environmental factors and characteristics come together to create an overall character for a region. According to the French, and indeed the French wine appellation d'origine contrôlée (AOC) system, this character then flows through to the unique qualities of the grape grown. Importantly, as noted in *The Oxford Companion to Wine*, the extent of terroir's significance is greatly deliberated in the wine industry. And as we will see, the mythical idea of terroir can be both a blessing and curse.

But back to the Sud de France region, where we had flown into from London (where we had spent a preparatory week at the London School of Economics). We were on the final leg of our Global EMBA journey together and, as per the curriculum's design, we were in Europe to immerse ourselves in the dynamics of rejuvenating and turning around heritage brands, and ensuring their continued relevance in a modern world. What better industry to explore than the heavily tradition-laden world of wines? In a family business. In France. This was the perfect storm. At least if you, like me, have a passion for disrupting and challenging accepted wisdom and orthodoxy. The idea behind the design of the Global EMBA (in 2015 voted the number one EMBA in Australia by the *Australian Financial Review BOSS* magazine, despite my girlfriend's facetious criticism) is that the intimate cohort of executives and entrepreneurs in the course study the various stages of the business life cycle – from the start-up ecosystem in Bangalore at the Indian Institute of Management, to the management of growth in the high-tech sector in Silicon Valley at the Stanford Graduate School of Business, to finally immersing ourselves in the 'fork in the road' dialogue that happens for mature businesses (to either transform or die) that we delved into at LSE followed by our intense period with the vignerons in Languedoc-Roussillon. Like Russell Crowe in the 2006 movie *A Good Year* by Ridley Scott, where the English protagonist Max Skinner inherits his uncle's wine estate in Provence, we would make this Anglo-French pilgrimage into an eccentric world of terroir, wine classification and appellation laws. In this context, one of the primary questions that I was obsessing about was how ideas of identity, location, heritage, provenance and tradition intermingle, and how their dynamic interplays with transformation, innovation and commercial success, and, ultimately, sustainability. What is the right balance between rear-view mirror and front windscreen, so to speak? And at what stage do these concepts become a mental fetter that hinders transformation?

These were all poignant questions on my mind, not just from a theoretical perspective, but also from a dually practical perspective. Firstly, my cohort team had been paired up with a sixth-generation Languedoc-Roussillon vigneron family and their new CEO, and were advising them on an innovative export strategy that we had to deliver to their board. Secondly, while travelling from Melbourne to London, I hosted three of my cohort colleagues on a detour to Stockholm, to get their insight into turning around the fortunes of my mother's mature menswear business, Georg Sörman. As it turns out, many of the challenges we encountered in France were echoed in Sweden. But before we get to this, let us dive into the questions on my mind when it comes to transformation, innovation, and rejuvenation. Let us scrutinise the old Latin saying 'in vino veritas' (meaning 'in wine, [there is] truth'), and let us do it in a context of a wine-growing region where speaking the truth, ironically, was not very abundant.

Mental fetters and identity imprisonment in Languedoc-Roussillon

A sense of place can be both a gift and a curse, and the location which sits at the core of provenance marketing can be a double-edged sword. Only champagne from Champagne can legally be called 'champagne'. Chicken Bega doesn't quite have the same ring to it as Chicken parmigiana, and Yunnanese pork doesn't whet one's appetite the way apple-smoked Canadian bacon does. A region has either built a world-class reputation for a particular produce, brand equity in its provenance and trust in its sourcing practices, or it hasn't. And while champagne, Parmigiano-Reggiano cheese, and Canadian bacon have all been blessed with the seal of approval from global foodies, this protection and communication of provenance can both bolster and hamper the individual businesses within such regions. Businesses can be bolstered in the sense that they can tap into the brand equity of the region, but the regulation associated with the intellectual property of place can also hamper innovation and development. On the flipside, for Languedoc-Roussillon, the sense of confused identity and provenance in this lesser known wine-growing region of France offers both opportunity and challenges as local winegrowers seek to unshackle themselves from commoditised brand associations and enter the imaginations of global foodies, whose sense of French geography is limited at best.

The successes of provenance marketing are numerous, and you can understand the aspirations of a region like the Languedoc-Roussillon, as it enviously gazes across the border into movie character Max Skinner's Provence, and further afield to Burgundy and Bordeaux. These are regions blessed with history, famous landscape paintings, and a tradition for artisanal and local craft; importantly, they have made a name for themselves globally as great local French brands. While these areas have entertained the upmarket aspirations and status anxiety of consumers around the world for decades, if not centuries, the Languedoc-Roussillon region has not been able to create the same kind of brand equity.

Historically, this was the region that focused on quantity, not quality – a reputation that was cemented during World War I when it supplied cheap and poor-quality wine for army use.

Such brand damage, no matter whether it is still apt 100 years later, has stained the region (excuse the wine pun). And Languedoc-Roussillon is seemingly desperate to recreate the successes of its neighbours, even if it is at the expense of reducing the use of its legal name, Languedoc-Roussillon, in favour of the more international-sounding 'Sud de France'. In a gesture toward identity conflict, certain lobby groups wish to let go of the poor brand associations of the Languedoc-Roussillon as the major contributor to the French wine glut, in order to start afresh by tapping into what the world knows, or thinks it knows, about the south of France and the French Riviera. These types of lobby groups, supported by the region's elite business families like the Mas, Bertrands and Bonfils, realise that location and how it is communicated in business is absolutely critical for a sub-brand that belongs to the region and tries to navigate its way through the regulatory maze, created largely to protect the local growers from international competition.

The irony of this attachment to place, and the obsession with marketing it as a (if not *the*) key asset, is that consumer knowledge of place is limited. Having grown up Swedish but having spent a lot of my time in the Anglo-Saxon world, I am still aghast at how many times people associate chocolates, watches and Roger Federer with my home nation. There are ostensibly two times in the year when non-French natives might care about French geography – one, if they are planning a holiday in France, and two, during the Tour de France, when we are bombarded on television with the names of French villages, and maps of the various stages of the tour. Yet, the wine brands and dynasties insist on marketing place, terroir and AOP as their key assets – to a consumer who doesn't know where the Languedoc-Roussillon is, doesn't understand the amorphous term 'terroir', and couldn't care less for French protectionism dressed up as unique provenance marketing. Whether the consumer is always right is another matter, of course, and one wishes perhaps that people were generally more interested in geography and the provenance of produce beyond the mainstream regions of the world that we all know about. And, of course, industry trends and consumer awareness, partly driven by the internet, digitisation and mobilisation of content, should all favour local storytelling. Foodie trends like 'farm-to-table', locavorism (the global word of the year in 2007), artisanship, story food, reality TV food shows, source and traceability should all buoy tradition and the local. If done right. However, the French wine industry as a whole has been slow to respond to consumer appetites for information.

Added to this confusion about just how important place and provenance really is, perhaps based in part on the French conviction that they are well placed to educate the world about wines, is the fact that most consumers in the New World and in non-wine-producing markets predominantly base their wine choices on grape varietal, rather than on a deep-seated trust in the chemical properties of the soil in an unknown region somewhere between the Alps and the Pyrenees. Taken together, you have the perfect recipe for consumer lack of savoir faire. This is, of course, to the great chagrin of the French wine producer who loves his soil, and who cannot fathom why the world doesn't understand the value of his unique terroir. Too many business owners, constrained by terroir terrorism, think local, but try to awkwardly act global in an international market, without asking themselves what the value chain actually wants, and so market the thing they have been told is most unique – the local terroir. A grating seam between vantage points, seemingly.

Breaking with tradition

This focus on the local, eccentric and unique is perhaps not surprising in the Old World, and Old World wines. It showcases the tension and dynamic in their competition with the New World, which has been somewhat freer from the regulatory and traditional burdens of place. I mean, Argentina, Australia, California and New Zealand had to earn a reputation in a global wine economy – a respect for the provenance of Mendoza, the Barossa, Napa Valley or the Marlborough had to be developed. And this had to start on a country level. If these producers had used small-scale place and location as the starting point for marketing Australian wines in the US, for example, where the consumer knowledge of Australian geography was (and is) limited at best (and the wine consumer at large in the US would be considered unsophisticated at best by international wine snobs), they would most likely have struggled in their provenance marketing efforts.

If, however, you went to market in a way that demystified wines, focused on fun labelling, zoomed out and associated the brand with the nation continent of Australia rather than a micro-climatic terroir, and went to market with a quirky point-of-sale focused campaign, you might do well. While this example from Australian wine brand Yellow Tail of a 'blue ocean strategy' is an interesting case in point of splitting with the traditions and competitive dimensions accepted by an industry, the larger lesson is that it focuses empathetically on the consumer first and foremost, something the French wine industry would do well to adopt. (For more on blue ocean strategy, see the book of the same name by Renée Mauborgne and W. Chan Kim.) Having spent time in the south of France and working with our family business client, I understand that this is not always easy. The shackles of tradition, passing on a legacy, family heritage and fierce local, dynastic rivalries sometimes take precedence over commercial nous, and place cognitive barriers around what is possible. The AOP regulatory framework further stifles innovation, and becomes an easy mental prison and an excuse not to market wines in a more user-friendly fashion.

It is perhaps illustrative that the French equivalent of the Yellow Tail example is a reverse innovation effort to market *Old-World wines* to the *New World* – taking on the New World at *its* own game, as it were. The strategy used by Jean-Claude Mas Arrogant Frog in its Australian and US marketing could be considered a simple duplicate of Yellow Tail's American go-to-market strategy, and it has been hugely successful in Australia, with one million bottles sold each year. Jean-Claude Mas's stroke of insight came from the anti-French sentiment during the early 2000s when President Bush called the French 'arrogant frogs', and he used this consumer insight into the minds of (some) Americans to brand a product line that could be accepted by the consumer, and interestingly also appealed to the Australian perception of the French. Importantly, this line of wines is branded significantly differently from the main family of Mas labels, helping to avoid brand confusion, and perhaps to avoid local French jealousies for his innovation in communicating the varietal and the brand identity, rather than the terroir and the appellation. This example is illustrative of the type of commercial success that is possible when you break with tradition, and empathise with a consumer who is bombarded with jargon, snobbery and micro-climate information, and who often doesn't even check out the back label, which the wine industry considers such a huge communication opportunity. At times, while we were consulting in France, we got a sense that many producers suffered a kind of artist's dilemma, where commercial success was akin to selling out, and many accepted 'foreign currency' instead of cash. In other words, write ups, features in industry magazines, critical acclaim, local respect and tilling the soil were sometimes substitutes for commercial success and revenue. Lifestyle, tradition, keeping up appearances and terroir came in the way of innovation, consumer awareness, and channel marketing.

Yet, as mentioned, local should have all the attributes of successful marketing, if done right. But this is where provenance marketing, as I experienced in the Languedoc-Roussillon, fell short. Most wine brands in the region fail to meet the consumer halfway. They communicate in the same way as other Old-World wine producers, in the same order and sequence, and trust that the quality of their grape juice will be noticed by the consumer. Focus has been on telling a story in the analogue world on their bottles and labels, and using images of chateaus, and less on helping the consumer make sense of the context of the bottle on the shelf. The branding messages get lost in the level of abstraction, at which the message is pitched. While the consumer when choosing a bottle of wine might firstly consider varietal (such as 'shiraz will go with my beef') and secondly price bracket (relative to the occasion) and thirdly general region, at the point of sale they rarely even consider the location or micro-climate. (See figure 1.7 to understand this friction between what the consumer wants and how the winemaker speaks.)

Figure 1.7: tradition as friction in the wine industry

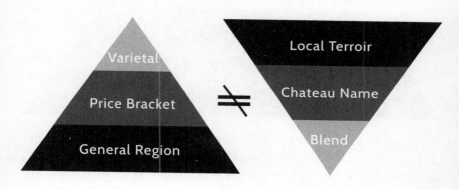

THEY SPEAK

Varietal

Price Bracket ≠ Local Terroir

General Region Chateau Name

Blend

WE WANT

The level of abstraction at which the Australian consumer, for instance, is operating is too high for the highly localised, terroir-focused wine producer who fails to capture any mindshare, given that the order they communicate in is totally inverted – that is, they focus firstly on the AOP, to indicate micro-climate terroir, secondly on the chateau location name and only thirdly on the blend of varietals determined by the appellation regulations. The consumer is lost. A better context or synced level of abstraction would be to get in line with consumer thinking, and provide valuable contexts at each level of abstraction to position the wine favourably in the minds of the consumer. This would be more seamless. For example, when advising our client on their export strategy in Australia we would suggest they focus first on the type of wine (shiraz, awesome for your Sunday BBQ), then on its price or ranking (included in a 'Six of the Best' list or the top 1 per cent of our wines), then on the region (Sud de France). (See figure 1.8, overleaf.)

Figure 1.8: branding wine seamlessly

They could then link the region back to something Australians know (like Tour de France personalities) and finally incorporate digital/mobile storytelling and video so that the consumer can attain status by telling their mates about a great wine they found and share via their digital and analogue networks. All of a sudden, the brand makes the customer a hero, because they are now speaking the same wine language.

On reflection, it is a great shame that regulation, sophistication, production categorisation and tradition stand in the way of innovation, transformation and commercial success. Seemingly intelligent people are not always commercially savvy, and some people from this region are a case in point. If I ponder the future for the region, and others like it, I imagine that the agricultural land might find a different use from wine growing in the future. Wine is a luxury, and on a global scale we have a wine glut but still see many food shortages, and with two billion more people entering the global food market over the next thirty-five years, traditions and lifestyles will increasingly come under pressure, and there will be new demands on the productivity of the terroir. Despite government protectionism, it is unlikely that many of the producers we came across will be able to tell the stories of their terroir in ten, twenty or thirty years, unless they transform, become less tradition-bound, change how they communicate and brand their produce in a way that captures the hearts and minds of a local, regional, national and international market.

Spilling wine on a textiles brand

From my own point of view I took away several lessons from this experience in Languedoc-Roussillon that have general application beyond the wine industry:

- *The value of outside advice in family business:* At our family business wine client, the non-family member CEO played a crucial part in professionalising and commercialising this sixth-generation family business. As CEO, he added an objective lens, and while still having to play politics and pull strings carefully, his nous for marketing and branding, and his international mindset was a strong asset for a family company, especially where none of the sons or the patriarch spoke English. In my own business (Thinque) I am trying to engage with external sources of influence, like the EMBA cohort, on a consistent basis, to invite challenge, ideas and new angles. In my associated family business (Georg Sörman Menswear in Stockholm) I realised external input from designers, management consultants, objective accountants, and extreme consumers and non-consumers, would be increasingly important in terms of how we rejuvenated this mature business and re-established its relevance in a disrupted retail environment.

- *Identity as baggage:* In a family business context, as well as in a broader business context, identity and industry boundaries can significantly hamper your perspective on how you do business, and limit your innovation. If a wine producer, like our client, thinks of himself as a farmer who gets rewarded on bulk and volume, this will affect how he brands the produce. If a person working for the oil and gas industry considers their industry boundaries as only extending to oil and gas, they might not take the outside threat of renewable energy, in the broader industry context of 'energy', seriously. Or if a bricks-and-mortar retailer considers their historical competitive advantage as being range, size and unique offerings for the 'big and tall' segment, as in the case of Georg Sörman, rather than client empathy, which I believe to be its true differentiator, this will affect their business model. This is especially the case in an age where 'long tail' economics holds that bricks-and-mortar stores should focus their efforts on the revenue-generating, profitable lines and sizes of clothing, while complementary digital services can more easily accommodate niche needs. From a personal point of view, whether I think of myself as a futurist, management consultant, or scenario planner will affect the kind of offerings I put in front of a client, and potentially limit my own scalability. Identity, how we think of ourselves, and the baggage that comes with that perspective, can severely limit our competitiveness. Thus, disrupting our own thinking on a consistent basis is crucial to ensure that we are open to new ideas and identities, shifting industry boundaries, and novel perspectives on what we should market and communicate about our competitive advantages. Identity is fluid, and we can always grow into a new suit as it were.

- *Differentiation, not quality:* While we as businesspeople frequently focus on doing things better, and improving quality, we sometimes forget that beyond a certain threshold, the customer may not care. As one industry pundit explains, 'we appreciate with our eyes, not our palate'. The law of diminishing returns applies in this regard. Beyond a certain point in quality, the more effort we invest in the product characteristics, the less the return on effort from that investment. A better approach would be to brand and package the differentiating factors of the product, and ensure the consumer really feels like there is a value proposition they can identify with. In part of my business as a futurist and keynote speaker, I have often been told that the keynote speech has to be 'world-class', and so my team and I always aspire to do our best to deliver on that brand promise. At the same time, the biggest investment for our clients is not in the keynote speaker at their conference, but rather taking their whole leadership team out of the business for several days, and flying them in globally for the conference. So we realised that the leadership team walking away from the session and doing even only one thing differently as a result of take-home value, is much more important than just listening to a polished story and quality presentation. This insight led us to a further focus on leave-behind value and a longer term impact arc, as opposed to just investing in better research, cooler slides, and polished presentation and thought leadership skills. For Georg Sörman Menswear in Stockholm, a need for differentiation would cause us to ask what this store can do that no analogue or digital competitors could do, and then package that. For example, for three generations of Sörmans, the store has looked after six to seven generations of Stockholm men. This expertise and enduring empathy cannot be replicated by a five-year-old digital disruptor, or even the other major menswear retailers in Stockholm. Or maybe it can?

The challenges and insights gained in the Languedoc-Roussillon deepened the conversation with my mum and, inspired by the mantra of 'in vino veritas', eventually led Mum to a call to adventure and an attempt at reinvention. Mum's ordinary world was in jeopardy, and while she wasn't yet able to fully comprehend the shifting tides of the world around her, she realised at some level that her very textile identity was at stake, threatened out in the extraordinary world of global, tech-enabled commerce.

As a child, I grew up in a family obsessed with antiques, whereas I was always more interested in technology, mobile phones, cars and Nintendo games. Yet, our parents used to drag us along to look at Swedish castles, old, dusty tapestries, fancy antique auctions at Bukowskis in Stockholm (just browsing), museums and moth-eaten flea markets. Their favourite TV shows are *Antique Roadshow* and *Downton Abbey*. They have a reverence for tradition, legacy and remnants that is quirky and admirable in a world of constant change and disruption. And while that reverence is potentially respectful to their elders, it does cause a suspicion of the new. I imagine that an obsession with the historical must be somewhat soothing, because it is largely static. The future, however, is a dynamic place. And the future was incurring on the territory of the past, in the present moment for Georg Sörman and its leadership.

CASE STUDY:
HOW WARBY PARKER REINVENTED THE EYEWEAR MARKET BY SEAMLESSLY INTEGRATING THE VALUE CHAIN

How do you identify industries that are too safe in their 'ordinary world' and are sticking too rigidly with their status quo? In other, words what industries are ready for disruption? No easy answers to this question exist, but three general signals do indicate if a market is likely to be disrupted:

- industries that are dominated by a few large firms with complacent leadership

- recurring and severe customer friction

- interchangeable middlemen or intermediaries who don't add value.

First of all, if an industry is dominated by a few big organisations that are self-satisfied, you can anticipate that disruption is near. And, secondly, industries that are experiencing recurring customer friction and frustration (think the insurance industry and consumer banking) are also under risk of being disrupted because customers will eventually start looking for other alternatives. This will, in turn, create a breeding ground for creative entrepreneurs who are willing to invest their time and energy into finding solutions that effectively address the real issues. (For more information on this, see Anna Johansson's article 'Shake it up: How to identify industries that are ready for disruption', available on Business.com.)

The third sign that an industry might face disruption is when intermediaries are interchangeable or don't add value. The kind of professionals I'm referring to here include travel agents, stock brokers, real estate brokers and photographer's agents. Digitisation has affected all of these sectors and more or less dramatically changed the relationship between the seller and the buyer.

All of these signs were in one sense or the other visible when Neil Blumenthal, now CEO of renowned eyewear company Warby Parker, started his business in 2010 (together with his MBA classmates Dave Gilboa, Andrew Hunt and Jeffrey Raider at University of Pennsylvania's Wharton School). Just like many other successful entrepreneurs, they started with identifying a problem – in this case, the problem they identified was simply that they thought glasses were too expensive.

When Blumenthal and his fellow entrepreneurs began their deep dive into the industry, they realised that the whole infrastructure behind the manufacturing of glasses was owned by a single company. As is common in industries dominated by a few very large players, they also saw rising prices for consumers and mediocre customer experiences.

And in 2009 and 2010, before they launched their business, they found out that less than 1 per cent of glasses were sold online while in other consumer goods categories online sales represented 10 and 15 per cent of the total market. It was out of these insights that the founders came to the conclusion that an entrepreneurial opportunity existed to reinvent the eyewear market.

Another insight they gained from talking to friends about their project in 2009 and 2010 was that people still were very hesitant about buying eyewear online, mainly because they couldn't see how the glasses would look on their face. To tackle this barrier Warby Parker first decided to offer free shipping and free returns. However, they thought that this offer wasn't enough to fundamentally solve the problem, so they decided to launch Virtual Booth, which is a feature that enables you to upload a picture on the website and then virtually try out different frames to see how they look on you.

Although the founders were happy with this solution, they were not completely satisfied, and they still asked themselves whether they would buy using this tool. After some time the founders came up with the additional idea of launching 'Home Try-On'. The idea behind this was simple: select five frames that you would like to try and keep them for five days. Then simply return the frames you don't want. Warby Parker pays for both shipping and return shipping, with no obligation to buy. The combination of free shipping and free returns, the Virtual Booth and the Home Try-On service not only helped customers to seamlessly overcome barriers and reduce pain points, but also elevated the whole shopping experience.

WarbyParker.com went live on February 2015 and two days later was featured in the renowned men's fashion magazine *GQ*, which called them 'the Netflix of eyewear'. During the same month they were also featured in *Vogue*. The publicity helped raise brand awareness and boosted their sales to such an extent that they reached their first year sales target within three weeks, and as a result had to manage a waiting list of 20 000 people.

Of course, keeping so many impatient people happy was a challenge, but they successfully managed this by being transparent about the delay in shipments and also explaining to customers what was going on. And, since then Warby Parker has heavily invested in seamless customer service and ensured that they hire people that are genuinely friendly and can deliver the kind of deep empathy that the founders wanted the brand to communicate.

An essential part of the brand's identity is their social mission, which is communicated under the slogan 'Buy a pair, give a pair' – and you can read more about the logistics and results of this promise on warbyparker .com. A company's social mission might not be the most important factor for consumers, but research from the global performance management company Nielsen suggests that consumers are increasingly willing to vote with their dollars. Consumers among the generational cohort Generation Y or Millennials are especially willing to pay more for products and services from companies committed to social responsibility. (See the article 'Global consumers are willing to put their money where their heart is when it comes to goods and services from companies committed to social responsibility', available on the Nielsen website, for more information.)

Another great benefit of having a social mission, according to Blumenthal, is that you attract people with the right skill set and, maybe even more importantly, with values that are aligned with your corporate culture. What's key here is that Warby Parker's social mission is seamlessly integrated with the brand and not just an 'add-on', thus making their commitment more credible and trustworthy. Another lesson you can take away from their way of working with a social mission is that they are making it easy for consumers to contribute to a better world. They're not demanding anything from their customers, but instead making every purchase a seamless act of kindness.

In the process, Warby Parker, of course, represents a problem in the extraordinary world of the future of retail that is severely encroaching on the ordinary world of the incumbents.

Ask yourself…

Think about the following to get some ideas on how you can apply the insights from Warby Parker to your business:

1. Do any signs indicate that your industry might be disrupted in the near future? How can you turn those future challenges into opportunities?

2. What assumptions about your industry (and your ordinary world) are you accepting without critical thought? Think about how you can question the status quo in your industry and create more value for your customers.

3. What problems and barriers might hinder or impede your customers from doing business with you? How can you turn these insights into creative ideas and solutions?

4. What sort of combination of different solutions collectively could address different aspects of a problem?

5. What do you do in order to ensure that the customer service that your business offers is top of the line? How can you better incorporate your brand values into your customer service?

6. What would a social mission look like for your company? How can you tie this mission to the core of your brand and make it seem credible to your stakeholders, allies, and fellowship?

7. How can your products and/or services seamlessly contribute to a more sustainable society in an extraordinary world?

STEP 2
HERO'S JOURNEY WHEEL FOR MAMMA SÖRMAN-NILSSON

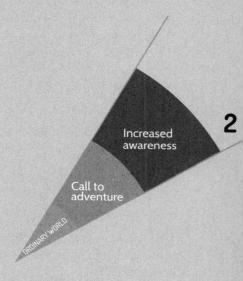

Increased awareness

Call to adventure

ORDINARY WORLD

2

Initial analysis, exploration and mapping of Georg Sörman and the impact of digital disruption in November 2012.
Birgitta becomes curious and contributes to fact-finding endeavours to find a constructive way forward, which leads to the strategic vision in *Digilogue* and 'Georg Sörman 100'.

Call to adventure

A call to adventure disrupts the everyday experience of the heroine. This disruption could be in the form of a direct threat to her family, physical safety or way of life, or a disruption of the intricate balance of her local community. In other words, the apple cart is deeply upset. This call to adventure may not always be as dramatic as a Gavrilo Princip shot (which triggered the 'adventure' of World War I), but could come in the form of a letter or a conversation about what the call to adventure is. Ultimately this will still rock the boat of the heroine's ordinary world and will highlight an odyssey which the heroine must undertake.

Here's how the call to adventure was issued in *Star Wars*:

- *Inner journey:* Increased awareness – R2D2 plays a portion of Princess Leia's call to adventure.

- *Outer journey:* Call to adventure – Luke is smitten by the vision and wants to help the maiden in distress.

And here's how it looked for my mother:

- *Inner journey:* Increased awareness – initial analysis, exploration and mapping of Georg Sörman and the impact of digital disruption in November 2012.

- *Outer journey:* Call to adventure – Birgitta becomes curious and contributes to fact-finding endeavours to find a constructive way forward, which leads to the strategic vision in *Digilogue* and 'Georg Sörman 100'.

2: Call to adventure

Disruption from within is better than disruption from without.

The love letter continues — a call to adventure

During the odyssey of the renaissance of Georg Sörman, my love letter to Mum has evolved and taken different shapes. In later iterations, the reinvention strategy for Aktiebolaget Georg Sörman – established in 1916 by my great-grandfather – was co-developed with my mother, Birgitta Sörman-Nilsson, and my father, Lars-Olof Nilsson, who at the time of writing jointly own this business; and their team of 11 staff. In its first iteration, the love letter took the form of my Global Executive MBA thesis, and was put to the test by some of the brightest professors and peers at the Stanford Graduate School of Business, the London School of Economics, the Indian Institute of Management, and the University of Sydney Business School.

The love letter, unfortunately by necessity and serious examination, took on a tone of tough love. When I began to write it in late 2012, the situation was already severe. For nearly a decade Mum had been injecting her life savings into keeping the unsustainable business model, which she 'inherited' from her father, alive. But the love letter also issued a call to adventure for Mum and her team. The analysis showed some slight hopes for the future, on certain premises. For example, the strategy we ultimately developed, and which we termed 'Georg Sörman 100' courtesy of the centenary celebrations in 2016, focused on the combination of 'timely technology and timeless traditions', and had to be followed and executed meticulously. We wouldn't be throwing out the analogue baby with the bathwater – useful traditions would be emphasised, and non-useful remnants would be discarded. By applying the best thinking and the most psychologically astute models on change management, external forces and disruption from the likes of John Kotter, Michael Porter and Clayton Christensen, we co-created the strategy with input from the owners (Mum and Dad), from the board (Mum and Dad), from the executive (Mum and Dad, again, this really does sound like a family business, right?), and the team of eleven staff. We mapped the psychometric strengths and capabilities of the team, built 'blue ocean strategy' canvases, and engaged a brand strategist with two Cannes Lions to her name to modernise the visual identity of the brand. The fact that our brand strategist – Hema Patel – was (and is) also a cherished ex-girlfriend of mine, and a close friend of the family would, I believed, create trust and buy-in the reinvention. And, of course, it was also the only economically viable choice, because we were granted much-needed 'mate's rates' for services my mum, majority owner, could otherwise ill afford. (More on Hema's impact later in the book.)

My mum's curiosity had been sparked during that fateful walk in the forest in 2012, when we agreed that I would put my mind to solving her business problems with her. The love letter evolved into a strategic form, and then into a book form, and the story of Georg Sörman and Mum's challenges started gaining international traction and media attention. All of a sudden, Swedish, English, Australian and American media outlets were curiously following the story of Georg Sörman's reinvention plan. As with any vision and plan, inspiration is important, as is execution. Mum has a knack for ignition and execution and, while strategy is not her strong suit, our dialogues led us to believe that I as the futurist could represent strategy, and she as the operator could represent execution. Part of the strategy had involved digging up old photos, stories, fabrics, archives and collections of Georg Sörman, and as we found out more about the origins, provenance and inspiration for the brand, this re-ignited Mum's curiosity in going on a quest into the future – a quest that would combine the best of timelessness and timeliness.

The fabric of adventure

It is 12 March, 2016, and I am racing down the mountain in my Norrøna and Atomic gear in Lech Zürs am Arlberg, Austria, with my metrosexual crew of Swedish skiing enthusiasts. Each year, we travel somewhere in the Alps for a week of downhill adventures and fresh air – and then carb offset all the health benefits of outdoor activities with beer and central European *le montagnard* (mountain) food. Depending on their level of skiing ambition, some members of the crew have longer lunches with more Stuben beer and schnitzel, while others carve up the mountain for longer. I belong in the latter category, and am also the geek-in-residence, which means I am responsible for recording both the geocontextual and health data on Trace Snow (to make us feel better about our after-ski bar tabs), as well as shooting films and photos of our epic adventures – which I then turn into an action edit for the inner circle.

What enables this action/adventure filming is a product from a company that understands the hero's journey (or the journeys of overzealous amateurs like us). With the GoPro Hero strapped to my helmet, I am able to effortlessly capture snow-capped peaks, powder, carving turns, and some epically silly tumbles. At the press of a button I am either recording with the fish-eye lens or not. I am either snapping a photo or not, and for extreme sports, or laymen's adventures among middle-aged men, this allows me and my mates to feel like Alberto Tomba for a few days, and have a good laugh at our memories of the day we hit top speeds of 86.6 kph in Lech Zurs, in 2016 (see figure 2.1, overleaf.)

Figure 2.1: Lech Zurs run, with top speed of 86.6 kph

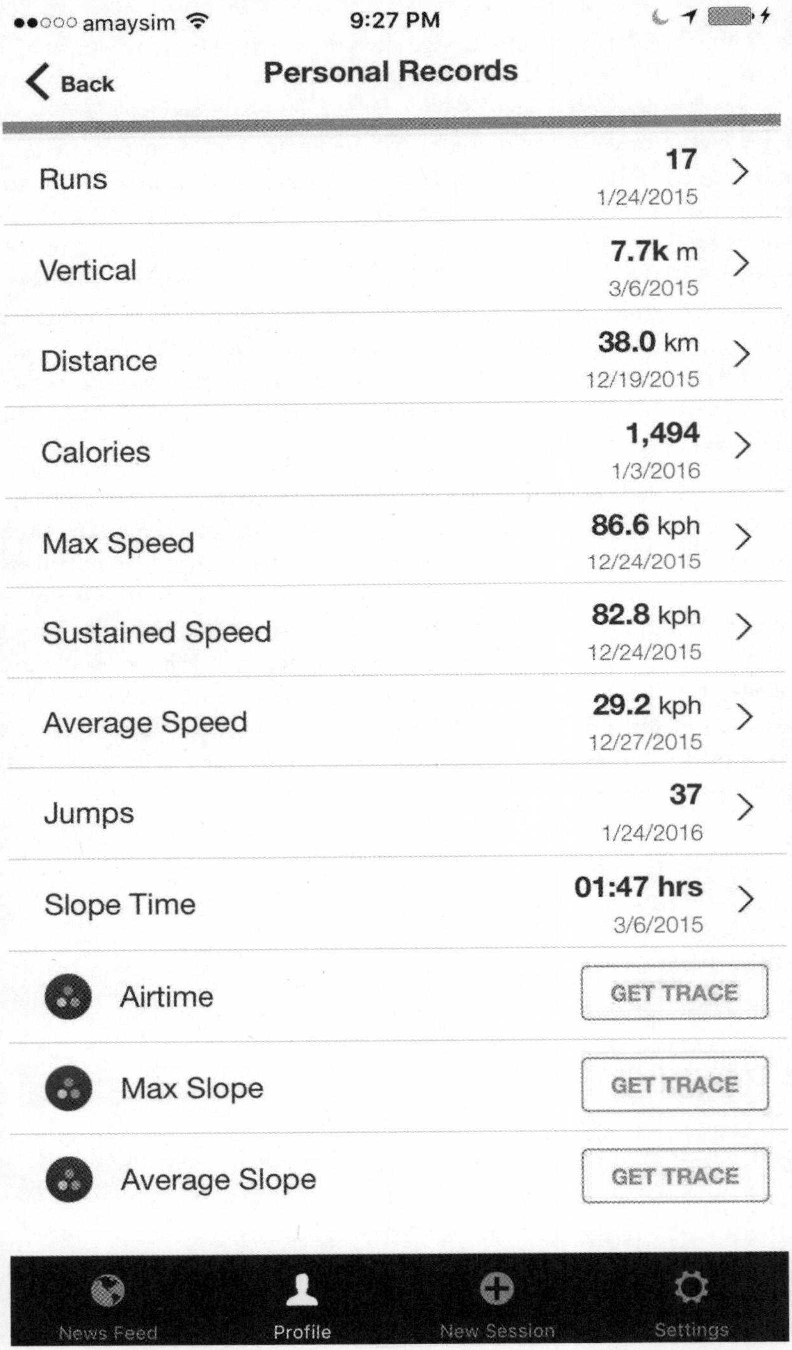

Source: Trace Snow by AlpineReplay, Inc.

The GoPro symbolises the success of brands that excel at digital storytelling. In March 2014, I keynoted at our client Sitecore's annual Digital Trendspot conference in London. The theme that year was 'The Art of Digital Storytelling', and the storytelling and themes of the event were based on classic stories like *Little Red Riding Hood*, *Hansel and Gretel*, and *The Three Little Pigs*, and how those stories (and hero's journeys) could be enabled – digitally. And while in the good old days brands might have thought of themselves as the hero coming to our rescue, increasingly, brands with foresight are starting to realise that *they are the mentors*, not the heroes. And that they need to inspire, guide and call upon us as consumers and clients to step up to the plate and become heroes.

In the wake of the collapse of traditional film producers and camera manufacturers, GoPro took a bold step in launching its digital camera. They did understand the Zeitgeist of our times, though, and decided to re-engineer the *Kodak moment* for the 21st century. Several things enabled their success, but one of the key aspects was elevating the user to the status of a hero, and turning us all into the directors of our own adventure and hero's journey (incidentally using this terminology in the naming of their device – GoPro Hero). All of a sudden, surfers strapped GoPro Heroes to their boards, triathletes mounted them on their bikes, skydivers wrapped them around their arms, and snowboarders attached them to their helmets. Without a viewfinder, filming your environment became effortless – or, seamless – and the unedited documentary style of recording turned you and your mates into the slightly tipsy mountaineers conquering some of the toughest slopes (the blue ones, of course) in the Vorarlberg Alps.

Storytelling as content marketing

The success of GoPro is partly that it is in the digital memories business, but also that it, unlike Nokia, had its finger on the pulse of the times, in that it tapped the narcissism, or urge to connect, among its clients, and their love of adventure. It thus staged a call to adventure – urging people to explore, to grow themselves, to go beyond their comfort zones, and to get creative while doing so. And their marketing campaigns and brand positioning around their core product, the Hero, are all about capturing and directing your own hero's or heroine's journey. While they may not necessarily play the active role of the mentor, they have built a platform for sharing extreme footage and amplifying user-generated content, to enable forms of peer-to-peer mentoring. And through their own content marketing, via YouTube, Facebook and Twitter, often created by fans for fans, they know that hero moments can go viral courtesy of their community. And they have flipped the conversation away from being focused on themselves, so that just like their lens, which is focused on what you see and experience – mountain tops, river valleys, friends (see figure 2.2) – they have become a companion on your journey.

Figure 2.2: the crew of Swedish skiing enthusiasts

GoPro is also highly adept at showcasing how adaptive the product is, highlighting in what areas of life it can fit and where it can document moments of heroism. And while they use a digital multichannel strategy, they also know which channel best lends itself to its action-oriented content (YouTube) where they actively engage in dialogue with their fans and community. GoPro not only shares videos, but also often goes to the source and story behind the video, sharing these details with its community, again driving the transparency and social aspect of the brand, making the community feel like GoPro is even more relatable. All this means the GoPro Hero becomes an accessory to your life and adventure, and to your global nomadism, challenges and obstacles. Ironically, by it taking a true client-first perspective, it has built a huge brand following as a result.

Turning the tables, in a positive way, and showcasing your clients and their stories of adventure is not just limited to brands like GoPro born in the digital age, however. On my 21st birthday I received a nice Swiss Army knife from my friends Mark and Evan, inscribed with a 'Happy 21st, Anders'. The knife was made by the heritage Swiss brand Victorinox. This brand, not unlike GoPro, produces an accessory that is highly functional and well thought through. The Swiss Army knife is nowadays so accepted it is a must-pack item on every camping trip, and a 'Doomsday Prepper' essential. It is much more than a spork, and its compactness and ingenuity packs a lot of punch. From opening cans, to slicing bread, to fixing car engines, to opening beer bottles, to cleaning your newly caught trout, the Swiss Army knife can do a lot of things. It can also be creatively used in non-intended ways by innovative heroes, and for its centenary Victorinox decided to highlight such customer stories on their storytelling platform. They made a call to adventure and action, asking their customers to contribute stories about how Victorinox products had helped them in sticky situations. Carl Elsener, CEO of Victorinox, stated at the launch of the digital platform for this heritage brand that:

> As a representative of the fourth generation of the Elsener family, I grew up with countless stories by and about Victorinox. As children, we shared in the thrill of our knives being allowed to come along on expeditions to the Himalayas, the North Pole or even to the moon.
>
> Later I realised that all the stories are a gracious thank you for our commitment to functionality, quality, innovation and design. They also show that Victorinox products are close to our customers' hearts. They rely on them. They have become lifelong companions.

With this in mind their inbound content and content marketing strategies focused on user-generated stories, which then provided their products with various archetypes. For example, the archetype of the 'helper', seen in the story of a passenger on a train who became a hero, thanks to his Victorinox pocket knife; the 'guardian' is another, seen in the story of a businessman who won a major contract thanks to his Victorinox travel bag; and the 'companion', seen in the story about a tourist who, without hotel accommodation, survived an icy cold night in Stockholm thanks to his Victorinox jacket. (See www.victorinox .com/global/en/Customer-Stories/cms/stories for more.)

Whether it is with video cameras, multi-purpose knives or fabrics, brands like Victorinox, and kindred spirits like Private White V.C., Filson and Barbour, are able to partner with their clients and empower them to be adventurous or everyday heroes. They have understood that the call to adventure and the art of storytelling are key in a world where every brand now must think as media and entertainment brands, and where you get to play the role of hero. One of the key questions for the future is how the digital and the physical aspects, tradition and technology, the timelessness of story and timeliness of the medium can be interwoven.

This call to adventure was what was enticing my mother, and in a way my love letter to her was the 'inciting incident' that got her started on her heroine's journey. In GoPro parlance, we were just yet to see whether she was going to strap the camera to her helmet and start climbing the mountain.

Tradition killed the radio star

For better or for worse, all business is local. The problem with this is that we are now living in a global economy and local eccentricities, unless well branded and communicated, can stand in the way of innovation, commercial success and the sustainability of tradition. That's right – local tradition and identity as a mindset could kill the sustainability of local tradition as a commercial enterprise. This is the irony, right? That by being so focused on identity, inheritance, family and the sense of place, those very things we treasure most run the risk of forever being lost. Because of this internal, and quite egocentric (you could even say arrogant) perspective, external competition, start-ups and customer-centric brands are perfectly positioned to disrupt you from your slumber.

At this stage, if you get caught out sleeping, it is likely to be too late. The early bird catches the worm, as it were. And 'early' here doesn't refer to who got up early 100 years ago; it pertains to who got up inspired, motivated and creative this morning. As a result, the question remains how heritage brands can stay relevant after being introspective for so long. And beyond this question of gaining commercial nous, can cultural language, legacy and traditional wisdom endure, if new forms of media, channels and amplification are ignored or discarded by brand owners and their leadership? Language loss, whether in business or in anthropology, is depressing because it decreases diversity, independence and variety of thought. And as a result of the loss of unique expression, cultures and lifestyles wither away.

I remember reading Jared Diamond's *Guns, Germs and Steel* while I was at university. In the book, Diamond argues that the three primary reasons the Europeans colonised large parts of the world (and not the other way around), and were successful in their market takeovers, were guns, germs and steel. That is, having better weapons, carrying germs (and partial immunity), and mastering steel and production were the primary competitive factors and differentiators. Over time, these led to huge inequalities, loss of diversity, genocide and victor's histories. In today's digital landscape, we stand on the precipice of a similar battle of civilisations, where old meets new. Where slow meets fast.

Language loss and the loss of wisdom

Let's look at language diversity as an example. According to Russ Rymer's *National Geographic* article 'Vanishing Languages', one language dies every 14 days, which means that by the end of next century, half of the world's 7000 languages will be extinct. Every two weeks, thus, a culture, a tradition, a way of seeing the world disappears. The whispers of elders will not be echoed by future generations. Nursery rhymes forever lost. Ancient knowledge of flora and fauna fading into oblivion. Rites of passage evanescing with the departing souls of the isolates who carry the last echoes of a way of life.

Imagine the solitude of being the last native speaker and sole survivor of an ancient tongue, with nobody to share it with. As Russ Rymer describes it in his article, 'with each speaker's death, another vital artery has been severed'. Rymer argues that the 'tongues, least spoken, still have much to say', and that the loss of biodiversity and species is an apt analogy for the loss of language. In other words, we lose our diverse richness as a human species as a result of language loss, and the replacement of 'long tail linguistics' by homogenous, conquering, colonial language behemoths like Spanish and English. In his article, Rymer points out that external linguists and anthropologists cannot 'save' languages from dissipating, but that salvation must come from within the imperilled cultures. Many languages die out because they are only verbal, and have no alphabet, and as such no written record. Some linguists and anthropologists argue that interventionist methods like creating alphabets, compiling a dictionary, or teaching native speakers to write has the effect of changing or influencing the language, and thus argue for the more hands-off approach of only recording a lexicon and grammar before the language is lost forever. The 'laissez faire' approach might appeal to those who believe in the old adage that 'you can lead a horse to water, but you cannot make it drink', and that change has to begin within. There is a lot of merit to this argument – we can't impose a willingness to save the language, and the method for doing so, on these speakers. Change needs to come from within, even if external forces may nudge us into seeing that adaption is a must for cultural and language survival. And when the rate of external change trumps the rate of internal change, adaptation and transformation, minority ways of seeing and speaking the world are in dire straits. Just like small businesses and cultures, and like that at Georg Sörman.

At the same time as laissez faire anthropologists have an important point in their non-interventionist stance, *National Geographic* is working closely with indigenous tribes around the world to help maintain, revitalise and record languages. Through the 'Enduring Voices' project, and using technology like video, audio, modern camera equipment and basic publishing tools, minorities across the world are now capturing oral and cultural traditions to ensure future generations can pass on the richness of ancient cultures. This is an important and urgent quest, given the rate at which languages are disappearing.

In other words, modern technology is giving relevance to ancient worldviews and customs. Amazing, huh?! In this way, unique perspectives on life, past, present and future may be maintained. For example, in the Tuvan language (235 000 speakers) on the steppes of Russia, the word *songgaar* means both 'go back' and 'the future', while the word *burungaar* means 'go forward' and 'the past' – because the Tuvans believe that the past is located in front of you, and the future is located behind you, as you cannot see it yet, while the past has already been witnessed with your own eyes. In Cmiique Iitom, the native tongue of the Seri in Mexico, the phrase *hant iiha cöhacomxoj* means the 'ones who have been told the ancient things'.

And understanding the ancient things can have modern scientific application. There is some science to the art of language, after all. For example, Seri call one sea turtle *moosni hant cooit*, or 'green turtle that descends', for its habit of seasonally hibernating on the sea floor, where the traditional fishermen were able to capture them. According to a 1976 *Science* article: 'We were skeptical when we first learned from the Seri Indians of Sonora, Mexico, that some Chelonia are partially buried on the sea floor during the colder months...however, the Seri have proved to be highly reliable informants.' And, of course, traditional knowledge of plants and herbs, as passed down through language, can have modern pharmaceutical application. For example, Australia's Aboriginal peoples traditionally used tea-tree and eucalyptus oils for healing, and these are now commonly used in modern medicines. (For more on this, see the article, 'Top 10 Aboriginal bush medicines', available on the *Australian Geographic* website. For global applications of traditional medicines, including treatments for malaria and asthma, see 'Traditional medicine for modern times: Facts and figures', available on the SciDevNet website.)

Language lost is a data loss of massive proportion, and often we have no cloud to back it up. This scares me enormously – and beyond the loss we suffer as humanity, imagine the emotional toll of losing your expressiveness and feeling like you let your elders and the spirits of past generations down. Tragic.

So beyond technology, what is required for cultural identity, as codified by language, to survive? Firstly, of course, we need a willingness to record and map the language. But secondly and equally importantly, we need a deep pride in the language itself. Without this pride – cross-generationally – a language will not endure, and certainly will not be rejuvenated. The pride cannot just be focused on the past, though, because languages are living things and can adapt with modern circumstance, as native tongues that add native descriptions of modern technologies like cars point out. For example, a Seri car muffler is called *ihíisaxim an hant yaait*, or 'into which the breathing descends'. But without the central ingredients of pride, cross-generational collaboration and technology, many of these minority languages will continue to disappear on the downward slope to linguistic monocultures. This feels like a terrible shame, given that the technology for cultural inheritance and codification exist. Darwinism will do the remaining work of sidelining lost languages to the dustbins of history, where we apply post-mortems and 'the benefit of hindsight' to 'wish' something had been done earlier. For sure, something could have been done earlier. Unfortunately, pride in identity and fluidity in technology adoption don't always go hand in hand. Trust me, I know from personal experience.

When do people change?

So, when do people change? Often, when it is too late – a very unsustainable proposition indeed. But when the rate of external change, whatever that may be, trumps the rate of internal change, adaptation and innovation, we find ourselves in dire straits. And while some may say, 'Live and let die', and bow to creative destruction or hail the idea of Digital Darwinism, even though I am a futurist, I also believe that there is a way for tradition to live on. And let us make no mistakes about it. Not all traditions are empowering or useful. Far from it. Whether it be female genital mutilation, the KKK, or orthodox beliefs about the flat world, traditions and unquestioned beliefs must be questioned and challenged. But, of course, in a post-Enlightenment age, and in the spirit of freedom of expression, dual obligation exists among listeners and speakers. Listeners must be tolerant and open to a diversity of ideas. This doesn't mean that we have to accept them, or that we must abstain from proving them wrong. If it is true that the best ideas and memes survive, a robust discourse will surely shine a light on mistaken beliefs or opinions. But I also believe an inherent obligation rests on those cultural flag-bearers who are at risk of extinction – an obligation to ensure that certain languages and modes of expression can live on. This often involves a certain level of openness to new forms of media, and reimagining the idea of identity. In other words, they need to listen to the call to adventure these new forms and ideas are offering. In this sense, Mum's curiosity for going on a journey together into the future was probably motivated as much by necessity and pure survival instinct as it was by any notion of self-actualisation. Whatever the motivation, the idea of cross-generational collaboration, and the prospect of a future for the family business beyond the third generation, the last acolyte, meant that Birgitta started dreaming of a better future for Georg Sörman.

CASE STUDY:
HOW HILTON'S DIGITAL APP CREATES SEAMLESS TRANSITIONS

Businesses – and especially digital businesses – have historically been good at solving human problems. Netflix makes it easy to stream your favourite movies and films, for example, while Instacart simplifies the process of shopping for groceries, Dropbox enables you to safely store, sync and share your files, and Podio makes collaboration and managing projects fun and easy. What makes these companies successful is their ability to not only identify and address real human problems, but also eliminate the friction points that slow the customer down, or impede the person from taking a certain action or completing a purchase. Friction doesn't necessarily stop your customers from doing something, but it negatively affects the customer experience and significantly reduces your chances of turning first-time customers into loyal followers.

Consider the following statistics, which highlight the importance of removing friction points and delivering empathetic customer experiences:

- Fifty-five per cent of consumers think that a frustrating experience on a website can negatively impact on their overall opinion of the brand (according to the Super Office blog '32 customer experience statistics you need to know for 2016').

- Poor service can cause up to 66 per cent of consumers to switch brand (according to the Huffington Post blog '50 important customer experience stats for business leaders').

- According to *Forbes*, 86 per cent of consumers are willing to pay a premium for a more satisfactory customer experience.

- According to American Express, nearly 80 per cent of consumers have not completed a purchase as a result of a poor service experience.

- Seventy-eight per cent of marketing professionals state that they use customer experience as a means to differentiate their brand from their competitors (according to Econsultancy).

- According to Oracle, nine out of ten customer experience decision-makers believe that a good experience is critical for their success.

A more analogue example of when you can experience friction is when you are travelling. It's a process that's often filled with small and big friction points. One friction point that may seem small, but can still have a bad effect on the overall experience of travel, is when you arrive at your hotel and have to wait in line before you are given access to your room. Of course, the reason you perceive this to be such a big issue is because you're likely tired after a long and exhausting day of journeying – but it's the hotel that cops all your negativity.

A study from Cornell University's Center for Hospitality Research suggests that the arrival process has a massive impact on overall guest satisfaction. The study, titled 'Lost in translation: Cross-country differences in hotel guest satisfaction', reports that when guests from the United States have to wait longer than five minutes, they reach a certain breaking point – and the effect of passing that point resulted in a 47 per cent decrease in guest satisfaction. The breaking point for guests from France, Germany, Italy and Spain occurred after waiting for fifteen minutes in line, while guests from the United Kingdom had a seventeen-minute tolerance and guests from Japan didn't pass their breaking point until they'd waited for thirty minutes.

One of our clients, the global hospitality company Hilton, has with their updated app Hilton HHonors turned this problem and friction point into an opportunity to seamlessly delight their guests. Hilton's app gives guests the opportunity to skip the line at the front desk and check in digitally via their smart phone. Additionally, the app enables hero guests to select both room type and exactly which room at the hotel they want to have. Other features include providing access to digital floor plans, the ability to purchase upgrades, make special requests and check-out. To sum up, Hilton gives their guests more insight and control over their hotel stay. The benefit for Hilton is that this app enables them to gather valuable data about their guests, which gives them an opportunity to optimise processes like cleaning, re-stocking of the minibar and much more. Moreover, they can use this data to build guest preferences, offer a better experience and get ideas for new services and offerings.

So what Hilton has done is replace an analogue touch point, the face-to-face interaction at the front desk, with a digital interface, the HHonors app. Apparently, digital solutions can sometimes be more empathetic than human service and can eliminate friction points in the analogue world. What's also worth keeping in mind in this context is that the customer doesn't think in terms of channels – he or she just wants to solve their problems and have a frictionless, or seamless, experience during their adventurous journey.

Ask yourself ...

To reduce or remove friction points, you need to have deep insight into why certain interactions can create a sense of frustration among your customers. For example, why does waiting in line for five minutes after arriving at the hotel irritate so many people? Small incidents like this might seem trivial, but they can significantly damage customers' overall experience and thus their attitude towards your brand. Think about the following in relation to your business:

1. Do you have any analogue touch points in your business that would deliver more value if they were to be digitised?

2. How you can you become better at gathering data throughout the customer journey? How would you use that data to improve your product and service offerings?

3. What can you do to make your customer experience unique and memorable? How can you use this experience to better differentiate your brand from your competitors?

STEP 3
HERO'S JOURNEY WHEEL FOR MAMMA SÖRMAN-NILSSON

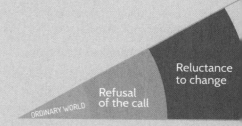

ORDINARY WORLD

Refusal of the call

Reluctance to change

Birgitta refuses to engage fully in critical analysis of the store and her brand, and then refuses to join Anders at Pitti Uomo in Florence in January 2014 to explore new brands and opportunities for Georg Sörman that are aligned to the new strategy. Birgitta refuses the call because 'somebody has to carry the milk' and manage the shop.

Refusal of the call

While on the surface the heroine may be curious about the future odyssey, at the current phase she still has fears and doubts that need to be surmounted. Deep personal doubts, crossed internal wires and introspective mistrust will ensue, relating to whether she is up for the challenge, and consequently the heroine will refuse the call somehow. The odyssey may seem too gargantuan and too difficult, and the comfort of the ordinary world may seem to trump the road of dragons and demons ahead. As this would also be our own human response, through this hesitation we are able to bond more closely with the reluctant heroine.

Here's how this stage looked for Luke in *Star Wars*:

- *Inner journey:* Refusal of the call – Luke refuses to follow Obi-Wan.

- *Outer journey:* Reluctance to change – Luke refuses the call because he feels obligated to stay and help his aunt and uncle on the farm.

And here's how it looked for Birgitta:

- *Inner journey:* Refusal of the call – Birgitta refuses to engage fully in critical analysis of the store and her brand, and then refuses to join Anders at Pitti Uomo in Florence in January 2014 to explore new brands and opportunities for Georg Sörman that are aligned to the new strategy.

- *Outer journey:* Reluctance to change – Birgitta refuses the call because 'somebody has to carry the milk' and manage the shop.

3: Refusal of the call

Being nostalgic is not strategic.

My heroine, my most reluctant mentee

As I cover in chapter 2, from late 2012 and through the first half of 2013, I worked on the first incarnation of my love letter to my mum – the thesis for my Global Executive MBA – which then evolved into the strategy we called 'Georg Sörman 100'. Through this process, Birgitta had begun to listen to the call to adventure this process represented. Her interest in the possibilities was piqued and she participated in forming future strategies. But then came the doubts.

At the time of the final delivery of the strategy in the early European autumn of 2013, the first red flag – that is, the first indication Birgitta was going to refuse the call – sprung up. Part of the thesis requirements for the Global EMBA was to deliver the strategy to the board, and to provide them with a copy of the presentation – which we did. Because of the tyranny of distance and the fact that I was working with some of our large corporate clients in Australia at the time, I had to do the presentation remotely. In preparation for this presentation, the task of the board (Mum and Dad) was to read through and reflect upon the strategy so they could then engage in a dialogue about the strategy findings during the presentation. The red flag sprung up when my cloud-based Box.com account showed that the 30-page pdf of the strategy hadn't been downloaded or read. Minor mishap I thought. They will probably read it later. Must have been a really busy week in the shop. Maybe a staff member had called in sick. Maybe the passionate tailor had been particularly detail-oriented about a stitch.

The love letter, seemingly, was still unread and unrequited. (My father did eventually read the strategy documentation, while Mum – previously an exchange student in Phoenix, Arizona, and a three-year resident of Canberra, Australia – claimed that her fluent English was insufficient for really getting into the text.) In the back of my mind, I was disappointed, and thought of different love languages to communicate the strategy. Maybe something more visual would work further down the line …?

After the initial lack of engagement during my remote presentation, in October 2013, while consulting with the CEO of a major Swedish listed retailer and his team in Stockholm, I grasped the opportunity to provide the Georg Sörman board, the executive team and the staff with another strategy workshop, and delivered the co-developed strategy paper in person. I thought maybe the digital interface hadn't been the ideal setting for a strategy presentation of this type and, in this setting, the participants were nodding along nicely. A sign of buy-in, perhaps? Buy-in was of course important, because earlier in 2013 my publisher had asked me to engage in a writing project to reformat my love letter to my mum into a book. The publisher and I were both enthusiastic about the future prospects of the cross-generational collaboration at Georg Sörman, and the co-developed strategy being put into action. We were, as it were, feeling very futurephile about the execution phase. In the European autumn of 2013, the resulting book – *Digilogue: how to win the digital minds and analogue hearts of tomorrow's customers* was released by Wiley. The marketplace and media took lovingly to the love letter. Interviews and articles in Sky News Business, *BRW, Australian Financial Review, Management Today*, Qantas Radio, *The Sydney Morning Herald, The Age*, The Drum, *Dagens Industri, CIO Magazine* and *CEO Magazine*, among others, followed. In the lead-up to the release, we did a sneak-peak launch of the book, symbolically and importantly, in Mum's shop in Kungsholmen, Stockholm, in July 2013.

This felt very important. Family and friends were there for support. Mum and Dad, and my brother, Gustaf, all had a chance to review, critique and provide feedback in the process of developing the love letter. They were all there during the Stockholm launch, which I came back to between jobs in Macau and Sydney. (And Stockholm is not on the way between those two points, for the geographically challenged.) The book now proudly adorns a special place on the 1930s wooden bench near the point of sale at Georg Sörman. In my parent's living room at home, it has a special place near their yellow Svenskt Tenn couch. But something is wrong. A second red flag. While media, business leaders, partners and clients have aligned themselves behind *Digilogue* after reading the love letter, the person it was meant for, Mum, still to this day hasn't read it. If you have ever written a love letter, no doubt you know that this hurts. You also know that when the solution to the recipient's woes is contained within that unread love letter, your love, contribution and help is both unrequited and unwanted.

Let me contrast this for a moment with one of our clients, Westpac, one of Australia's largest banks, and one that describes itself proudly as a '200-year-old start-up'. Westpac's general manager for retail, Gai McGrath, credits the ideas of *Digilogue* with the turnaround of the bank's retail division. In a 2015 article in the *Asia-Pacific Banking & Finance* magazine, she tells of how Westpac went from the bottom-placed retail bank of the four Australian majors to the leading main financial institution in customer satisfaction. In the interview, Gai paraphrases Mum's love letter by referring to 'global futurist Anders Sörman-Nilsson who said, "The key thing for companies tomorrow is to balance a digital mind with an analogue heart". That is core to Westpac's strategy of helping its customers to prosper and grow.' If they were good enough for Westpac Retail, I had been hoping that the merits of the Georg Sörman 100 idea would be good enough for my heroine.

In the summer of 2013, in association with our book launch in Mum's shop, I sat down with Mum and we had a tete-a-tete about how we would collaborate together. I had long had a dream of moving my business to New York and, at the time, my girlfriend, Zhenya, was living in Manhattan and I had had in-depth conversations with immigration lawyers about heading over to the Big Apple. But something was gnawing at me. I knew that the ideas in that love letter deserved to be implemented and put into practice. On the ground. In Stockholm, not from New York (at least not yet). My mum reiterated her curiosity and gratefulness that I was re-considering my move to New York, and that basing myself in Stockholm was an option.

All of a sudden, it became a very viable option. Zhenya and I split up (caused by the tyranny of distance and a few other Russo–Swedish conflicts), and I decided to set up a new base in Sweden. There was work to be done and, according to the strategy we were building, the mission for the family was to restore Georg Sörman to its glory days and stage a renaissance for the business, not unlike the rebranding exercise that Languedoc-Roussillon (covered in chapter 1) has to go through. We wanted to go back to the start, and reignite the design and customer empathy elements of the Swedish Grace period, when Georg Sörman first came into being. As a result, we had to reignite our *Fingerspitzengefühl* – our intuitive flair, or instinct – and our curation of our collection.

The strategy consisted of restoring glory to a faded brand, and clawing back our position as a premium brand relevant for both a younger and an older silhouette, cross-generationally. The place to travel outside of Mum's ordinary world into an extraordinary, international world of savoir faire? Pitti Uomo – the world's pre-eminent twice-yearly sartorial menswear fair held (fittingly) in the capital of the Renaissance, Florence. The renaissance for Georg Sörman would begin in the epicentre of *the* Renaissance. We would make a dedicated effort to start new collaborations, work with genuine family businesses with great provenance, and help instil a new confidence in the brand of Georg Sörman. I started sowing the seeds of making this journey in the European summer of 2013, but come January 2014, Mum refused to join me in Florence, stating that 'somebody has to carry the milk', meaning someone has to work 'in' the business.

Saying 'yes' but doing 'no'

Maybe I shouldn't be surprised by this initial refusal of the call to adventure. There was a precedent, an earlier red flag. We grew up in a household where Mum smoked, and Dad occasionally joined her. As kids do (evidently still to this day), we worried about the health and future prospects of our parents. So we used to pester our parents to give up smoking and their tobacco habits altogether (Dad, like most military men in Sweden up till the 1990s, was a long-time user of *snus*, Swedish chewing tobacco). I remember both my brother and I being convinced that our parents' habits would kill them. As a result, we staged fear-based PR campaigns and shed lots of tears in our manipulative attempts to drive changed behaviours. We used all the health information at our disposal in the early 1990s, believing that surely an evidence-based approach would work. Nope. So we used the money angle – surely the economically rational angle would work. Nope. We pointed towards our beloved Grandma Ingrid, who suffered through her life because of her 50-year relationship with cigarettes and her bouts with cancer. Finally, in the mid 1990s, Dad caved in and changed. He made a New Year resolution and had the strength of character to stick to it. Kudos and respect, Dad. Mum made the same resolution at the same time, and Gustaf and I were so relieved. Finally, our parents would lead healthier lives and so hopefully be with us for a long time.

While they both said yes, however, my parents didn't both 'do yes'. My mum did 'no'. The head nodded yes, but deep inside, she hadn't yet bought into the behavioural change. Of course, I wasn't initially aware of this. But I remember vividly the day when my trusting bubble was burst. I came back from school in Stockholm, and went to the bathroom. I did what us men do, and then reached for the flush, just like my mum must have done earlier that morning, and as I did, I noticed the incriminating evidence – two yellowing, bleak Marlboro Light cigarette buds in a melange of uric acid. I didn't flush. This was evidence that she had said yes, but had done no.

Of course, my mother is far from the only person to say yes but do no. In 2006, Kodak released an internal video called 'Winds of Change'. Don't worry, I'm not about to launch into a full analysis of Kodak's failure to digitally transform in the face of digital disruption. That analysis was done in *Digilogue*. But one thing bears mentioning here. And that is this same evidence of saying yes, but doing no. This internal video prepared not long before the release of the first iPhone, and later released by Chief Marketing Officer Jeffrey Hayzlett to the public, spoke of the things that Kodak was going to do. The video is surprisingly futuristic as it takes us through the future of photography – we hear about shareability, facial recognition, biometrics and metaknowledge. As smart phones, Instagram, Facebook, SnapChat and GoPro have become commonplace, we realise that Kodak's internal communications team really knew what was going on. They saw the future.

In the video, the key message, delivered in a self-deprecating and humorous manner, is that 'Kodak's back'. (If you'd like to see the video, you can check it out on YouTube – just search 'Kodak winds of change'.) Now, we all know it didn't quite work out that way, but if you enjoy schadenfreude, check it out anyway. And I am sure, just like we have heard of a celebrity or two trying to get their 'accidental' home porn movies removed from the internet, Kodak's executives are likely also wishing that some embarrassing moments could be eternally forgotten in the digital era. But no. This digital video will endure. In the extraordinary world of the internet, things have a capacity to live on – forever. Because, while we were promised by the video that 'By God, you were a Kodak moment once, and by God you will be one again. Only this time it will be digital!', we are still left hanging. Kodak was invested in the past, and despite seemingly saying yes to the future in this video, the executives kept doing no. Culture, as we know, eats strategy for breakfast. And unless there is a genuine willingness to say yes, and do yes to transformation, change management programs are a fool's errand.

And so it was with my mother and her smoking. In the meantime, our Grandma Ingrid's health kept deteriorating, and between the late 1990s and early 2000s she developed cancer, leg wounds and eventually chronic obstructive pulmonary disease. Grandma Ingrid gave up smoking on the advice of the medical doctors – because it was a case of life or death. For Grandma, however, it was too late. Her body wasn't able to recover fully, and eventually she passed away in 2006 with a silent last gasp for air. For my mum, it wasn't until she moved with our family to Australia in 1997 and so shifted contexts, and saw the agony that Ingrid experienced with her leg wounds, that she gave up smoking. The message from the future, which Ingrid sadly broadcast to her daughter, was the straw that broke the camel's back (no cigarette pun intended). As a family, we are incredibly grateful that our mum eventually made the change. When it comes to my mum's business survival, I knew she also needed to make a change before it was too late, like it was with Grandma Ingrid.

Being nostalgic is not the same as being strategic

I fundamentally and at my core believe that the future is the promised land of milk and honey for the ones who are curious, agile in spirit and flexible in mind. I equally believe the future is purgatory for the lazy, the ignorant and the complacent. Change doesn't care whether we like it or not, and it will always happen without our permission. And when the rate of external change and upheaval trumps the rate of internal adaptation and agility, any brand, including my mum's and dad's, will find itself in deep troubles. The examination and analysis of the business we engaged in through 2012 had shown that Mum's business model was perfectly prepared for a world that no longer existed. So I was dumbfounded as she refused the call to adventure and action. If what you are doing is clearly not working, why keep on doing it? Maybe I am a simpleton, but my approach has always been that if what you are doing isn't getting you results, change your approach. Just being nostalgic certainly isn't the same as being strategic.

This makes me reflect on the futurephobia and resistance I consistently came up against with my parents as we tried to implement new strategies at Georg Sörman. I often describe the awkward intergenerational dance with my parents as a case of taking two steps forward, one step backward – and then one step forward, two steps backward. While I am not a psychologist, a joke about psychologists and light bulbs is pertinent here. The question goes, 'How many psychologists does it take to change a light bulb?' With the answer being, 'Only one but the light bulb has got to want to change'. In other words, again, you can lead a horse to water but you cannot force it to drink.

On the other hand, we have all experienced times in our lives when people we love have engaged in self-sabotaging, cyclical behaviour, and even when we offer them a new approach, we see them reverting to the behaviour they know, often hoping for a different result. While it is tempting to pull out a saying like, 'The definition of insanity is doing the same thing over and over again and expecting a different result' (which happens to be a falsity and, according to *Psychologist Today*, may be the 'dumbest thing a smart person has ever said') in our family contexts, I do believe when we are trying to help loved ones break out of perseverating behaviours we must ask ourselves whether the person actually wants our help. According to dictionary.com, perseveration, as opposed to noble perseverance, is the 'pathological, persistent repetition of a word, gesture or act'. Perseverance, on the other hand, is the 'steady persistence in a course of action in spite of difficulties, obstacles or discouragement', according to the same source. The latter has a sense of stoicism to it. The former is, according to *Psychology Today*, a troubling issue needing clinical attention. While I am not fit to make such a diagnosis, I have learnt that no matter how frustrating it is for a change agent to observe alleged perseverating behaviours and to provide change strategies, unless the light bulb wants to change, your efforts will be in vain. So far, my perseverance simply hadn't been able to cure the perseveration.

Let me give you another illustration of this. As a long-time believer and practitioner of the inbound methodology of marketing (and avid HubSpotter), I am convinced (and the evidence backs me and other inbound strategists up) that great content, in context, helps any brand build a loyal tribe of followers who opt-in to listen to your message. This approach is sustainable, educational, generous and engaging, and drives pride among the brand's staff and clients. For Georg Sörman, digital and social media have always been a major part of the renaissance of the brand. And as marketing innovators, one of my companies – Thinque Digital – has always investigated ways of personalising messages that are of interest to particular psychographic niches. What is psychographics? Psychographics – as opposed to demographics, which is the study of statistical data relating to the population and particular groups – is the study and classification of people according to their attitudes, aspirations and other psychological criteria. This is an incredibly personal and human approach to marketing, because messages are only sent to those who are already interested in what you have to say. Facebook is an example of a platform that enables this high level of targeting. And on behalf of Georg Sörman, Thinque Digital, as its outsourced marketing and branding agency, has been using Facebook since 2013 to build Georg Sörman's renaissance brand and connect with new client pools who may be interested in our brand story. The statistics show us that this is an economical and wise investment as we have amplified social conversations but, importantly, also converted these social conversations into commercial conversations, and new business for Georg Sörman. But my technophobic mother is at times fact-resistant. So I alerted Mum to a personal connection to try to awaken her interest in Facebook. If the data doesn't convince, try speaking to the heart, right?

First let me now give you some background to the personal connection. In 1969, Birgitta was an exchange student in Phoenix, Arizona. Based on her stories – involving parties, a first boyfriend, weird host families and life-long friends – it seems like my mum had a great time. In fact, during my trips to the United States I keep in regular contact with Mum's host families and friends, and their children, who tend to be around my age. This is kind of nice for (positive) nostalgic reasons. There are, however, some friends who Mum lost touch with. People move, change address, split up, change surnames, or simply don't respond to analogue letters. Or, in other extreme cases, positive intent to stay in contact goes by the wayside because of fires. Let me explain. In the late 1970s, before I was even born, Mum received a Christmas card from Cheri, one of her best friends from her days in Phoenix. Back in those days, you used to pull the Christmas card from the envelope it was stuffed in and if you wanted to continue the correspondence, you had to manually copy the return address on your own fresh envelope, and then stuff a card or other paper into it, so that the cycle could be continued at the other end. In Sweden, we have a social proof tradition of taking all received Christmas cards and placing them above our mandatory open fireplace mantles. So, when Mum got home from work and saw Cheri's lovely Christmas card, she read it and allegedly felt an urge to respond immediately by writing a nice letter back in front of the cosy open fireplace. The only problem was that my dad had used the envelope with the return address to ignite the fire. That was not the only fire he ignited that Christmas. For thirty-eight years, Mum has been upset with Dad for burning the return address, and getting in the way of her positive intent to write back to Cheri.

Enter Facebook – which Mum (until May 2016) refused to use because she doesn't have time for it, and she prefers old-school methods of communication from the good old days when communications were human and easier. Please note a sarcastic tone. In 2015, my Facebook Business page (make sure you subscribe to www.facebook.com/thinquetank when you get a chance) received a message from a Cheri R, asking me whether my mother was Birgitta Marie Sörman and whether she had lived in Arizona in high school. She also let me know she thought she had met me in Massachusetts when I was a baby.

I responded to this message (knowing full well Mum would never respond to Cheri via Facebook, but thinking maybe she still wanted to write that unsent letter), confirming Birgitta was indeed my mother and that I would let her know Cheri had been in touch.

Cheri responded a few short hours later with the following (reproduced as originally typed):

That would be great. You were a little guy when you came and visited with us in MA. My daughter's name is Birgitta Marie after your wonderful Mom. I love seeing her pictures and you young men as well. I see you are in a very interesting field.

My mum's full name is Birgitta Marie Sörman-Nilsson. While Mum tells fond tales of how the Arizonians used to call her 'bird-shitter', which I guess has some phonetic similarities to her name's Americanisation, here at least was one of her friends who admired Mum so much that she named her first-born daughter after her. Mum must have made a good impression! And luckily, Cheri clearly wasn't too pissed off with the fact that Mum never responded to that Christmas card thirty-eight years ago (while Dad had been bearing the brunt of Mum's rage for the same period of time for igniting that birch wood log with an airmail stamped envelope). So, forgive me for getting a little excited about this digital reunion.

Around this time, I tell Dad about what has happened on Facebook, and because he is Facebook literate (with a strong digital immigrant accent, mind you), he understood the connotations – and that no longer was there any excuse for Mum to hold a grudge against him. Armed with this good news, we approach Mum with our excitement. Mum's reaction was a bit unexpected and somewhat underwhelming. She said she still had no physical address for Cheri, and asked whether Cheri could perhaps reach out via email like normal people do (because Facebook was a 'new' media that Mum had been hoping she wouldn't have to learn before retiring from the business world). At the time of writing (months after the digital, semi-magical near-reunion), Mum has still not responded to Cheri, despite multiple attempts by Cheri to reach out via my personal and business Facebook pages and my father's personal page. When I asked Mum why she hadn't responded, despite a multitude of communication channel opportunities, she answered that she'd been too busy.

To Mum, the digital world is dehumanised. While it is not entirely worthless, to her mind it is certainly worth *less* than the real, or ordinary, world that she knows so well. This is despite the evidence that the solutions to many of her woes around digital disruption might actually lie within digital technology. One example of these possible solutions is the VIP nights for Georg Sörman clients that Thinque Digital has been marketing and organising for the brand. These are semi-annual events when core VIP clients get invited to a day of entertainment, food and nibbles, and shopping. In October 2015, for instance, we organised an omnichannel campaign with handwritten letters, a beautifully printed invite, a tailored website, landing pages and pre-scheduled autoresponders courtesy of our technology platforms HubSpot, MailChimp and Unbounce, as well as in-store jazz, gourmet sausages and craft beer tastings – suitable for the Autumn lifestyle collection in Sweden being showcased. At the time, our co-curation revenue was up 47 per cent compared to 2014 – a nice success. The combination of omnichannel marketing, a great cross-generational musical event and psychographic messaging in our communications led to a fantastic success – through smarter communications that were deliberately on brand. And as we say in Sweden, the 'results came as a letter in the post', meaning the results correlated directly to the smart investment.

Beyond that, a curious and insightful event happened in the lead-up to this particular VIP day: a Baby Boomer lady had come in a few weeks prior to the event and photographed clothing in the store. My mum, ever on alert to thieves and people price-comparing in real-time, didn't like what she saw, and told the story to the family. It was left at that. A few weeks later at the VIP event, a man came up to one of Mum's sales associates and showed her pictures of twelve items of clothing, including Barbour jackets, Oscar Jacobson slacks, Inis Meáin jumpers and Eton shirts that his wife had photographed for him prior to the event in the store. He bought everything that she had recommended for him. His wife – of course – was the same lady who Mum had complained about. Maybe we shouldn't be so fast to judge new consumer behaviour enabled by technology.

Reluctant heroines may need a little nudge

On a trip to the Netherlands to consult with one of our clients, ABN-Amro Bank, I stopped at the urinals at Schiphol Airport, as I usually do after a long intercontinental flight. As I approached the urinals and did what men do, I noticed that a fly was sitting on the wall of the urinal. *Easy target*, I thought. As I hit the bullseye, I realised that the fly was not a real fly, but rather painted on. I had been nudged into a new focused behaviour – a behaviour that benefitted my conscience, the airport, and the cleaning staff. Many other users of these toilets have been similarly nudged, and because of this nudge, cleaning costs have dramatically fallen (by as much as 80 per cent), and cleanliness and general care of the bathrooms has improved. According to Wikipedia, 'nudge theory' holds that positive reinforcement and indirect suggestions to try to achieve non-forced compliance can influence the motives, incentives and decision-making of groups and individuals at least as effectively as – if not more than – direct instruction, legislation or enforcement. It is an important concept in behavioural science, political theory and economics. And inspired by this concept, I have spent three years trying to nudge my mentee, and this book's heroine, Birgitta, into behaviours that will help her thrive in a disruptive future. But, yes, 'as a letter in the post', there has been a regular reluctance to fulfil the journey of adventure.

The antidote to futurephobia?

If you listen to the news, you'd think that we – you, me, the species, our planet – are headed straight for disaster. The volatility of the share market, Brexit, jobless recoveries, terrorist attacks, religious fundamentalism, extinction, robots taking our jobs, immigrants challenging some people's sense of national identity, the latest PISA education scores, ADHD, diabetes, the divorce rate, civil war, global warming, polar bears, ebola, cybercrime, starvation, school shootings, racist attacks, the Kardashians. Yes, it is a scary world. Anything from the preceding list will definitely raise your blood pressure during the 17.30 news. You'd be forgiven for thinking that Armageddon is nigh. You'd also be forgiven for thinking that now is not the 'good old days', and that the future will be even worse. If you listen to the short news and the drama. Read the clickable news items and the headlines that spike adrenaline. The news stories that give you a rush of blood to the head. That trigger your lizard brain, and fear-based reactions. If you do this, it's very tempting to become a futurephobe.

Media contains a lot of noise, and very little signal. And as people we tend to get carried away by the noise – we don't see the forest for the trees, as it were. We focus on the short news, and of course this is in the interest of the media, because they are reliant on clicks, interest, engagement and reactivity. However, the effect of these stimuli is to stupefy us, to paralyse us, and diminish our cognition that the long news is usually good news. (We will return to this idea of the long news later.)

For the moment, let us explore this idea of 'futurephobia', because it is seemingly all around us at the moment. But let us start by acknowledging that this term is not strictly a scientific term for a known phobia (I made it up). As Wikipedia tells us, a phobia is a type of anxiety disorder, usually defined as a persistent fear of an object or situation that the sufferer goes to great lengths in avoiding, typically disproportional to the actual danger posed, often being recognised as irrational. Rather, let me use this term in a pop-psychology fashion, for those people who seemingly have a misplaced fear about the future, which in turn hampers their actions in the present, and results in them living their lives looking through the rear-view mirror of nostalgia. The definition of nostalgia, on the other hand, from dictionary. com is that it is 'a wistful desire to return in thought or in fact to a former time in one's life, to one's home or homeland, or to one's family and friends; a sentimental yearning for the happiness of a former place or time'. Futurephobia, in the way we will use it for the purpose of this book, is also distinct from 'chronophobia' – the fear of time – which is, in fact, a diagnosed phobia. In her book *Chronophobia: On Time in the Art of the 1960s*, Pamela Lee describes chronophobia as 'an experience of unease and anxiety about time, a feeling that events are moving too fast and are thus hard to make sense of'. This is an experience you can perhaps relate to. Have you got kids? Are they growing up too quickly? Are you an octogenarian? Do you feel like more of your life is behind you than in front of you? Perhaps you're a technophobe? Is the world of digital devices spinning you out? I am not trying to diagnose you here; rather, I am just saying we probably have all had an experience of feeling like time is moving too fast at times.

A chronophobe, if you'll indulge me further, is distinct from a 'chronomentrophobe', which is someone who has an irrational fear of clocks and watches. This would not be a popular condition for Swiss timepiece manufacturers, in other words. A Disney version of a chronophobe would be kind of like Captain Hook, who was constantly tormented by Tick-Tock the Crocodile, who had swallowed an alarm clock and would torment Hook, seeking his second, delicious arm. Luckily for Hook, his own paranoia, combined with the constant ticking in the crocodile, would alert him to the impending danger of potential future encounters. So, in other words, Hook might have well been a 'chronomentrophobe', or at least had a Pavlovian response to the ticking stimulus.

Nostalgia and Ostalgia

The 2003 movie *Good Bye, Lenin!* provides us with a good example of resisting the future. The narrative is set in East Berlin around the time of the fall of the Berlin Wall. It is a tragicomic film that focuses on a family's efforts not to upset the family matriarch, an ardent supporter of East Germany's ruling Socialist Unity Party of Germany who suffers a heart attack and lapses into a coma prior to the fall of the wall. Alex (played by Daniel Bruehl) lives with his sister, Ariane (Maria Simon), his mother, Christiane (Katrin Saß), and Ariane's infant daughter, Paula. During Christiane's coma, the wall falls, Erich Honecker resigns from office, the East German police start to lose their power, and Western norms and capitalism infiltrate East Berlin. After an eight-month coma, Christiane awakes, but her doctor warns the family that she is severely weakened and that sudden news of the recent disruptive events might cause another, possibly fatal, heart attack. As a result, the family decides to carry out a well-meaning deception that nothing has changed, and to retain the 'Ostalgia' (which was one of the inspirations for the film and is a fusion of 'Ost', German for east, and 'nostalgia'). They retro-fit their apartment with drab East German interiors to sooth their mum's delusion, throw out their new Western clothes in favour of their old Eastern garb, and repackage new Western food in old East German jars.

Their deception plan is successful, but becomes more complex with the continuing changes, such as the unveiling of a huge Coca-Cola sign outside their mother's window, and with Christiane's wish to watch television, which results in Alex editing old East German propaganda newscasts that he plays from a VCR in a neighbouring room to bring his mum the 'latest' news. Things become even more complicated as Christiane regains strength and ventures outside the apartment block and sees her neighbours throwing away their old Eastern furniture. Alex tries lovingly to cover up these developments by recruiting a taxi driver who he believes looks like the famous Sigmund Jähn – a German astronaut and pilot who in 1978 became the first German to fly in space as part of the Soviet Union's Interkosmos program – to say that he is the new leader of East Germany and will be opening the borders to West German refugees. *The movie is a heartening account of a son's attempts to look after what he believes is his mum's best interests.* It is also a powerful reminder that we cannot hide away from the present or the future, and that being nostalgic is not very strategic in a world of constant change and upheaval. And that, perhaps, *disruption is only really disruptive if we are not mentally adaptive.* And yet around the world, wherever we turn, we meet people who long for the 'good old days', which is a fact-resistant way of viewing present reality and future developments. This nostalgia is also a strong reason these sorts of people refuse the call to adventure when it is offered to them.

It's not that I am an optimist. I am factivist. And while I am as much of a romantic as much as the next Bollywood tragic, nostalgia, or 'Ostalgia' in the case of Germany, doesn't provide me any comfort for creating better futures. The reunification of Germany made a strong impression on me as a youth, and I remember the excitement we, as young people, felt at the time. As a student from 1988 of the Deutsche Schule (German School) Stockholm, my classmates and I vividly lived through the end of the Cold War through our immersion in this microcosm of Germany at Karlavägen in my native city. I recall the bomb threats, the security guards, and the general sense of change that swept through the school in the late 1980s and early 1990s. My school class included children and friends from both sides of the wall, both sides of the Iron Curtain in Europe. I grew up with refugees from Latvia (the children of anti-Soviet activists), the kids of Polish refugees and Eastern bloc capitalists (read into that whatever you like), the offspring of alleged Stasi (East German secret police) deserters, as well as next-generation West German car magnates. In a class of 27 I was one of only two kids who had two Swedish parents. We read news reports of East German families smuggling their children in rolled up carpets across the border into West Germany, and my first girlfriend, Therese, had lived at the Swedish Embassy in Berlin during the divided era, telling me vivid tales of life in Berlin from the mid-1980s. The sense of joy and predestination was strong within us as we watched the Berlin Wall come down, and as the reunification of families and a nation unfolded in front of our young, innocent eyes. We had a hunch, a strong sense, an intuition, that the past was not good, and was instead divisive, backward – even evil – and that the future, guided by integrative thinking, promised something better.

Everywhere around us we felt like the future was in the air. And we knew, instinctively, with more future ahead of us than time behind us, that what had just occurred was of historical significance, and that this momentous event was laying the groundwork for a better future. Of course, change always has winners and losers. And the incumbents who prefer the status quo, who refuse the call to adventure, have the most to lose. The winners are those who are curious and ambitious, who are thirsty, who have an appetite for the future. It is not just a matter of being optimistic or pessimistic. How we view the future also comes down to our level of objectivity and whether we are factivists or fact-resistant. (For further proof on how the future is better than the past – and why we all need to be futurephiles – see figure 3.1, and 3.2, overleaf.)

Figure 3.1: child mortality* by world region

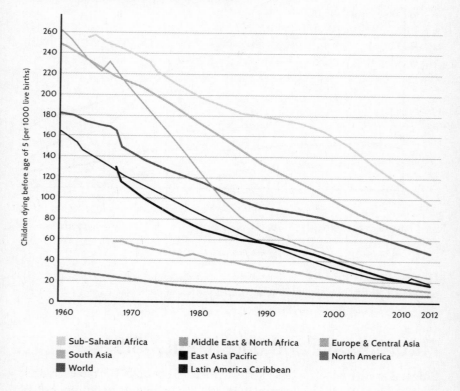

* Children dying before the age of 5, per 1000 live births.

Source: World Development Indicators, The World Bank

Figure 3.2: living in absolute poverty

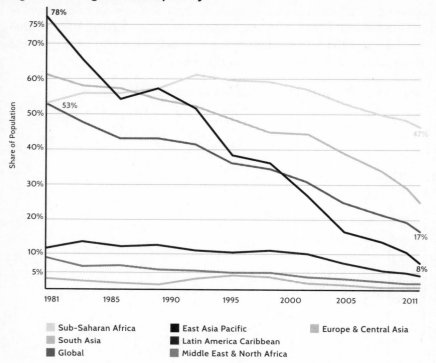

Sub-Saharan Africa	East Asia Pacific	Europe & Central Asia
South Asia	Latin America Caribbean	
Global	Middle East & North Africa	

*The absolute poverty is defined as living with less than $1.25/per day. This is measured by adjusting for pricechange over time and for price differences between countries (PPP adjustment).

Source: WDI Poverty Headcount, The World Bank

Futurephobia and Daesh/ISIL/ISIS

Progress and development is too much for some people. The radical Islamic death cult of Daesh belongs squarely in the category of futurephobes. Inspired by misplaced seventh-century ideas of the Caliphate, their barbaric ways have been partly enabled, ironically, by modern weaponry and digital media. In a similar vein to people who voted for Brexit, the world has moved too quickly and in a direction they don't like. Daesh, also called ISIL or ISIS, is not merely a bunch of psychopaths who throw homosexuals from towers, stone non-believers to death, and film executions of burning journalists. According to Graeme Wood in the article 'What ISIS really want' from *The Atlantic*, it is a 'group with carefully considered beliefs, amongst them that it is a key agent of the coming apocalypse'. Wood goes on to say we can gather that

...Its religious views make it constitutionally incapable of certain types of change, even if that change might ensure its survival; and that it considers itself a harbinger of – and headline player in – the imminent end of the world.

This group aims for the realisation of a dystopian alternative reality where they wield power over a population almost as big as Sweden's. Its nature is medieval religious, and its philosophy highly regressive. In his article, Wood continues that '...in fact, much of what the group does looks nonsensical except in light of a sincere, carefully considered commitment to returning civilization to a seventh-century legal environment, and ultimately to bringing about the apocalypse'. Truth is that the Islamic State is Islamic. Some pundits in their political correctness would doubt that this barbarian crew is religious, but, as Wood notes, they often literally follow a historic text, and most major decisions and law promulgated by the Islamic State follow what it calls 'Prophetic methodology', which means applying the prophecy and example of Muhammad, in 'punctilious detail'. As a result Western leaders like Major General Michael Nagata, the Special Operations commander for the United States in the Middle East, concludes that 'we have not defeated the idea...we don't even understand the idea'.

Innovations and modernity flies in the face of these 'pious forefathers' (who are adherents of Salafism, after the Arabic *al salaf al salih*, meaning exactly 'pious forefathers'). Today's versions of extremist Sunnis model themselves on the prophet and his early crew when it comes to all behaviour. As a result, they have made proclamations of *takfir*, which is an edict against people who they view as apostates because of their sins. Behaviours like selling alcohol, wearing Western clothes, shaving one's beard or voting in an election all qualify one for apostasy, and consequently death, which purifies the world according to the Islamic State. As I have committed three of the above sins, I am an apostate. Equally though, Shiites are also apostates in the eyes of these Sunnis, because they are an innovation on the origins of Prophet's teachings, and to innovate on the Koran is to deny its initial, supposed seamlessness (as in supposed perfection). Talk about futurephobia. Wood points out that this means that 200 million Shia Muslims are thus marked for death by the Islamic State, as is any willing Muslim participant in democratic elections, because this stands in contrast to laws made by Allah.

George Orwell once said about fascism in Nazi Germany, that it is:

> Psychologically far sounder than any hedonistic conception of life … Whereas Socialism, and even capitalism in a more grudging way, have said to people 'I offer you a good time', Hitler has said to them 'I offer you struggle, danger, and death', and as a result a whole nation flings itself at his feet … We ought not to underestimate its emotional appeal.

Many Islamists have answered the call to this novel version of preposterous adventure, to the great dismay of the thousands of fellow Muslims and other citizens around the world who have innocently lost their lives to pave the way for the Islamic State's futurephobic vision of apocalypse (which means the end of time as we know it). Futurephobia – whether in the sense of ISIS' attempt to bring us a seventh-century caliphate, 'Ostalgics' wanting a return to the 'magnificence' of the Iron Curtain, or business leaders espousing that 'we have always done it this way' – denies the virtues of futurephilia, development and innovation. Worse, futurephobia is blatantly dangerous, for the proponents, the people willing to listen and the broader world. Thus, it is critical to differentiate between positive tradition, and mere mouldy remnants or leftovers. Train your critical mind, and have faith in developing a future that is better than the present, as well as the past. Every day you create the evidence that the future can be a better place. You decide, just like my mum, every day, whether you want to wake up a futurephobe or a futurephile.

The real antidote to futurephobia — the long view

Plenty of good news is available. If we look beyond the trees we can see a magnificent, enchanted forest of possibilities. We don't have to be stuck in the woods if we don't want to. Yet most people chose to live in fear. I am guilty of this, too, on occasion. For example, I live on the magnificent Pittwater on Sydney's Northern Beaches. It is an enchanted place and, courtesy of the fact that I live in Ku-ring-gai Chase National Park, the wildlife is rich. We have our own jetty and, in summer, I use it to jump in for a dip each morning. I love it. It's like the best of the Swedish summer and the Stockholm archipelago, but for nine months of the year, courtesy of the Australian climate. In Sweden, at my parents' house outside of Stockholm, I like to spend my days in the water at Lake Malaren, true to my Piscean nature. It's aquatic bliss. And no sea creatures to think about.

So now, at Elvina Bay, I have the chance to have extended 'Swedish summers' (which are only a few, intense weeks in length), in a place that is reminiscent of my Swedish youth's summer holidays. Yet my cousin Daniel and my brother, Gustaf, love to alert me to the dangers of Australian wildlife. They like to remind me of the presence of bull sharks in my local waters. Do you think this, combined with a certain Steven Spielberg soundtrack, is a spoiler? You bet. Yet, it's statistically irrational, right? Fewer people die each year globally as a result of shark attacks than from bee stings, champagne corks, cows and falling out of bed (individually, not combined). Yet, I am not as relaxed in the water as I would be in Stockholm. Despite the data.

The data does show us, however, if we step back for a moment, that we are living in historically great times, and that things, on balance, are likely to get even better, by many measures. A directional movement indicates that the future will be much better than the past for a great proportion of people in the world. My Swedish colleague, Dr Hans Rosling, does a fantastic job around the world helping people move away from being futurephobes to being futurephiles by pointing to and visualising data. And the data today shows that, for example, poverty in the United States has halved in the last twenty years, that more girls go to school now (and stay for longer) than at any time in history internationally, that childhood mortality is at a historical low, our life expectancy is higher than it has ever been, and that despite the spikes in media interest (and my thoughts, of course, go out to the victims and their families of woeful terrorist attacks) fewer people are dying in international or civil conflict than at any time during the twentieth century (see figure 3.3).

Figure 3.3: number of deaths from conflict, 1940s to present day

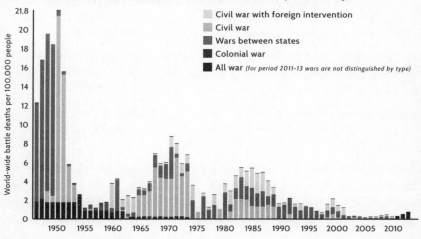

Source: Our World In Data by Max Roser

But if we are constantly living in the moment, tuning in to the short and sensationalised news each night, getting caught up in quarterly reports and profit warnings, and following the short-termism of democratic election cycles, our vision is likely to get distorted, and this can prevent us from implementing better, long-term decision-making. We need to zoom out, and look at data from a longer term perspective. We need to embrace the 'long now', on our individual hero's journeys into the future.

The essence of futurephilia is a love for the future. A belief that things can be better tomorrow, and that decisions today can create more fruitful futures. I am a proud futurephile. And as such I am a member of a foundation called the Long Now Foundation. This organisation seeks to create a counterbalance to what it believes is a 'faster/cheaper' mindset, and to promote 'slower/better' thinking. The Long Now Foundation takes a long-term perspective, into the next 10 000 years, and has abandoned four-digit dates in favour of five-digit dates to address long-term challenges and opportunities. Try this on for a moment. What would happen if you were able to focus twenty, forty, 125 or 1000 years into the future? How would this affect your decisions? On the foundation's website, Stewart Brand, one of the founders of the movement, has the following to say about the inspiration behind the Long Now:

> Civilization is revving itself into a pathologically short attention span. The trend might be coming from the acceleration of technology, the short-horizon perspective of market-driven economics, the next-election perspective of democracies, or the distractions of personal multi-tasking. All are on the increase. Some sort of balancing corrective to the short-sightedness is needed – some mechanism or myth which encourages the long view and the taking of long-term responsibility, where 'long-term' is measured at least in centuries. Long Now proposes both a mechanism and a myth.

On the website, co-founder Danny Hillis also reflects on what he calls 'an ever-shortening future' proposing a new clock, one that moves people's focus beyond this ever-shortening future:

> I would like to propose a large (think Stonehenge) mechanical clock, powered by seasonal temperature changes. It ticks once a year, bongs once a century, and the cuckoo comes out every millennium.

Unlike Captain Hook, the members of the Long Now foundation are not chronomentrophobes. Their project to build the Clock of the Long Now consists of building a timepiece that will operate without human interference for ten millennia. The first prototype of the clock began working on 31 December 1999, just in time to display the transition to the year 2000 – or to show the date change from 01999 to 02000. Since then, the two-metre prototype has been on display at the Science Museum in London, and the first full-scale prototype is being funded by

Jeff Bezos and located on Bezos' land in Texas. The purpose of the clock, in the words of Stewart Brand, is to 'embody deep time' for people, reframing the way people think in the same way as seeing photographs of the Earth taken from space helped people change the way they thought about the environment.

On the death of my grandfather Per, of Georg Sörman fame, in 2003, my grandmother gave me a gift. It was my grandfather's gold Movado watch. A beautiful Swiss timepiece. For me this watch signifies something enduring, something timeless. A longer term perspective. Cross-generational heritage. For me it also signified that some day, the baton of restoring the brand Georg Sörman to its former glory would be in my (and my mother's) hands (or at least on the wrist). My grandmother had one complaint, though. And the complaint was with my grandfather. Per liked wearing this watch on special occasions in the latter stages of his life (and when the downward spiral of business fortunes had begun). So, by the time I inherited this watch, it was neither accurate nor (when it actually did wind up), would it keep running for very long.

Since then, to restore it to working condition (and probably imbuing the mechanics and engineering of the Movado's movement with a deep business symbolism) I have been on a search globally for the missing piece that led to its mechanical breakdown. Given that the watch is from the 1950s, suffice to say it has been an odyssey to find this missing piece – a 90M movement/setting lever – which seemed to have disappeared from the archives and tool sheds of horologists and watchmakers in Europe and Australia. It wasn't until December 2015 that I managed to find a watchmaker who was able to fix the issue at the core of the watch. As a horophile, I am pleased to say that the mechanics of the timepiece are now working again. And this timepiece, mentally, emotionally and symbolically, connects me with my past, present and future. And in this sense, I believe the project of the 10 000 Year Watch, with a cuckoo that comes out every millennium, can hopefully make an impact on our collective thinking about time and the future as well. There is something quite meditative about this longer term perspective, isn't there? The design principles certainly have a horizon that is liberating, and de-stressing. (Check out the Wikipedia page for the 'Clock of the Long Now' for a rundown of some of the design and maintenance considerations.)

What if we all thought about our businesses, services and products in this way? And how might this longer term, futurephilic perspective shape how we deal with global problems, or view every day events? What things might we want to create or focus on preserving because of their inherent qualities? For example, the Long Now Foundation goes beyond time, clocks and expanded perspectives, and in their educational programs focus on long-term policy (beyond three-year electoral cycles), scenario planning (which we at Thinque are big believers and practitioners in) and the idea of singularity (which I cover in chapter 5). It has also taken an interest in the preservation of world languages in its Rosetta project, because it sees language loss (discussed in chapter 2) from a long-term perspective. The Rosetta project focuses on preserving languages with a high likelihood of extinction over the period 2000 to 2100, with samples of such languages being inscribed onto a disc of nickel alloy. And, while the future of the language of our family business is still in jeopardy, its history, its brand and its values can still be preserved in writing, audio, visualisations and in modern media. This is worth preserving in a multitude of forms – including in book format, as in the lines you are reading now – for future generations and other heroes who may learn from the road less travelled.

CASE STUDY:
HOW SWEDISH FUTUREPHILE TINK MADE MANAGING YOUR PERSONAL FINANCES FUN AND SIMPLE

Two industries that in the last five years have gone through disruptive changes are banking and finance. We've seen financial technology companies like Lendico, TransferWise, FutureAdvisor and Tink revolutionise these industries and the ways consumers do their banking. Banking today has, thanks to digital technologies, become increasingly democratised and mobilised.

One of the start-ups in this space that fascinates me the most is the Swedish financial app Tink, which was founded in 2012 by Daniel Kjellén and Fredrik Hedberg and has over 350 000 users in Sweden as of 2016. At first glance, that might seem like a low figure, but with only around ten million people living in Sweden that becomes a decent number of users. What FinTech (short for financial technology) players like Tink have in common is that they are decoupling consumers from their primary financial and banking relationships, and enabling a more empowering future for adaptive futurephiles.

In a 2015 interview with the technology media site TechCrunch, Sebastian Siemiatkowski, founder and CEO of Swedish e-commerce company Klarna, made the following statement about disruption in the (largely futurephobic) finance industry:

There has been no innovation for years, and now the EU has opened up these markets, new companies are taking advantage of the poor competition and creating new services.

The founders behind Tink had one simple idea: they wanted to help people to gain a deeper understanding about their spending habits and thus educate them on how to be better at saving money, to create better futures. This is a challenging mission when many people find dealing with personal finances a mundane and tedious task. Many people also find the experience of managing their money stressful and difficult, which explains why they avoid financial planning. What founders Daniel Kjellén and Fredrik Hedberg decided to do in order to tackle this problem was to create a 'gamefied interface' and a user experience that made it fun, easy and practical to keep track of your expenses, create budgets and analyse your financial situation in real time. The app is free and it automatically connects with all your banks and financial services, and they use the same kind of security solutions as the world-leading banks so users have no need to worry about hacking (we hope). The central mantra comes down to 'what can be measured can be managed', and if you add beautiful visualisations for the numerically illiterate (and finance-phobeic), real-time measurements and projections, these can help consumers be futurephiles instead of futurephobes – seamlessly.

The key behind Tink's success is the way that the app can visualise and automatically organise your spending into different categories so that you as a user can track and compare your spending over time. The app also enables its users to set up savings targets and initiate payments and transfers. This means that with Tink you can easily identify which shopping habits you might need to change to be able to save those extra dollars that over time can build up to a significant amount. Because they are able to find these valuable insights themselves, these users are then more likely to feel a sense of pride, responsibility and, perhaps most importantly, a sense of control over their financial situation.

Tink makes managing personal finances a task that users can do spontaneously on the go, and it does so without demanding too much of the user. It's not surprising that the app has been so widely adopted in Sweden and internationally recognised by media outlets. Today's consumers crave simplicity and want solutions like this that empower them to make smarter decisions about their futures, and encourage them with a call to (responsible) financial adventure.

This kind of user experience and interaction is very different from what you would have with your bank manager or through a traditional banking app. It's becoming increasingly clear that our relationships with banks are shifting – the results of a recent Gallup poll that surveyed over 9000 American adults indicate that visiting physical bank branches has become a thing of the past. The survey results showed that people today are less likely to call or visit a physical bank branch, but more likely to engage with the bank digitally via desktop or mobile channels. (For more on the results of this survey, see 'Risks to banks from rise of digital banking', available on the Gallup website.) This is a development that start-ups such as Tink and the Australian Acorns app have capitalised on. The interesting question here is how the battle between big banks and financial technology companies will play out in the next five or ten years. Will big banks manage to futurephobically fight back with their new 'customer-centric offerings' or will start-ups continue to hold the edge?

Ask yourself ...

Making processes and interfaces fun and simple doesn't just relate to the financial services industry. Think about the following with regard to your business:

1. How are you providing value through your interface and does it entice a call to adventure? Is it a combination of analogue and digital touch points? How can you enable smarter decision-making for your customers by improving your interface and enabling better futures for your clients?

2. What can you learn from the user-friendly interfaces used by financial start-ups? What makes them unique and compelling?

3. How can your product or service simplify your customer's life? How can you help them visualise data?

STEP 4
HERO'S JOURNEY WHEEL FOR MAMMA SÖRMAN-NILSSON

Anders moves back to Sweden to collaborate with his mother and father on the cross-generational renaissance of Georg Sörman. Birgitta wants to collaborate on the revitalisation of Georg Sörman, and starts seeing the value in the reverse mentoring with Anders.

ORDINARY WORLD

Meeting with the mentor

Overcoming reluctance

Meeting with the mentor

This is a 'fork in the road' moment. The heroine needs guidance if she is going to undertake the odyssey potentially ahead of her, and the mentor is a figure who gives the heroine something she really needs. This could be an object of great importance, a critical insight or foresight to overcome a dilemma the heroine is facing, sage advice, some practical training or even self-esteem. Whatever it is that the mentor provides to the heroine, it helps dispel doubts and uncertainties, and enables the heroine to move forward with the odyssey.

Here's what happened during this stage for Luke in *Star Wars*:

- *Inner journey:* Meeting with the mentor – R2D2 plays the entire message, revealing that Luke holds the plans of the Death Star. Obi-Wan gives Luke his father's lightsaber and tells him of his heritage.

- *Outer journey:* Overcoming reluctance – Luke wants to help.

And here's what happened for Birgitta:

- *Inner journey:* Meeting with the mentor – Anders moves back to Sweden to collaborate with his mother and father on the cross-generational renaissance of Georg Sörman.

- *Outer journey:* Overcoming reluctance – Birgitta wants to collaborate on the revitalisation of Georg Sörman, and starts seeing the value in the 'reverse mentoring' with Anders.

4: Meeting with the mentor

The past is a full stop; the future is defined by smarter questions.

Opening hearts and minds

In 2005, my brother, then living at home in our parents' house at Färingsö outside Stockholm, gave me the most profound movie recommendation I have ever received – for the wonderful movie *As It Is in Heaven*. As an atheist, the title didn't inspire me. But my brother insisted. He even managed to convince my parents to watch it. I was living in Balmoral, Sydney, at the time and had the opportunity to eventually watch the movie at the nearby Art Deco Orpheum theatre in Cremorne on Sydney's North Shore, where incidentally it ran for 103 weeks straight, and (as documented in a 2007 *Sydney Morning Herald* article) beat *Titanic* in box office takings. The movie still gives me goose bumps just thinking about it, and anytime I hear 'Gabriella's Song' from the soundtrack I start uncontrollably crying tears of joy and inspiration. Ew, I know. (If you have seen the movie, you will know exactly what I am talking about, though.)

I know from the times I have spent with clients in the United States that audiences there can be very appreciative and will occasionally break out into standing ovations. During my executive education in Bangalore, I also sat among Indians who clapped and expressed engagement throughout a Bollywood blockbuster. This wearing of hearts on the sleeves is not something that usually comes as naturally to Australians, but what emerged after the climactic finish to *As It Is in Heaven* moved me – deeply. The entire cinema audience stood up and broke out into a standing ovation that lasted for what felt like an eternity. A collective sigh of emotion had gripped our hearts and minds and we all stood in awe at what we had just experienced. I also came to feel a more personal message from this movie; I felt a calling, I cannot describe it any other way, to move home to Sweden to complete a mission.

Let me return to the narrative of the movie, which was nominated for Best Foreign Language Film at the 77th Academy Awards, was directed by Swede Kay Pollak, and starred Michael Nyqvist and Frida Hallgren. In the film, Daniel Daréus (Nyqvist) is an internationally celebrated composer whose life ambition is to 'make music which opens people's hearts'. He lives the intense high life on the global music scene and is in high demand, but his own heart is not in good health, and at the beginning of the movie he suffers a heart attack on stage. This leads him to retire back to his native village in Norrland, in the north of Sweden. There he buys the abandoned old school and, as he re-explores his old town and its surroundings, memories of his traumatised childhood, the loss of his mother at an early age and schoolyard bullying re-emerge. Soon after arrival, the local pastor visits and asks Daniel whether he would come to listen to the church choir. Grudgingly, Daniel, who wants a break from music, caves in, even though it is obvious the choir and the pastor want his help in coaching and leading the choir. While reluctant at first, Daniel slowly develops an excitement in helping the choir, and in the unlikely setting of Norrland, far away from the global stage, he rediscovers his own love for music.

The choir consists of a diverse mix of locals, with their own secrets, aspirations, internal dynamics and emotional baggage. Daniel learns to appreciate each and every one of them and helps them to find their unique voice, tone and expression, and together they find harmony in the diversity. Gabriella (Helen Sjöholm) is particularly talented, and Daniel writes her a solo performance – 'Gabriella's Song' – which helps her regain her self-esteem and stand up to her physically abusive husband, Connie (Per Moberg), who incidentally was Daniel's own tormentor as a child. The choir's success grows, and as Daniel grows more confident in his role as the leader of the choir, he applies for the vacant role of cantor, and confidently steps into the role as an employee of the pastor. As a visionary, Daniel employs unconventional methods that are seen as heretical and challenging to the pastor, who originally asked for Daniel's help and who feels like his authority is compromised by the charismatic composer.

A romance slowly develops between Daniel and Lena (Hallgren), which is used as a pretext by the pastor to start a church investigation into the blasphemous practices of Daniel. Eventually, the pastor suffers a mental breakdown because of the changes brought in by Daniel and the fact that church attendance is lower than the choir concerts. This culminates in the pastor threatening to kill both Daniel and himself as a result of the changing status quo. As you're likely starting to see, the narrative is in many ways a story about the friction between futurephiles and futurephobes, and the dynamics of change.

Unbeknown to the rest of the choir, Arne (Lennart Jähkel), the choir's unofficial brand ambassador, registers the choir to compete at the annual 'Let the People Sing' event in Innsbruck, Austria. Daniel is hesitant as he doesn't believe that people can compete in music, and he is cautious about re-emerging onto the global stage, considering his own heart's health. However, his reborn love for music, finding an outlet to write 'music that opens people's hearts', and the persuasion of the group lead him to accepting the challenge, and the group sets off on a transformational odyssey to Austria together. The final scene of the movie shows Daniel dreaming about rushing towards his own younger self in a field of wheat, fulfilling his life's ambition of writing music that opens people's hearts.

So why does this movie speak so strongly to me? I mean, every time I watch it (and as you can likely tell from my preceding description of it, I have watched this movie in the double-digits), I am literally not able to *not* be moved to tears of joy. And I am not one who cries easily (unless called for ...). Even though I know this sounds grandiose or even deluded, I feel like in some ways this movie was written for me. In my more megalomaniacal moments, I get a sense that, just like Daniel, I have built an international reputation – as a futurist, mind you – and like Daniel I have always had an ambition to open people's hearts (and minds) to the world of possibility and become their best selves – to drive progress, discovery and growth. For ten years I have had an opportunity to do that on the international stage – from Sydney, Singapore, Shanghai and San Francisco to Stockholm. Combined with an ambition to move home to my own native village, I wanted to reconnect with my roots, and help change the fortunes of my mum and dad's choir at Georg Sörman. Like Daniel, employing heretical methods, changing processes, and occasionally going against the wishes of the established leadership (Mum and Dad) has not always been easy, and certainly anybody that ever tried changing the status quo will be able to identify with this experience.

Reversing roles: mentor son, heroine mother

Since shifting base from Sydney to Stockholm in 2013 (and back again in 2016), I have asked myself why I embarked on an uncertain odyssey of implementation in Sweden. My brother advised me against this 'fool's errand', and my Global Executive MBA cohort warned me of the downside of engaging with family business, especially during a particularly successful phase of my own business, Thinque. My dad told me that I was better off staying away.

There is a smorgasbord of reasons why I persisted, some of which I have already covered in earlier chapters. And 'no' is not usually a good counterargument when you are talking with a change agent. Ultimately, I also knew my work wasn't done with just writing text on a page in a strategy document. The ideas we had generated together between the generations after I first issued the call to adventure deserved to see the light of day in a practical way.

And this quest wasn't just about restoring Mum's honour. I also wanted to help my dad, who retired as a colonel in 2006 at the age of 55 from the shrinking Swedish defence force, and who had been complaining about how the business, and Mum's micromanagement of it, stood in the way of the retired life he had imagined. Not only this, but he had also complained about how the reactive injections of life savings to meet payroll needs was draining his and Mum's joint future life design. Passive aggressive comments had been uttered to me and my brother many times about the impact of the business on his (and family) life. He often commented that if he had known retired life away from the professional forces would mean unpaid slave labour for the family business without a sliver of a hope of a financial dividend, he would never have retired in the first place.

In 2006/7, Dad's acquiescence had been secured with a 40 per cent stake in the business, and in many moments of weakness since that time he has expressed his exasperation by asking that the business doors get locked and the key thrown away. I don't believe he fully means it when he says this, but the emotional sentiment of the supporting partner in so many family businesses is encapsulated in this comment. Of course, the problem with that solution is that it is not really a solution. Locking the door doesn't lock out all future problems. I was convinced that Dad's future ambition for peace and quiet, a life beyond the business and for a future payout for his 'sweat equity' and support for the family business and of Mum since 1979 provided me with an invitation to help him on his quest to climb Maslow's ladder of retiree self-actualisation.

The conversations with my dad have often reminded me of Cat Stevens' epic 'Father and Son'. In this, one of my all-time favourite songs, the cross-generational exchange hones in on a son's desire to break away and create his own destiny, while the father advises his son that it's too early to make these sorts of changes. Instead, the father tells his son he's still young and has plenty of time, that he should take his time to think more, marry, settle down. The heartaching pre-odyssey dialogue is sung magnificently by Cat Stevens in two different registers to represent each of the characters interchangeably, and to bring alive their unique generational perspectives on life. (You can check out the online version by going to YouTube and searching 'father and son Cat Stevens'.) In a relationship where, statistically, Dad has more of his life behind him than in front of him, and, statistically, with me having a longer future ahead of me than a past behind me, the phrases speak to our family dynamics. Unlike the son in 'Father and Son', however, I did not now face the choice of going away and creating my own destiny. For many years I had already done that successfully around the world. Contrary to the younger generation in Stevens' song my destiny was to lean in, to come home, and to support because I could see that neither Mum nor Dad were 'old, but happy'. Rather than keeping all the things inside, I decided that while it might be hard, it was harder to ignore all the things I knew. It was time to help my parents overcome their futurephobia.

You might well be thinking now that Anders is trying to play Holden Caulfield's character from *Catcher in the Rye*. And, yes, my psychologist may say the same thing. I wanted to ensure that my parents' future retirement would be lived happily and financially stress-free, and with no sense of regret. And I also wanted to stop hearing complaints about the business during social gatherings of our small family unit of four. Something had to be done. I couldn't watch them in this destructive rat wheel anymore. The love letter hadn't been read, the instruction book for a better future had been ignored, and the complaints kept coming. Enough was enough. I had to stand with my mother (see figure 4.1, overleaf) and join the quest as its mentor, and 'lift some milk' (as we call 'executing on stuff' in Swedish).

Figure 4.1: my mother and I, working together at Georg Sörman

This quest was not purely selfless, as you can likely tell from some of the reasons I have run through for starting it and issuing the call to adventure. I have no intention of pretending that the success of the 'Georg Sörman 100' strategy was devoid of self-interest. However, I believe that my aspirations were fully aligned with the spoken objectives, goals and ambitions of my parents – at least their verbalised and overt ambitions. My transparent and selfish reasons also included the aligned objective of seeing through the implementation of our strategy with positive financial results, and ensuring that the business would be professionally managed and in 'saleable' condition (in a family business context, this doesn't mean that we would necessarily sell, but that the business would be attractive to a potential suitor). The business's success would benefit its two shareholders, Mum and Dad. Importantly, this success would also give them peace of mind and pride – and, from my perspective, help their relationships. And I knew that the involvement of the fourth generation in a family business selling menswear would be viewed positively by the market and help attract a new generation (my generation) back to the brand, while also strengthening the authenticity of a brand known for timelessness and timeliness. The collaboration with my parents, who are baby boomers, would also send a signal that we are as committed to the baby boomer clientele as we are to gen X and gen Y. In this sense, again, our interests aligned.

From a personal credibility perspective, there was also an element of wanting to 'walk the talk'. Over four continents thousands of people have heard me speak about Georg Sörman and its struggles with change, technology and digital disruption. In many ways, I as part of the fourth generation have become a brand ambassador and spokesman for the modernised brand. If the implementation failed, what would it say about me as a management consultant, strategist and futurist? Would I lose all credibility? And if we failed, where would it leave my parents? How could we inspire other small business owners, independent businesses and family operators that a viable business future existed in a globalised world of scale, speed and automation? For too long, I had been preaching to appreciative clients and audiences seeking innovation, change and agility. Now it was time to help my difficult, (occasionally) futurephobic and ageing parents. It was time to come home. And unlike the parable of the prodigal son, I had nothing to be ashamed of – I was returning home from international success. And yet I was soon to discover that it is challenging to become a prophet in your hometown.

Fool's errand?

My brother has often described my mentor's journey to Sweden to help in the renaissance of the family business as perfectly fitting the definition of a fool's errand – that is, a task or activity that has no hope of success. I am not sure I agree with either the definition or his analysis.

Firstly, let's look at the definition, and my issue with it. Fools have historically been so much more than comedians or archetypes of ridicule. In fact, court fools, or jesters, have played an important role in royal courts around the world since time immemorial: speaking truth to power. According to Beatrice K Otto in her book *Fools are everywhere: The court jester around the world*, they have played crucial roles in negotiations, diplomatic disputes and in challenging both nepotism and military strategy. Because of the fool's use of wit and humour, rulers would often turn to them for advice, particularly in situations where they felt threatened by the noblemen or aristocracy around them, or in situations where they were surrounded by yes-men, with little to contribute. In other words, a fool's errand may in fact be taken to mean successful negotiations and strategic results if we dig a bit deeper. And I believe that in the curious case of Georg Sörman, the errand can still be completed by the heroine of this story.

'Three generations from shirtsleeves to shirtsleeves': are all families psychotic?

You have likely heard these sayings: 'Don't get into business with friends'; 'You can choose your friends, but you cannot choose your family.' So if you shouldn't do business with friends – who you may actually like, and who through a process of elimination and recruitment you have carefully vetted – how on earth could you ever successfully be in business with your family, who are handed to you by default? Yet, according to trusty Wikipedia (quoting figures from the *International Encyclopedia of Organizational Studies*), family business is the most common form of entrepreneurship globally. And no matter how dysfunctional we may seem and truly be on the inside, the marketplace seems to enjoy the idea that families are somehow holding it (the business) together, at least on the surface.

A sense of continuity and pride, for example, exists in ideas like 'Georg Sörman & Sons', 'established 1916', 'family owned and operated', 'Stockholm's oldest gentlemen's outfitter'. Just like being a locavore diner (or sourcing produce locally) soothes a particular consumer's heart, so 'shopping small', preferably with a family who has had to endure the hardships of intergenerational succession, painful buy-outs, hostile takeovers and leadership by dictatorship, for whatever absurd reason, seems to appeal. And the families who run these artisanal shops, hotels, cottage industries or large-scale multinationals seem to see the benefits of 'keeping it in the family'. My favourite magazine, *Monocle*, which I am proud to say featured my first book *Thinque Funky: Upgrade Your Thinking* as one of the 'Top 10 Things to Improve Your Life', obsessively romanticises the artisanal skills handed down from a Japanese mother to her daughter in Kobe, or the *Fingerspitzengefühl* passed from a Swiss watchmaking father to his Alpine son. And as consumers, we suck it up, hook, line and sinker. The notion is bizarre, yet somehow appealing. And yes, there is something very romantic about this intergenerational storytelling.

In 2015, after taking stock of how my futurephile odyssey with Georg Sörman was tracking (not good enough – my mother was still refusing the call, in any number of small ways), I finally managed to convince my parents of the merits of becoming members of the Family Business Network (FBN). This is an international network and education association that specialises in generational collaboration and succession. The PR campaign for joining FBN took three years, after which Mum and Dad finally succumbed to participating in FBN's Owners Program. Glacial excitement. My mum's resistance to FBN was perhaps best summarised in her rhetorical question, 'Why would I volunteer to sit in that gynaecologist chair and expose our family in front of the world?' Given that was her association or mental imagery surrounding FBN, I'm sure you can empathise with her lack of enthusiasm, unless you really enjoy your visits to the gynaecologist or urologist. Most of us don't. For his part, Dad resisted by claiming that FBN was too expensive to join, and that the courses were a massive investment. I countered by saying that we couldn't afford *not* to do this program together. In the end, my PR campaign to join FBN wasn't so much a PR campaign as an ultimatum. I made it a condition of continuing the collaboration. (Stay tuned for the results of this ultimatum.)

Failing to succeed — a family business' self-fulfilling prophecy

What we were up against is the generational prophecy of family business (see figure 4.2, overleaf). Across cultures and contexts, there is a saying which in Swedish holds '*förvärva, ärva, fördärva*'. In English, this means 'acquire, inherit, poison'. (In Swedish, it rhymes.) In other words, the first generation starts and builds the business, the second generation nurtures and brings the business success, and the third generation ruins the business. The English-language equivalent holds that 'it is only but three generations from shirtsleeves to shirtsleeves'. How convenient, given that Georg Sörman sells beautiful Eton shirts! According to Boston's Family Firm Institute, one study shows that only 30 per cent of family businesses succeed in shifting to the second generation, and only 13 per cent manage to shift to the third generation (my mum's generation), and that when it comes to the fourth generation (my brother and me), only 3 per cent are controlled by the founder's family. While controversial, this is sometimes known as the 30/13/3 rule in a family business context. So, not only was I up against a very tradition-bound culture and the disparate interests of the owners, but I was also facing the gargantuan task of going up against the generational prophecy to see if we could get Georg Sörman beyond the hump and into the 3 per cent.

Figure 4.2: the generational prophecy for family businesses

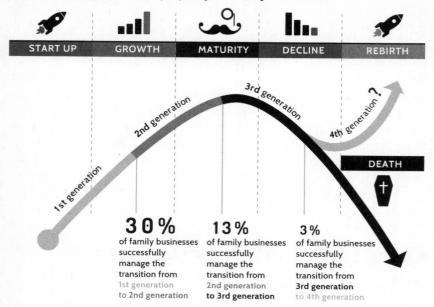

By way of comparison, here are the short- and medium-term prospects of small businesses in the United States, according to the US Bureau of Labor Statistics:

> About half of all new establishments survive five years or more and about one-third survive 10 years or more. As one would expect, the probability of survival increases with a firm's age. Survival rates have changed little over time.

Yet, something highly disturbing seems to be happening around the third generation in a family business context. And according to researchers and experts in family business, like Annelie Karlsson from FBN Sweden, if you get beyond the third generation, the family business can become a 'crown jewel' that doesn't cause an intra-family disruption, but becomes a cherished treasure which combines rather than divides. This is what I wanted my family to achieve. Were we failing to succeed and, if so, why? Why wasn't I, like the fictional Daniel Daréus (in *As It Is in Heaven*), able to fully open Mum's and Dad's hearts? How was it that the futurist, who is able to successfully package a wonderful yet challenging view of the future for tens of thousands of unknown people around the world each year, was sucking at it in a family business context? Was this a case of the plumber's taps always leaking? (Or, as we say in Sweden, the shoemaker's son having the worst shoes?) We needed to cross the chasm to the fourth generation, yet the collaboration was failing. I was back in Sweden and was 'lifting the milk' – I was meeting with new suppliers, going to procurement meetings, collaborating with the accountants and lawyers of Georg Sörman, implementing the Georg Sörman 100 brand strategy by updating customer touch points, training the staff, meeting with media outlets, creating corporate partnerships and enabling sponsorship opportunities. And I was starting to see some changes in Mum (such as her joining FBN, for example). But as soon as it came to rolling up our shirtsleeves and implementing the 'Georg Sörman 100' strategy and investments, I saw evidence of sabotaging behaviour – little metaphorical cigarette butts like those I mentioned in chapter 3 – which flew in the face of the strategy. By extension, this made the prophecy of 'from shirtsleeves to shirtsleeves in three generations' all the more likely.

CASE STUDY:
AIR NEW ZEALAND'S HUMAN-CENTRIC REDESIGN OF THE FLYING EXPERIENCE

The dream of flying is perhaps the oldest of man's dreams, writes the Swedish author Maria Küchen in her book *Att flyga* (translated in English as *To Fly*). For Maria, her love of flying began when she saw glider planes fly soundlessly across the sky at Ållebergs flight centre in the small town of Falköping, south-west of Stockholm in Sweden.

These days, the global aviation industry has made the world more connected than ever before. We can travel to distant places and experience cultures and see sights that we've only previously seen in movies or read about. Flying has become a way of fulfilling our dreams and hopes. But as flying has become a viable travel option for the masses and low-cost airlines like Ryan Air have changed the industry, we can see that the attitude towards air travel has changed.

Air travel is no longer perceived as a glamorous and alluring experience – like it was during the 'Golden Age' of aviation, between the end of World War I (in 1918) and the beginning of World War II (in 1939) and during the postwar era in the 1950s and 1960s. Back then, when travel was considered to be a luxurious experience, people dressed up before flying. It's easy to become nostalgic when you see vintage photos of people travelling in the 1950s and the characters in series such as *Mad Men* and *Pan Am* (which both portray life and work in the 1960s) travel by air. However, the fact is that flying today is much better than it was during the so-called Golden Age of aviation. Today, flying is cheaper, safer, faster and actually more luxurious, and the statistics show that there is much money to be made in business and first class services – in 2012, premium seating accounted for 8 per cent of passengers, but 27 per cent of total air travel revenue, according to the International Air Transport Association (and reported in *Business Insider*).

So why do so many people still see flying as something they have to endure and not as an experience they enjoy? A few common reasons might be that the seats are too close to each other, the leg space is insufficient, the meals are bad, the bathrooms tiny...and the list goes on. With the aim of tackling some of these challenges and friction points, a few years ago Air New Zealand teamed up with the renowned American innovation and design agency IDEO – their mentor on their journey of transformation.

Air New Zealand provides domestic services within New Zealand and international flights to and from Australia, the South Pacific, Asia, North America and the United Kingdom. In preparation for the launch of their new Boeing 777-300 aircraft in 2010, they decided to modernise and update the long-haul offering, and consequently they asked IDEO to rethink the complete flying experience with them.

One of the first phases in this project was to research and gather insights about the friction points that reduce the quality of the flying experience and customer journey. One of the first insights they gained was that some people think of the long-haul flight as an opportunity to be social with the person sitting next to them, while others prefer to keep to themselves (like me). This is, of course, problematic because it creates a situation where people who just want to keep to themselves feel like they are being disturbed by the person sitting next to them, and the more socially inclined people perhaps feel like they are being ignored or can't connect with the person sitting next to them. In other words, friction will appear between the two.

Together with IDEO, Air New Zealand addressed challenges like this one by building up a 1:1 scale prototype of the interior in a Boeing aircraft. In that environment, they started experimenting and workshopping with different design solutions that could reduce or completely remove the pain points that frequent flyers experience. IDEO used what's called a 'human-centred' design approach, which can be described as a process that's inspired by behaviours instead of demographics. Furthermore, human-centred design is empathetic, collaborative, optimistic and experimental. As highlighted by Tim Brown and Jocelyn Wyatt in their article 'Design thinking for social innovation' (published in *Stanford Social Innovation Review*), it's an approach that's been adopted by a wide range of industries, and can be applied to any challenge, regardless of whether it's about developing physical product, space, service or a system.

Human-centred design (not dissimilarly to the phases of design for Georg Sörman) can be divided into three phases:

- inspiration
- ideation
- implementation.

The first phase is about gathering insights about the people you are designing for. It's important in this phase to keep an open mind and respect the needs and desires of the people who will ultimately use the service or product you are designing. After you've gathered enough data and insights, you move forward to the ideation phase, where the purpose is to be creative and come up with a range of different ideas about the problem you're trying to solve. This phase is also about turning your idea into something tangible and testing it so that you can receive more feedback. The ideation phase is very iterative, which means that you are trying to reach the goal by doing a lot of testing and repeating the analysis several times. The purpose of the third and final phase is to implement the solution, but before you do that you need to define what success is for your product or service and also how you will measure and evaluate this success. These aspects are crucial if you want to turn your concept into a real and viable solution.

After a month of gathering insights, collaborative workshops and testing new design solutions, IDEO had created full-scale seating prototypes and produced a video where they and Air New Zealand presented new service scenarios and opportunities, including its creative storytelling safety videos, and the premium economy space seats. As an aside, I was travelling back from Los Angeles to Sydney on Air New Zealand in business class a couple of years ago when, in association with the launch of *The Hobbit*, I found myself in the midst of hobbits, dwarfs and wizards. Air New Zealand truly does extraordinary world storytelling – and hero's journeys – magnificently.

These innovations eventually meant the airline's customer journey and strategy was transformed so that Air New Zealand could offer future passengers a world-class experience that was both memorable and distinctive, and, of course, free from the friction points – seams – that passengers often encounter. As a result of their hard work on innovative thinking when it comes to passenger comfort, and them listening to the mentors at IDEO, they've been acknowledged as a one of the world's most prominent airlines, winning Airline of The Year in 2010, 2012 and 2016 on the world-leading product rating review website AirLineRatings.com.

Ask yourself...

Think about Air New Zealand's human-centric redesign and the following with regard to your business:

1. How can you apply a human-centred design approach in your business, and to your clients?

2. Do you fully understand the needs and desires of your customers? Are you implementing insights about your customers when designing your customer experience?

3. What ideas have you not yet had the courage to test on a small scale? How can you turn those ideas into tangible prototypes that are ready to be tested?

4. How would you define a successful customer experience? Think about which metrics and results would be worth measuring.

STEP 5
HERO'S JOURNEY WHEEL FOR MAMMA SÖRMAN-NILSSON

Birgitta sees positive developments for her business from the mentor's attendance at Pitti Uomo and Copenhagen Fashion Week 2014 and frees herself up mentally to the idea of attending Pitti Uomo in June 2014. Birgitta joins Anders on a pilgrimage to Pitti Uomo in June 2014, and a retail inspiration trip to Tokyo in October 2014. It seems that she is stepping up to the plate.

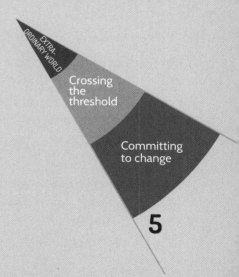

EXTRA-ORDINARY WORLD

Crossing the threshold

Committing to change

5

Crossing the threshold

The heroine is now ready to commit to the call to adventure. This odyssey could be a mental, spiritual or emotional journey, and can be a voluntary quest or the heroine may well be pushed across the edge into an extraordinary world. Either way, the heroine finally crosses the threshold between the ordinary world and the magical world of possibility. This threshold could be something as simple as leaving her cushy home for the first time in her life, or doing something she has always been scared of doing. The threshold involves a paradigm shift and a Crossing the Rubicon moment, which symbolises the heroine's commitment to her journey and whatever the future holds.

Moving from the ordinary world to the extraordinary world creates a paradigm shift both internally and externally. It requires the combination of a mental belief that something better can exist, and the willingness to commit to and invest in the actualisation of this change. While our heroine, Birgitta (and her 'co-conspirator' Lars-Olof), has dabbled in the extraordinary world, she has had a tendency to retreat into the ordinary world, so while Luke's journey has inspired generations of *Star Wars* fans, it is at this transition moment in the real world where friction starts occurring in a very real way for heroes and heroines.

Here's how this stage looked for Luke:

- *Inner journey:* Crossing the threshold – Luke's aunt and uncle are killed. He and Obi-Wan travel to Mos Eisley to hire a ship for their journey.

- *Outer journey:* Committing to change – after his aunt and uncle's deaths, Luke is free to deliver the secret plans to Alderaan.

And here's how it played out for Birgitta:

- *Inner journey:* Crossing the threshold – Birgitta sees positive developments for her business from the mentor's attendance at Pitti Uomo and Copenhagen Fashion Week 2014, and frees herself up mentally to the idea of attending Pitti Uomo in June 2014.

- *Outer journey:* Committing to change – Birgitta joins Anders on a pilgrimage to Pitti Uomo in June 2014, and a retail inspiration trip to Tokyo in October 2014. It seems that she is stepping up to the plate.

5: Crossing the threshold

Science fiction is fast becoming science fact.

Moving into the extraordinary

'So, when is the next Pitti Uomo, and how do we coordinate with Gustaf's wedding plans?' The question surprises me as it comes from my mother's mouth as we walk down from the big road on Färingsö, outside of Stockholm, towards my parents' house. This 1.2-kilometre road was unpaved when I was a child and spending my summers at what is colloquially known as 'Svartsjölandet', and it used to seem eternal as we walked it to collect my grandfather, Per, on his arrival home from Georg Sörman in the late afternoons. It was a road I had walked holding my mother's hand many times. But now, our grip on the future seemed further cemented. She seemingly wanted to plan six months into the future and ensure she would see the following year's collection, and seemed to be acknowledging that Pitti would become a central pillar in the yearly rhythm.

After refusing to come to the January 2014 Pitti Uomo, my mother had finally visited Florence and Pitti with me in June 2014. The event had made an impression on Mum as we secured new vendors that were aligned with the renaissance direction of our family brand's strategy, and Mum was genuinely excited about the future possibilities and promising new collaborations with brands like Barbour, Eton, Filson, Woolrich and Derek Rose. We had mingled with textile greats and icons in castles and estates, enjoyed great bonding dinners, and sipped cocktails on the roof of the Westin together with our friends from Eton. I was equally enthused because I could see that Mum had crossed the threshold into a bigger, more extraordinary world.

So I told Mum the next Pitti Uomo was in January 2015, and we booked our travels to Florence shortly thereafter. But we would manage to take another adventure trip together before then.

In 2014, Mum 'turned even' (a Swedish expression for women who don't want to expose their age). Given that I was keynoting for a financial advisory client from Australia in Tokyo, I thought, *Why not gift Mum a business class ticket and four nights at the Westin in Tokyo?* So we made it happen. The day after an 'open house' luncheon, Mum and I left for Arlanda airport to catch our Turkish Airlines flight to Tokyo via Istanbul. After being in business for nearly ten years at the time, this would also be the first time that my mum would hear me keynote to a global client, and partly about our joint collaboration at Georg Sörman at that. This was big and momentous.

After a long trip and a refreshing night's sleep, Mum and I launched in, joining the client's various events each night – which, among others, included the CEO participating in sumo wrestling and dining in a restaurant that had famously been featured in *Kill Bill*. Mum became a bit of a hero to the rest of the attendees, particularly after they had heard about her business challenges. And I believe Mum even shed a tear or two during my presentation. After the work was wrapped up we stayed on for a couple of days to explore Tokyo's retail scene, and began plotting the next steps of implementing the strategy for Georg Sörman's menswear store, as well as figuring out what we would do with its sibling store, located in Stockholm's Old Town. Given my mum's wish to concentrate efforts; the value of focus and brand recognition; the opportunities of the island of Kungsholmen vis-à-vis Old Town (largely one-time visiting tourists frequent this area, which makes strategic marketing challenging); and the differences in collections between sartorial menswear, and unisex knitwear (in Old Town), the family had agreed to divest the shop in Old Town (see figure 5.1). Unfortunately, the landlord had made this impossible (I talk more about this in the next chapter), which sparked my mum's and my creative minds into thinking about new possibilities in this extraordinary world of possibility. Mum had stepped across the threshold.

Figure 5.1: Stockholm geocontext and Georg Sörman

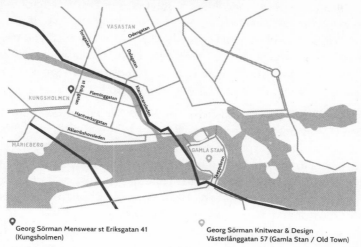

Georg Sörman Menswear st Eriksgatan 41 (Kungsholmen)

Georg Sörman Knitwear & Design Västerlånggatan 57 (Gamla Stan / Old Town)

What is science fiction and what is reality?

When I am not travelling around the world and exploring urban melting pots, spending time with start-ups who are creating tomorrow, or advising clients on the agility required to succeed in the future, my happy place is my home at Elvina Bay in Pittwater, on Sydney's northern beaches. Something about the energy and the vibe at Elvina Bay ensures awesome serenity, as Darryl Kerrigan from *The Castle* would call it. I live offshore, which means you can't reach my house by car. The closest convenience we can offer if you want to pay a surprise visit by land is that you embark on an epic seven-hour bushwalk from West Head Road, through the Ku-ring-gai Chase National Park. On the way, you may meet some of my friendly neighbours, like diamond pythons, red-belly black snakes and various arachnids, while being mesmerised by the cockatoos, rosellas and king parrots that come for a visit each morning. To get home, I cross the bay either in our boat, *Rita*, via water taxi or the rustic Church Point Ferry. Once I have departed the Australian mainland across the moat, a feeling of bliss, and reconnectedness through digital disconnection sets in. The cadence of life slows down, and slight inconveniences like lugging food, groceries and Vinomofo-sourced wines across from Australia to Elvina Bay are offset by the convenience of my post box at the heritage Church Point General Store, friendly neighbours and a local community who are always willing to provide us with a lift or some muscle. Life around Scotland Island, Lovett and Elvina Bay is idyllic, if not paradisiacal, and couldn't get much more analogue. Another plus is that as a wannabe Doomsday Prepper and occasional zombie-apocalypse fearmongerer, I'm fairly well placed here for future eventualities. If you have a similar prepper mindset, you know what I am referring to. If you have no idea what I am referring to, ignore everything I just said. Either way, trust me that Elvina Bay in its unspoilt, national park location couldn't get much more analogue. That is until Pokémon Go entered our worlds.

Now, my backyard and the peninsula on which I live between Lovett Bay and Elvina Bay is an enchanted forest of Japanese-designed objects. And my avatar 'Swedishfuturist' (a pubescent Japanese anime-looking character – see figure 5.2) gets to explore the national park's extraordinary world. And yes, I also now look like a zombie as I do so. Yesterday, I ran into my neighbours, Angie and Roger, and their bulldog Ralph as 'Swedishfuturist' was coming down the hill from my house toward North Elvina Ferry Wharf.

Figure 5.2: a Pokémon Go avatar

I realised that I was looking like a zombie walking down the muddy hill with the Pokémon Go theme music playing in the background, while taking my iPhone 6+ for a walk, so I approached them and re-introduced myself (as Roger had been away on an extended business trip to Singapore). About five minutes into the conversation, they asked about the subtle soundtrack in the background, and so I told them that I was out for a 'research trip'. Having grown up with dogs, I realise that one of the benefits of having them is their correlation with exercise and walks. They will let you know if they want to get out and about, so to speak. And Roger gladly pointed out this analogue truism – to which I friendlily responded along the lines that now you can have the same benefits of dogs without the trimming and grooming requirements and the musky smells and drool, courtesy of Nintendo (which hasn't yet designed anything for snuggles in front of the fire during cold Pittwater winters, though).

We hadn't walked more than 500 metres before a Magikarp jumped out at us 10 metres up from the Lovett Bay beachside of the peninsula (see figure 5.3). I quickly collected 200 Stardust and three Magikarp Candy from this 10.77 kg and 0.97 metre virtual beast. After parting ways (maybe I was freaking out Ralph the dog, because he was starting to feel redundant?), and a search for more Pokémon up towards our local waterfall, I returned with only a Magikarp to show for my seamless scavenge. Luckily for me, just outside Angie and Roger's fence I was cornered for a moment by a Para, which I quickly neutralised. It remains to be seen whether this bug will catch on among the rest of our neighbours, but suffice to say Nintendo and brands which are able to provide entertainment at the seamless intersection of the physical and the virtual can indeed create sticky brand experiences, turning their customers into avatar heroes.

Figure 5.3: catching a Magikarp

Pokémon Go, released in 2016, is perhaps the first time a brand has been able to do so successfully, and seamlessly, bridge the analogue–digital divide. And you can bet that other brands will design for this convergence between science fiction and non-fictive life. In fact, what we are witnessing today is the blurring between virtual reality and reality. Such an interplay now exists between virtual world games and our physical environment that the 'digital divide' (in this sense) is becoming a meaningless expression (with regards to physical–technological differentiation). Science fiction is becoming a reality. The mobile interface, gamification and geocontextual data are enabling us to move between ordinary worlds and extraordinary worlds, seamlessly. Our ordinary world can instantly be enchanted with digital objects, and we can seamlessly move along on our hero's journeys during digital scavenger hunts. Indeed, it is the movement between these two worlds that can lead to major change. Parents who are sick and tired of their kids being glued to computer screens playing first-person shooter games, and who have gently nudged them to go out and play 'like we used to in the good old days', will now see their kids walking around zombie-like in parks, school yards and beaches looking for Pokémon. And if we look at the initial hype around Pokémon Go, the market clearly responded with jubilation at the seamless blend of analogue, ordinary worlds, and digital, extraordinary worlds. Nintendo's share price (at the time of writing) had doubled since the launch of Pokémon Go (even while receding as the initial momentum wore off).

What is virtual and what is real is now debatable. Even for traditionalist parents. Consider a scenario in which you live in a regional area and your child needs surgery. In the past you would have had to travel, in the analogue world, to see a specialist, and then waited to book in with the right surgeons. Now, thanks to the robotic da Vinci Surgical System, doctors can remotely carry out the surgery in 3D HD interfaces, executed in your local community hospital via your local robot's four robotic arms. This gives you access to world-class expertise, remotely and virtually, executed by a robot in your regional community, with real-world benefits for your child. The surgeon, or surgeons – who may work in different analogue locations – receive real-time feedback via haptic touch, to ensure surgical success. Now, do you care what is real and what is science fiction, or can you see how the boundary is starting to blur? To add to this phenomenon, a study at Beth Israel Medical Centre in New York has shown that doctors who play computer games for a minimum of three hours a week carry out another form of surgery – laparoscopic – 27 per cent faster and with 37 per cent fewer mistakes than their non-computer-playing colleagues. The more hours of computer games they played, the better the performance. The conclusion from this study was that:

> Video game skill correlates with laparoscopic surgical skills. Training curricula that include video games may help thin the technical interface between surgeons and screen-mediated applications, such as laparoscopic surgery. Video games may be a practical teaching tool to help train surgeons.

Now, I am not saying that Pokémon Go will make your kid a better doctor when they grow up; I am just saying that our artificial, mental barriers between what is real and what is science faction must be challenged as the ordinary world and extraordinary worlds start converging.

Seamless convergence and hero enablement

One of my modern-day heroes is Max Harpham. *Who?* you might ask. Well, Max is 11 years old. You may not know him. Yet. He lives in leafy Thornleigh, Sydney, and is the son of my colleague and business manager, Emma Harpham (based at Thinque's Sydney office) and her husband, Aaron Harpham. Max has blond locks and blue eyes, and while he doesn't care much for the 11-year-old girls at his school, his mum has told me that they swoon over little Max, which makes him a little embarrassed. Bless. Max is into his extreme sports, loves his longboard skateboard, and enjoys games and challenges based on speed. His preference is engine-powered pursuits. He does well at school, and has for the last few years running won the best and fairest award for the Normanhurst Eagles Football Club. All of this is pretty cool, because Max Harpham was born profoundly deaf. If a freight train went past behind him, he wouldn't be able to hear any analogue evidence of it. In a world filled with noise, there was none for Max Harpham when he was born.

But because of a great Australian innovation, the bionic cochlear implant, Max Harpham perceives a synthetic, digital signal bilaterally where there was no analogue signal whatsoever. This bionic cochlea is a surgically implanted electronic device that provides a sense of sound to a person who is profoundly deaf or severely hard of hearing. Because of a perceptive healthcare system, and compulsory screenings of newborns, Emma and Aaron discovered early that their firstborn son suffered from a severe disability – yet one that could be solved with modern technology. For those of you who might be fans of *Boardwalk Empire*, you'll know that it portrays Al Capone as being severely disappointed and disheartened when he realised his son was deaf, because to him it meant a godly punishment, shame and that nobody would be taking over the lucrative family business. In one particular scene, Al Capone sees that his son Sonny, born in 1918 and not 2006, has had his face bruised at school, and tries to teach him to defend himself from the bullies. Sonny gets scared by Al Capone's demeanour, and the next evening when Al comes home he changes his approach with his son, and instead plays Sonny a tune on his mandolin, putting his son's hand on his throat so that the boy can feel the vibrations of his singing. Only a few decades later, modern technology has changed the game for deaf people and their families.

For the Harphams, there is no shame. In fact, they are proud of their little cyborg, Max. (According to the Merriam-Webster dictionary, a cyborg, from cybernetic + organism, is a person whose body contains mechanical or electrical devices and whose abilities are greater than the abilities of normal humans.) In some ways, Max might be one of the early trendsetters on the path to transhumanism, an international and intellectual movement that aims to transform the human condition by developing and creating widely available technologies to greatly enhance human intellectual, physical and psychological capacities. (For more on this, see Nick Bostrom's article 'A history of transhumanist thought', published in the *Journal of Evolution & Technology*.) Max Harpham didn't choose his condition. But technology, converged with his human body, offers him a sense where none was before. That is the closest to magic we may come as a species. To add to that, in 2015 Max was chosen as one of twelve Australian children to speak in Parliament to federal members on the 'Power of Speech', saying that 'Whatever I dream I can be, it's a possibility.' Thanks to modern genomic testing, Emma and Aaron have also found out that if they were to extend their family to a third child (beyond Max and firstborn India), that based on their genetic combinations, they have a 25 per cent chance that any future child of theirs might also be born profoundly deaf. In the meantime, this little cyborg is walking proof that the future is already here.

Max Harpham, like others who have benefited from modern technology and implants improving health and lives, is part of a development that futurist-in-residence at Google, Ray Kurzweil, calls 'singularity'. Kurzweil borrowed the term from science fiction writer Vernor Vinge, who used the term in his 1993 essay 'The Coming Technological Singularity' to describe a point in the future when humans and technology would effectively merge. At this point, human biology and modern healthcare would seamlessly integrate, and modern healthcare would extend the physical abilities of humans. In Kurzweil's work, which builds on Vinge's idea and Kurzweil's previous works 'The Age of Intelligent Machines' (1990) and 'The Age of Spiritual Machines' (1999), he outlines the law of accelerating returns, which holds that the rate of change in a variety of evolutionary systems tends to increase exponentially. These systems include computers, genetics, nanotechnology, robotics and artificial intelligence, and the law will contribute to a point of technological singularity becoming a reality in the year 2045, where progress is so rapid that it outstrips the human ability to comprehend it. In the year 2045, Max Harpham will be what we used to consider 'middle-aged'. I will be 64 and, according to Kurzweil, potentially eligible for eternal life. Max, however, is already part and parcel of the convergence between human biology and technology. In the exponential future, we may all be seamlessly converged with technology.

Every day, the lines between virtual and reality are blurred. The distinction between the ordinary and the extraordinary withers away because of empathetic and smart technologies. We are able to cross the threshold into a magical world – and as Arthur Clarke pointed out, 'Any sufficiently advanced technology is indistinguishable from magic'. Be it a technological threshold, or a mental barrier between ordinary and extraordinary worlds, heroes – including Max Harpham and Birgitta Sörman-Nilsson – have to cross the threshold to explore the magic and possibilities available in a tech-enabled world.

The interface with technology and the internet

With the emergence of the internet and our reliance on it, the user experience has transformed over time. Remember trying to access the internet via WAP, Blackberry, or dial-up a few years ago? But even at the time of writing, the human interface with the World Wide Web is still clunky in many ways. We access the internet, not like cyborgs, but in socially awkward ways. Think about the experience of sitting on a bus and observing the people around you. You will not see eyes. You will see the top of people's heads. You will not be making eye contact. You cannot flirt. Instead you will find people around you swiping left or right on Tinder in their attempts to meet humans. And that's okay. The occasional glance from someone may happen when they have an ill-designed crack at doing neck yoga to cure the fact that they have been unergonomically staring at mobile screens all day. Again, I am not one to judge, as my smart phone is one of my greatest productivity and social tools – at least to socialise with people who are not there with me in the present moment. As I travel around the world, my clients and partners often complain about the fact that seemingly a whole generation, or two or three, are dissociating from physical reality by escaping to digital reality. When I show them pictures of folks travelling via lightrail and subway in the

1930s, all reading the morning newspaper, I do point out that nothing, other than the screens, has changed. Our screens, in the digital world, are a lot smarter than the analogue interface of the broadsheet we used to access the wide world with prior to the World Wide Web. The point here is to say that while smart phones are bringing us closer to the online world from our offline worlds, the distinction between online and offline will seize to exist in the future.

In 2011, Google attempted to solve the anti-social behaviour of looking down at screens in public when it announced Google Glass. These smart pieces of eyewear were rolled out to innovators and early adopters in a beta trial, in a dedicated effort to bring the internet to users in a seamless fashion. Much can be said for Google Glass. Many of us already use eyewear, and glasses have become both a functional fashion accessory and a socially accepted tool for curing visual conditions like myopia, astigmatism and hyperopia. I was first prescribed glasses as a thirteen year old and remember my mother sitting me down to pre-frame responses (no pun intended) to the bullies at school who would inevitably attack me on my next day of school. Luckily, I didn't really need these responses as my environment was quite accepting of my novel gaze. Maybe things were different when my mum got her first prescription. Either way, being able to see properly, and avoiding the headaches caused by squinting as I tried to make sense of the blackboard at the German School in Stockholm were viewed as legitimate reasons to sport a pair of fashionable tortoise-shell spectacles.

Most people are now equally accepting of glasses. Indeed, a 2011 survey by the British College of Optometrists found that one-third of Brits thought glasses made someone look more professional and 43 per cent believed they made people look more intelligent. Now, while this study might be attacked for being biased, you could at least argue that I was a bit of a trendsetting thirteen year old – and several of my pimply mates soon turned up in school with their own versions over the coming months. Evidence of social proof, perhaps? Either way, Google was hoping that the fact that wearing analogue glasses is seen as socially acceptable would mean that their investment in augmented, digital frames – Google Glass – would be an equal hit. It hasn't.

Their idea has merit. We already use glasses to correct certain human flaws. Why not help us avoid unergonomic posture, socially disrespectful behaviours like incessant messaging during a family catch-up, or risking falling over (or being hit by a car) while walking. The problem was that people distrust other people who have the ability to Google search them in real time, and Google Glass adopters were quickly labelled 'glassholes' as a result. (For more on these ideas, see Will Butler's article 'People don't like Google Glass because it makes them seem weak' in *The Atlantic*.) Of course, if you are looking for YouTube humour dealing with this subject, visualisations of how the world views Google Glass users, and the top 10 reasons not to get them, the search results are only a Google click away. So in some ways, I should be thankful to my mum for dragging me to the optometrist in the analogue 1990s, and that she didn't order me Google Glass for Christmas in 2014.

As someone who wears glasses, and is okay with my own geekiness, I have, of course, given Google Glass a go. At a retail banking conference in Melbourne where I was keynoting, I took off my Moscot frames and replaced them with Glass. My lenses correct for the fact that I am near-sighted and have astigmatism. Without them I don't see very well when I am out and about and need to make sense of objects or words that are distant from me. If I had to, though, I would be okay to read a book that is up close. The problem with Glass is that people who actually wear glasses need to switch to contact lenses, because Glass has no prescription, just a small screen in the top right corner. So I couldn't see any of the content displayed because of my optical condition. And it made me feel awkward. Hyper-aware of my uncoordinated stroll, my continuous bumping into objects, and my ramblings to the 'assistive technology' attached to my face. Sarah Hendren, a thought leader on assistive technology quoted in Will Butler's article, analysed the situation poignantly by saying that technology designed poorly is a flag that marks us as 'culturally designated as needing special attention, as being particularly, grossly abnormal'. I don't know if the people at the banking conference would have described my appearance in equally strong terms, but they very well might have.

So what is the difference here between Max Harpham with his cool cochlear implants and Anders Sörman-Nilsson's digital version of having two left feet? Is it the fact that Max was born with a loss of hearing, and I just wanted to improve my access to information and media on the go? Maybe it is a generational thing? Will the kids of the future be more at ease with assistive technology that goes beyond the analogue canes, wheelchairs, and orthotics we use today? Will they have a greater sense of social acceptance of bionics and the integration between technology and biology? Certainly, Google would argue that as the technology evolves and is adopted, greater societal acceptance will ensue. In his article, Will

Butler noted that, in its defence of Glass, Google has argued that Glass has the same image problem as the original daguerreotype cameras, which were shunned until public figures started appearing in front of them (and so dispelling myths that the new technology was harmful). As such, it has announced a partnership with Luxottica to integrate Glass technology with fashion. Whether this will be the silver bullet remains to be seen, but suffice to say that Glass has an image problem, and that until they find a seamless design and application for the technology, the market seems unlikely to rush to this augmented reality.

It may well be that Google's go-to-market strategy was ill-conceived. Glass was conceived of as a consumer product, and its future may lie more in the business and enterprise space. Going hands-free and having an augmented picture of patient health may be useful for surgeons, for example, while security and insurance firms might value real-time footage and video stored in the cloud, and video-conferencing – a frictive experience if there ever was one – might go through a paradigm shift with the use of wearable technology like the Glass. According to Barclay Ballard's article 'Google Glass' future is in the enterprise', available on betanews.com, studies have shown that employees who use wearable devices exhibit an additional 8.5 per cent productivity and a 3.5 per cent increase in job satisfaction, so enterprises have reasons to be bullish about this device. So freeing up our hands is a bet that Google has right. The user interface with technology and the internet is not going to be entirely dictated to you by your digits. And who knows? Maybe Glass will make the some journey from enterprise technology to omnipresent social technology that the mobile phone has made over the last thirty-five years. So while the initial judges and jurors have voted down Glass as a consumer device in its first iteration, the exponential future may well see Glass-like devices being added to our transhuman toolkits.

Every wo/man's home is their intelligent castle

Consider the following facts about how we are continuing to incorporate technology into our everyday lives:

- According to *Forbes*, the Internet of Things (IoT) market is expected to expand from $78 billion dollars in 2015 to $1.68 trillion dollars in 2020.

- According to research by Intel, the number of IoT devices is predicted to grow from 15 billion in 2015 to 200 billion in 2020, and most IoT-devices will be installed in factories, businesses and healthcare. services. And as a result of installing these smart objects, businesses will get vital data to track inventory, increase efficiency, save costs and even save lives.

- In 2015 GM announced that every one of its new cars in the United States will be equipped with 4G LTE, contributing to the emerging trend of the connected vehicle and indicating that connectedness will be the norm for all new cars worldwide (according to the World Economic Forum).

'A man's home is his castle', goes an old English saying. This proverb was incorporated into the title of the 1997 Australian hit movie *The Castle*, about the working-class Kerrigan family. The Kerrigans live in a simple makeshift home filled with love, next to an airport, and because of a planned airport extension, developers approach the Kerrigans with a notice of compulsory acquisition. Darryl Kerrigan shows the hired property agents his spontaneous extensions to his house and the house's flaws (which Darryl enthusiastically believes will heighten the perceived value of the property) and is told that the house is valued at AU$70 000. Darryl and his family wrongfully believe that the government cannot evict them from their 'castle' and try to rely on weak legal advice from a local conveyancer to argue that the 'vibe' of the Australian Constitution is on their side. Finally, by chance, Darryl runs into a retired Queens Council barrister, Lawrence Hammill, who takes on their case pro bono, and who eventually successfully argues to the High Court that the Kerrigans have the right to just terms of compensation for acquisition of property under Section 51 (xxxi) of the Constitution. In his persuasive closing, Hammill QC refers to a quote by Darryl Kerrigan that his house is 'more than just a structure of bricks and mortar, but a home built with love and shared memories'. Many of us, at least if you have a heartbeat, would share Darryl's sentiment. In his case, the whole of the house was a lot more than the individual pieces that went into building it. Anyone with a home or a place they call home would agree, based on this idea that the sentimental whole is larger than the sum of its parts. And while that has probably always been true, the idea of a home, its bricks-and-mortar physicality and its notions of shelter, are about to undergo a significant shift – as your castle is becoming increasingly intelligent.

The smart home has always been a dream of futurephiles. Think of the Jetsons. The connectedness of things, or what's been labelled the 'Internet of Things' (or even more extreme in our client Cisco's parlance, the 'Internet of Everything') is upon us in a big way. What is this IoT? Well, no longer will humans just connect to the internet via a touch screen, laptop, smart phone, or desktop. Instead, the internet will be embedded ubiquitously into every thing, or as Cisco holds it, *everything*. This means that no longer are just you and me – or people, as in the old Nokia ad – connected. We have moved beyond Nokia's biblical imagery of stretched out arms and digits. Tomorrow, it will be about machine-to-machine connectivity. Everything will be connected and, as a result, will be communicating – your fridge, your Nespresso machine, your bed, your fitness devices, your scales, your car, your entertainment system, your shower. And this calls for re-designs to our current user experience of the internet. While you have been nesting like Darryl Kerrigan and setting up your home with the latest from the IKEA catalogue, Nest Labs has been busy amplifying, augmenting and integrating your home. Nest Labs sprung out of the design division at Apple, meaning their user interface has a high aesthetic quality. And now that Google has bought Nest, the company has access to the most brilliant data scientists and engineers in the world. This gives them the form and functionality nous of seamlessly converging the physicality and utilities of your home. Their go-to market product? (Drum roll...) A thermostat.

The Nest Learning Thermostat is essentially a glorified thermostat. You know the old-school (mostly ugly) analogue device that ruined the minimalism of your Scandinavian design aesthetic at home? The surprising truth about thermostats is their power – on average, they control 50 per cent of your energy bill. So why has the user experience always sucked? Add the fact that old-school programmable thermostats were only actually programmed by 10 per cent of consumers, and you see that this part of the energy sector was ripe for disruption. The Nest Learning Thermostat, on the other hand, is sleek, elegant, even sexy. A beautiful digital interface with touch capability integrates your home's utilities and energy consumption. Program it to power the AC on fifteen minutes prior to your arrival back home on a hot New York summer's day, for example, without wasting power while you're out and about. If you feel a little like the princess in *The Princess and the Pea* and you have a particular temperature that supports your REM sleep, you can program the Nest accordingly. And the Nest keeps learning. Its intelligence observes your family's patterns, so in a few days your coaching and tweaking may no longer be necessary. Instead, it can coach you on how to lower your energy consumption, save money and be more environmentally friendly. It also lets you remotely monitor your house, and provides data visualisations to help you make smarter decisions about your home. This is why future-minded energy companies around the world are giving away Nests to their customers.

But Nest Labs is not just a one-product company. Nest Labs believes your smart home shouldn't be dumb, which is unfortunately what most homes are like. While writing this book, I took one month off for a writing retreat in the French Rhône-Alpes region, staying in the Le Jorat Chalet near a city called Sainte Foy Tarentaise. My Swedish background has embedded in me some bad habits (given our minimal amount of sunlight in the winter months, we love having every light on in the house, including the rooms we are not physically in) and I kept up this wasteful behaviour while at the chalet – which drove my French girlfriend at the time, Clementine, insane. Unfortunately this chalet, an old converted Alpine farmhouse, didn't have a Nest Learning Thermostat installed, which meant that Clementine instead tried a system of 'nudging' me into compliance. She designed a simple system – a white paper sheet in landscape format scotch-taped to the dumb fridge. For every 'leaving-the-toilet-(or-other)-light-on-when-Anders-is-not-in-the-room' transgression, I received a negative transgression mark, with each transgression mark being worth a total of €5. At the time of writing, my total transgressions, despite the nudging and the motivational efforts by Clementine, equalled sixteen. Sixteen transgressions! I accidentally left an unnecessary light on sixteen times, despite the transparency and the negative impact on my personal finances. Now you understand better why Clementine might be my ex-girlfriend. Clearly, I'm an annoying boyfriend. And if you extrapolate this silly behaviour to billions of people around the world, who behave in similar ways, the big data would show you that Nest Labs has a huge opportunity in front of them.

The opportunity goes beyond pedagogically 'nudging' the inhabitants of millions of homes to interact with the Nest interface. It extends to the Nest Learning Thermostat potentially becoming the central brain of the smart home. As a result of this insight, Nest Labs realised that this central brain needed to speak to the rest of the nervous system of the home, and its associated machines and devices. So in its 'Works With Nest' efforts,

Nest Labs is actively collaborating with, and enabling your Nest Learning Thermostat to communicate with your ChargePoint-connected electric car, your Philips Hue smart light bulbs, your Whirlpool washing machine, your Jawbone Up wrist band, your Big Ass Fans, your Mimo Smart Baby Monitor, your PetNet pet feeder and your LG HomeChat, among others. Now the only thing missing is your coffee delivery when you wake up ten minutes earlier than normal – your Jawbone Up could alert Nest of your alertness, and it just needs to send a signal to your Nespresso machine and ask George Clooney to hand-deliver your arpeggio shot to you in bed. Now, that's a caffeinated dream, ladies! Bring on the smart, romantic home. Jokes aside, this connectedness means that your Whirlpool can do your washing load off-peak, that your smart light bulbs can warn you of a fire, and your Nest Learning Thermostat can turn off the electricity to your stove if that is what is causing the fire. A dumb home could never do this. Thank you for transforming our home into smart castles. Because of Nest Labs and the Internet of Things brands, the closing argument in *The Castle* takes on even more meaning, as we are now able to monitor and see the whole as well as the individual parts of our castles.

Nesting in action

My love affair with Nest began when part of the Thinque team and I went for a work trip to New York and Boston. Just like the chalet in Sainte Foy Tarentaise, our apartment in Williamsburg was booked on Airbnb. In this case, our lovely host Mai left us an immaculately looked after fourth-floor penthouse. When we arrived in NYC from Europe and Australia, the city was hot and humid. It was a true Indian summer. I have been an avid Airbnb user, for personal and business travel, since 2011, and the brand's promise of 'belong anywhere' is something that resonates for someone like me who averages 240 international travel days a year. The downside of NYC is that very few apartment blocks have elevators. Not good when combined with heavy Rimowa suitcases, 33°C and the hygrometer showing 88 per cent humidity. Luckily, our colleague Anton, who had flown in from Stockholm before the rest of us, had already figured out the intuitive Nest Learning Thermostat so that by the time we entered the apartment in hip Williamsburg a cool 67° Fahrenheit (around 19.5°C) was chilling us back to normalcy. We were then beautifully coached by the green leaf indicator on the thermostat so that we could optimise our energy consumption during the stay. While we did our bit for the environment and for creating sustainable futures, another synergistic winner was Mai, who by encouraging her guests to use the Nest was able to save on her quarterly energy bill, meaning her margins on the Airbnb business became a little more lucrative. As you can likely tell I am a bit of a technophile, so my colleagues often had to remind me to come back to physical reality and human conversation in the apartment instead of continually being mesmerised by Nest's beautiful interface and intelligence.

This and other associated types of computer intelligence are not necessarily natural, human-style intelligence, but instead fall under the umbrella of artificial intelligence (AI) or machine learning. Artificial intelligence is the intelligence exhibited by machines or software, and is also the name of the academic field of study that looks at how to create computers and computer software that are capable of intelligent behaviour. Major AI researchers and textbooks define this field as 'the study and design of intelligent agents', in which an intelligent agent is a system that perceives its environment and takes actions that maximise its chances of success. After working with our friends at Cisco in Miami, during their and Tech Data's Ignite program, Cisco's Internet of Everything gently made its way into my alpine retreat in France. How? Well, courtesy of these clients, I received a Christmas present in the form of an Amazon Echo. This looks similar to the multitude of wireless music speakers on the market, but the cloud-connected Echo is different in fundamental ways. It doesn't just project sound, for example, but also listens to its surroundings. Constantly. While Amazon allays privacy concerns by saying that its voice-activated system 'Alexa' needs a voice command like, 'Alexa, play The Beatles', to be able to hear this first command, you have got to be listening in the first place. Or perhaps different rules apply to our future robot family members in our futuristic homes? Either way, Alexa is now 'alive' and well (after a couple of little hacks that enabled me to use it in Europe), and we have been using her (to great delight) to check on the weather, listen to news, ask trivia questions, wake us up and write Christmas shopping lists, along with coaching her on our music tastes. My only moment of freaking out was during dinner when we were talking about the Amazon rainforest, and Alexa magically woke up and asked me whether I wanted to shop anything on my Prime account. Someone had been eavesdropping! I am not sure whether my Amazon Echo should be counted as an 'intelligent agent' quite yet, despite the fact that it/he/she is capable of natural language interaction with humans, but I feel like I had to tell you a little bit about this product, because 'she' represents a definite move by AI into our homes. We might have gotten used to having Siri answer trivia questions in our back pockets on the go, but now our homes have an intelligent agent helping out the family in Jetson-esque fashion. And the more you engage with it the smarter it will get.

While you, the human, may at times sound like you are trying to teach your old dog new tricks, Alexa is removing the border between science fiction and reality. Amazon Echo is bringing us closer to the vision of HAL in *2001: A Space Odyssey*. (By the way, if you make Space Odyssey-related jokes, she will respond in somewhat snarky fashion. I dare you to try. I know, a programmer did that, but it is a cute way of having humans like me anthropomorphise this black cylinder in my temporary Airbnb alpine kitchen and ask her probing questions about how foie gras is made.) Over time, frighteningly so, she, just like another science fiction AI protagonist, Samantha (Scarlett Johansson) in *Her*, might learn my tastes and my low intellectual rigour when it comes to responding to her jokes. The worrying thing for us humans is that artificial and computer intelligence doubles every eighteen to twenty-four months. This might be helpful but also poses the question of how quickly we as humans, used to linear growth, are able to develop and upgrade ourselves. I don't believe my personal assistant Alexa will take over my home in the near future, but she may well scare a few human personal assistants around the world into re-thinking their career choices. So, the old dogs learning new tricks may be us humans after all.

Artificial or organic intelligence?

And time is not on our side. On 7 June 2014, a computer named Eugene Goostman passed the Turing test in an event organised by the University of Reading at the Royal Society in London. *What is the Turing test?* you might ask (or perhaps not, if you've seen *Ex Machina*). The Turing question-and-answer test, entitled 'Can Machines Think?' is named after the computer genius and code-breaker Alan Turing, who during World War II was instrumental in breaking the Nazi's Enigma encryption. Before 7 June 2014 no computer had passed the test successfully, with success defined by whether the computer could influence the human judges to think that it is human 30 per cent of the time (or more), during a series of five-minute keyboard conversations.

It's essentially a test of a machine's ability to exhibit intelligent behaviour the same as, or indistinguishable from, that of a human. And the Russian chatterbot, named Eugene, during a series of five-minute-long text conversations, succeeded in convincing 33 per cent of the contest's judges that it was a human thirteen-year-old Ukrainian boy. René Descartes (1596–1650) once said, 'Cogito ergo sum', or 'I think, therefore I am'. The Turing test, both widely heralded and criticised, asked a similarly philosophical question – if computers can think, do they truly exist? Or can they at least influence us to think they exist? Now, they can.

This is a vastly different world from yesteryear. My grandmother Ingrid Sörman, married to my grandfather Per Sörman, was born in 1919 in Västergötland (West Gothland) on a farm. She was the eldest daughter and performed well at school. My grandmother was a beautiful woman with a huge heart, but toward the end of her life she opened up about one of her big regrets: that she was unschooled. While she could read and write, Ingrid had been forced out of school after year six by her parents, because while she was the oldest child of a sibling pair, she was not the oldest son. Her younger brother, Karl-Erik, was the one who was destined to take over the farm. End of discussion. Ingrid became farm labour, and told my brother and me horrific stories of the 5 am milking sessions with the cows in the middle of Swedish winter. That milking, necessary for family survival, was the reason she had been pulled from school. So, instead of helping her learn, nurturing her bright and curious mind, her young hands froze and shivered every morning while massaging Daisy's teats.

My grandmother's 'unschooling' was thus a chip on her shoulder for life, and she looked in admiration at the educational opportunities my brother and I have had. And I remember vividly visiting a modern dairy farm in the early 1990s with my grandmother, and the way her eyes lit up when she saw the technology strapped to the cow's udders. She told us afterwards that this was 'marvellous', and that a part of her wished that this technology had existed in the 1920s, because it might have kept her at school, and so redeemed her shame at being unschooled. We love our grandmother dearly, and this was my first encounter with the idea that robots and technology could replace humans, and free us up for other more meaningful endeavours. Now we have entered an era in history when not only my grandmother's brawn is challenged by technology, but increasingly all of our brains as well. (We will come back to human displacement a little bit later.)

Artificial intelligence is starting to replace human intelligence, or brains. But the notion, and phrase, is also linguistically challenging. Artificial intelligence belongs to a collection of words and phrases known as 'retronyms'. These are words created to differentiate between old and new versions of something. Think of watches, for example. Before digital watches emerged, watches were just watches. Then we invented the retronym 'analogue'. Advances in technology are often responsible for retronym coinage – related examples include 'paper money', 'genuine leather', 'natural flavour', 'straight marriage', 'handmade shoes', 'acoustic guitar', 'snail mail', 'bricks-and-mortar shop' and 'dumb phone'. As William Safire, who popularised the term 'retronym', says in his 1992 article 'On language; Retronym watch', 'The idea of a retronym is to downdate: to modify a familiar term in a way that calls attention to its not being the updated version.' This makes sense in the case of the technologies I've listed as examples, but what about when it comes to human intelligence? At what stage does artificial intelligence stop being artificial, and when does it become 'real' or 'human' intelligence? The lines between science fiction and reality are blurring. Clearly, Eugene and robots that are engaging in machine learning are figuring out how to make us humans think that the intelligence they are displaying is not a retronym, but organic.

So, while taxi drivers around the world have been attacking Uber drivers, should other human beings really be the targets of their aggression? Are we likely to need human drivers in the future? Or will cars, trucks and vans be self-driven? I would hazard a guess and say it will be the latter. For several years, Google and Uber have invested in self-drive automation – which makes total sense. Human beings suck at driving. I remember reading a report from *The Wall Street Journal* on the island nation of Samoa, which switched from right-side driving to left-side driving in 2009. (You can still find the report – 'Shifting the right of way to the left leaves some Samoans feeling wronged' – online.) The switch was brought about because the Samoan government wanted to bring the nation into alignment with New Zealand and Australia, which have left-side driving rules, and compatible cars. With sizeable groups of Samoan migrants in New Zealand and Australia, many Samoans had imported cars from family members in these nations, and large numbers of domestic Samoans preferred the lower prices on imports from Australia and New Zealand. Unfortunately the switch was not a case study in optimal change management and communications. Many school buses, for example, optimised for right-side driving, had not yet been retro-fitted with doors on the opposite sides. Instead, they retained their original doors, meaning kids had to exit and enter the school buses from the middle of the road in oncoming traffic. And if you have ever made the trip from continental Europe to England, or the other way around, you know the mental agility required to switch between left- and right-side driving. Nearly forty-two years prior to Samoa, Sweden made the switch from left to right, with encouragement from their change management campaign to 'Smile a little in the right-hand traffic. We are all beginners.'

And while some humans believe they are highly skilled drivers, no matter what side of the road they drive on, the reality is that a lot of us suck. According to CNN's article 'I'm the good driver, you're the bad driver', an American Allstate study has shown that two-thirds of drivers consider themselves as excellent drivers while at the same time admitting to using unsafe driving practices. The same study revealed that about one-third of drivers have sent a text message or email while driving. Another interesting insight from the study is that almost half (45 per cent) of the interviewed people admit that they have driven while being very tired, to the point of nearly falling asleep. The study indicates that among drivers there seems to be a tendency to overrate your driving behaviour while blaming your own poor behaviour on circumstance. So, maybe it is time to welcome our new robot overlords.

In 2015, I was invited to share a stage with the general manager of Uber Australia at the Westpac Business Trends Forum in Sydney. After my keynote on digital transformation, David Rohrsheim joined the panel discussion, which focussed on digital disruption. We spoke about aspects like the sharing economy, smarter utilisation of assets, environmentalism, civil disobedience and the backward notion of car ownership, as well as the fact that a correlation (or causation, depending on who you ask) existed between uberX's presence in cities and lower rates of driving under the influence. According to the US Centers for Disease Control and Prevention, every day in the United States, almost 30 people are killed in motor vehicle crashes that involve someone drink-driving. In 2014, 9967 people were killed in crashes caused by alcohol-impaired drivers, which accounted for 31 per cent of all traffic-related fatalities.

Uber released a report into the drop in drink-driving arrests and said in a subsequent press release that 'when empowered with more transportation options like Uber, people are making better choices that save lives'. David Plouffe, Barrack Obama's former campaign manager said at the time of the release of the report that 'Since we launched uberX in California, drunk-driving crashes decreased by 60 per month for drivers under 30'. Plouffe added, 'That's 1800 crashes likely prevented over the past two and a half years'. If you're a statistician, you might have doubts about the verity of Uber's causality claims. Nonetheless, if Uber services are contributing to people not drinking and driving, that's a good thing. The claim does make intuitive sense, and while data scientists and statisticians in Silicon Valley are fighting this one out, the reality is that drink-driving weaponises already sucky drivers. Uber is now the designated driver we couldn't afford in the past, and that is seemingly having a correlative or causal effect on young people's behaviour. If we can just nail voice-to-text messaging soon, maybe we can also start having an impact on crashes caused by human error while texting. Again, humans often suck. Now, imagine if Uber replaced these human drivers with self-driving cars.

For Mum, she is proud that she knows how to email, and she has figured out texting. Even in small letters (meaning she's not always digitally screaming at me and my brother). Recently, she even joined Instagram. Georg Sörman uses MailChimp, HubSpot and Facebook. Geocontextual marketing tools like Google Maps and Foursquare are driving traffic into store, and her inventory has been tagged courtesy of one of our clients' GS1 global barcoding standards. Mum has crossed the threshold into the extraordinary world of digital... well, at least she is dipping her toe in.

CASE STUDY:
HOW THE NORTH FACE USES AI TO MAKE ONLINE SHOPPING SMARTER AND MORE PERSONALISED

One of online shopping's biggest challenges is how to give every customer the right personal attention. When you walk into a bricks-and-mortar store, you are usually greeted by a person who is supposedly there for you. He or she can help you to pick the right size and style, can answer your questions and respond to your thoughts about the properties of the garment's material, and much more. This level of interactive and intimate experience is something that e-commerce has so far failed to achieve.

To address this challenge, the American outdoor clothing brand The North Face decided in 2015 to launch a new interactive online shopping tool. The shopping tool is based on IBM's Watson artificial intelligence system and is developed in partnership with Fluid, a digital commerce agency and software solutions provider. The idea behind the initiative is to better guide customers through the online store and give them personalised recommendations that are based on their individual needs and preferences.

The online shopping assistant enables The North Face's customers to use natural language (question-and-answer) as they try to find the right gear.

Todd Spaletto, president of The North Face, said in a statement:

> By tapping into the power of IBM's Watson, we can ensure our customers get the best jacket for the activities they love, whether that's ice climbing in Montana or skiing in Vermont. This not only improves their online shopping experience; it ultimately maximises their outdoor experience.

By asking the user questions about their planned outdoor activity, destination, temperature and weather conditions, the system is able to give relevant and personalised recommendations. In other words, The North Face is digitising the analogue in-store interaction that usually happens between a sales associate and a customer.

The desktop version of the online shopping tool has showed promising results. During the two months of testing (which formally ended in January 2016), 50 000 people had used it and the average engagement time was two minutes. The overall experience was rated 2.5 out of 3 from the users who provided feedback, and 75 per cent said they would use it again. Because of these promising results, The North Face decided to launch a mobile app that's based on the same powerful artificial intelligence software as IBM's Watson. The North Face's new online shopping experience is enabled by customer insight, and wouldn't be as immersive, intimate and seamless if it didn't provide the right advice, at the right time.

This kind of intelligent digital personal shopper can enable more refined and accurate recommendations, and also contribute to an interactive, personal and seamless customer experience. Most online and offline retailers don't have access to these smart technology solutions; however, you can gather valuable data about your customers in other ways. For example, if your business has a Facebook page, you can get both demographic and psychographic details about your customer base. And if you have Twitter you can get an insight into what topics your followers are tweeting about. Moreover, through HubSpot you can retrieve information about how your customers have found your website and what content they interact with. This is probably no news for you, but the real challenge here is to store the data, analyse it and know how to turn it into more profitable actions in an extraordinary world, across the digital threshold.

Ask yourself...

Think about the following with regard to your business:

1. What digital initiatives can help you deliver a more personalised experience to your customers?

2. Do you have a strategy for collecting, analysing and turning data into meaningful customer insights?

3. What digital tools can help you get a deeper understanding about the psychographic data on your customers?

STEP 6

HERO'S JOURNEY WHEEL FOR MAMMA SÖRMAN-NILSSON

Birgitta and Anders hire brand strategist Hema Patel to visualise the rejuvenated brand. Georg Sörman attempts to divest its second, smaller design store in Old Town, Stockholm, but faces a greedy landlord.

Hema presents the brand concepts, and after failing to reach an agreement with the landlord for the divestment, a brother brand, Georg Sörman & Sons, is developed by the mentor for Old Town.

EXTRA-ORDINARY WORLD

Tests, allies and enemies

Experimenting with first change

6

Tests, allies and enemies

The heroine is now finally out of her comfort zone but as soon as the threshold has been straddled, an even more difficult series of challenges will test her. The obstacle becomes the way forward, and challenges are strewn across the path into the extraordinary world. These may be physical in nature, or people hell-bent on slowing down the heroine's progress. As a result, the heroine has to triumph against each challenge she comes up against on the odyssey to the rainbow. As she does so, the heroine must uncover who can be trusted and who can't. She may create alliances and enemies, all of which in their own way help in shaping the heroine for even greater challenges in the future. Strength, agility and skills are challenged and each mountain to climb provides the heroine with fundamentally important insights into her character and weaknesses, and increases our bond with her even more.

Here's how this stage looked for Luke in *Star Wars*:

- *Inner journey:* Tests, allies, and enemies – Luke and Obi-Wan hire Han Solo and Chewbacca, who become their allies. They evade Imperial Stormtroopers who try to prevent their escape.

- *Outer journey:* Experimenting with first change – in the cantina, Luke is saved by Obi-Wan's use of the Force.

And here's where Birgitta was up to:

- *Inner journey:* Tests, allies and enemies – Birgitta and Anders work with brand strategist and Cannes Lion winner Hema Patel, to visualise the rejuvenated brand Georg Sörman 100. Meanwhile, Georg Sörman attempts to divest its second, smaller design and knitwear store in Old Town, Stockholm, but faces a hostile and greedy landlord. Birgitta prepares to make the mental leap to letting go of part of the business, in order to invest in the core menswear business. Birgitta and Lars-Olof prepare to join mentor Anders at the Family Business Network.

- Outer journey: Experimenting with first change – brand strategist Hema presents brand concepts for Georg Sörman 100 and, after failing to reach an agreement with the landlord in Old Town for the divestment, a brother brand, Georg Sörman & Sons, is developed by the mentor and his allies for Old Town. This store will synergistically play with the main brand by specialising in Scandinavian menswear. Thinque and Georg Sörman agree to a one-year retainer to implement the Georg Sörman 100 brand across all digital and analogue touch points to symbolise the renaissance of the business.

6: Tests, allies and enemies

Disruption is a signal from the future that it is high time to change your business approach. Today might be too late.

Navigating the path into the extraordinary

Author Haruki Murakami says it so well: 'Unfortunately, the clock is ticking, the hours are going by. The past increases, the future recedes. Possibilities decreasing, regrets mounting.' And this is certainly the case for my mum and the family business.

Of course, all family businesses have pros and cons. One benefit is that staff members are treated with love and respect, and are included in the inner circle. A downside is that staff members are treated with love and respect, and are included in the inner circle. Since 1916, Georg Sörman has had a physical presence in Old Town in Stockholm. The original store was located on Stora Nygatan 21, and the current store has been located around the block on Västerlanggatan 57 since 1928. Old Town was, as the name suggests, the old centre of Stockholm and for many years the centre of commerce, as ferries and boat traffic from both the Baltic Sea and Lake Mälaren congregated to barter and trade in Stockholm's heart. It was a great place for business, once upon a time. But times change and, like so many similar areas around Europe, the main shopping streets in Old Town have lost the stores known for their quality, aesthetics and craftsmanship, helped along by the transitory nature of one-day tourists looking to buy a fridge magnet or a Viking helmet produced in Thailand.

To keep up with the shifting nature of retail in Old Town, my grandmother Ingrid managed the store proactively and reactively, successfully introducing Scandinavian knitwear as a quality differentiator (which both the *Los Angeles Times* and *Qantas Magazine* have highlighted over the years). As is common in old towns around the world, successful concepts quickly get copied, and instead of competing on quality, many of today's vendors pitch 'Scandinavian' knitwear produced cheaply in China, and some unsuspecting tourists don't know the difference. Our heroine has always refused to budge on quality in Old Town, and hadn't wanted to update the collection strategically in any particular direction.

Because of legacy and status quo relationships, little had changed in this sibling store in the Old Town, and even the shopkeeper/general manager at the time of my return to Sweden looked and felt frail. I am very proud that my family for generations has had a positive, caring and fruitful relationship with refugees and immigrants in Sweden, and the shopkeeper until November 2015 was a Lebanese refugee – let's call her Sara – who had arrived in Sweden in the 1980s. Over the years, Mum had employed three members of this family, and they have been an important part of the business. The challenge was that Sara was starting to become frequently forgetful.

Over time, Sara began to act irrationally and emotionally with team members. Mum does have a lot of empathy but it had devastating results. As a consequence, and because of a lack of transparency, our family initially decided that maybe we would be better focusing our efforts on the main sartorial haberdashery in Kungsholmen and letting go of this side of the business. As Dad said about the situation, 'When a branch of a tree is rotten, cut it off for the benefit of the whole'. Thus, we engaged a commercial realtor to assist us in the divestment of this side of the business, and so ensure that necessary funds could be freed up to invest in the turnaround/ renaissance strategy of the core business. We felt like we had a plan and purpose for Georg Sörman at Kungsholmen, and this was also HQ, and the store Mum had worked in for many years. This store was also responsible for 90 per cent of revenue and had more jobs attached to it – jobs that our heroine was intent on protecting.

In Sweden, the divestment of a commercial rental contract has a financial component to it, and under Swedish law you can divest a shop lease – and this was one we had had as part of a synergistic and respectful relationship with our landlord in Old Town since 1928. Swedish law also states that the landlord has to agree to and bless the transfer of the rental contract to a new tenant. In this case, the chairman of the strata of the building (the acting landlord) refused to seal the deal, obstructed the negotiations with the prospective buyer/tenant, asked for a bribe to seal the deal, and finally offered us a new rental contract at 30 per cent higher rent as our best option – or we would be kicked out. This guy had clearly gone to the Business School of Hard Knocks. And while I respect that this guy's job was to get the most money into the strata's kitty, he showed zero respect for Georg Sörman having been a faultless tenant for eighty-seven years. None. Ahhh, the enemies you meet.

So, what to do? As a family we regrouped, and decided to continue with the rental contract for another three years, essentially to buy us some time. One month later, Mum and I departed on our adventure to Tokyo (as I talk about in the previous chapter), and in a Sendagaya café, Mum and I started brainstorming creative solutions for the smaller shop. Given the emergence of our digital agency, Thinque Digital, and the marketing and branding services it was providing to Georg Sörman, Kungsholmen, and multinational clients around the world, Mum and I came to the conclusion that Thinque could finance a refurbishment of the kitchen and storage area of the store, turning it into an office, and the Thinque staff could also manage the store. The store's surface area of around 40 square metres retail space and 20 metres storage and kitchen would ideally lend itself to such a pursuit. Our minds went to work, and I promised that we would come up with a strategy for a new collection and brand direction that would create synergies with Mum's shop. The brand – Georg Sörman & Sons, selling Scandinavian menswear, design and lifestyle brands – was born shortly thereafter.

While Georg Sörman at Kungsholmen has more of an Anglophile, earthy, estate-like persona, the persona of Georg Sörman in Old Town would add to the renaissance and gentrification of the area by celebrating the youthful Scandinavian lifestyle of marine/aquatic, and the Old Town's history of being the meeting place between salt and fresh water, at the convergence of the Baltic Sea and Lake Mälaren.

Unfortunately, the remnant of this idea is now a few business cards on superb paper stock (see figure 6.1), and the beginnings of amazing partnerships with Danish and Norwegian designers such as Andersen-Andersen, S.N.S. Herning and Livid Jeans. While Mum, Dad and I met the external enemy, the acting landlord, in a united front, our internal divisions were evident from the beginning. And while Dad liked the idea of a clear strategy and the Scandinavian identity for the shop (which would appeal both to Stockholmers and tourists), and the immensely lowered cost of new management (with no shift in ownership), later hearsay from Mum's closest co-workers indicated that she never believed in the idea or the new direction, or the team that would manage it – us. Ouch. (What is it they say about your mum's belief in you? You can do twice as much as you yourself think, and three times as much as your mum thinks...) Anyway you get the idea.

Figure 6.1: Georg Sörman & Sons business card

Despite feeling like Mum never really bought into the idea, we got cracking on this project in December 2014. We sourced Scandinavian suppliers at Pitti and at the Copenhagen Fashion Shows in January 2015, I received three competitive quotes from architects, and Mum and I sat down with the bank to look at financing options for Thinque's management and investment in the business. We had in-depth talks with our accountant, and initial proposed management contracts were worked on to see if we could find a good way of collaborating together. Given the seasonality of retail and the need to place orders in line with the strategy at least six months prior to the stock being available in store, we agreed we would place a curated and small order at the beginning of 2015 for delivery in the late summer (last week of August 2015). One condition for the management transfer, and the launch of the new 'younger brother' brand of the Georg Sörman brand family, was that no new stock from the old collection (unisex, and all ages) would be bought, and that all old stock would be cleared during the summer, prior to our team moving into the store. Grudgingly, our heroine said 'mmmyes' – but, again, did no.

In a July 2015 meeting with the accountant who was helping us negotiate our potential management agreement, Mum ultimately got so worked up about these proposed conditions that one of the blood vessels in her eye burst. She had literally 'seen red'. While this was only one of many factors that highlighted that our heroine wasn't ready to cede control to her futurist son (and reverse mentor) and his team, it was a symbolic landmark, and one that made me realise that if we took further steps into this 'collaboration' things would go from bad to worse. So, we never reached an agreement for the proposed management transfer of this shop, which was sad. I would have loved to have been able to successfully collaborate on this project, and realise the vision of the 'younger brother' brand. (Indeed, this positioning of the collection is such a good idea that I still wish someone else would take it on, and so highlight its merits to my slightly suspicious and distrustful mother.)

The downside to our failure to negotiate terms and a direction that we were both happy with was that the smaller order of Scandinavian menswear turned up in September 2015, which Mum directed to be sent to the main store at Kungsholmen instead. As Mum had continued to buy the old collection stock for Old Town, an additional outlay of around €15 000 was needed for the brands we sourced. At the time of writing, out of the five new brands we sourced, Mum is still collaborating with and selling three.

As the Hollywood movie saying goes, 'With friends like this, who needs enemies?' It is true to say that this stillborn early-stage project was a disappointment for all involved, but I am happy things didn't go further. The friction at the negotiation stages, and the absence of good will to find a common ground for a future agreement, highlighted that any future investment into the project would most likely have been wasted. In the meantime, status quo and ordinary world continues in this part of Stockholm. And while I am not a huge believer in status quo as a matter of principle (unless everything is working harmoniously, of course), re-focusing solely on the sartorial, Anglophile side of the business for the store in Kungsholmen brought us back to the original idea, and enabled everyone at Thinque Digital and Georg Sörman to focus on the renaissance strategy.

Neo-luddites and technophobes

People around the globe are engaging in neo-Luddite discourse focused on technology-caused unemployment. The original Luddites were nineteenth-century textile workers who feared the end of their employment in the face of labour-economising technologies. Their modus operandi consisted of smashing and destroying machines like the stocking frames, spinning frames and power looms that were introduced during the Industrial Revolution, and which threatened to replace the textile workers with lower skilled operators. (If you have been following the taxi industry's lobbying against Uber, you might see connections.) The movement formed the crest of a wave of increasing working-class discontent in England during the Industrial Revolution, and emerged during the harsh economic conditions of the Napoleonic wars. And the Luddites, thought by some to be named after Ned Ludd, a young man who supposedly smashed two textile frames in 1779, were well organised – to the point that, at one stage, more of the British forces were fighting the Luddites than were fighting Napoleon in the Iberian Peninsula. The response of the Luddites to new technologies prompted not only military responses, but also legislative changes. Machine-breaking had been criminalised by the Parliament of Great Britain as early as 1721, with the penalty being penal transportation to North America (and later Australia), but as a result of continued opposition to mechanisation, the *Frame Breaking Act 1812* made the death penalty available. (Now you know some of the types of people who originally settled Australia.)

Several decades later, Karl Marx noted in *Das Kapital*, Volume 1, that it would be some time before workers would be able to distinguish between the machines and the form of society that utilises such instruments. David Ricardo, in *The Principles of Political Economy and Taxation*, said that 'The instrument of labour, when it takes the form of a machine, immediately becomes a competitor of the workman himself.' Scottish essayist Thomas Carlyle called this age 'the Mechanical Age', analysing that the technology was causing a 'mighty change' in people's 'modes of thought and feeling. Men are grown mechanical in head and in heart, as well as in hand'. Over time, the term 'Luddite' has come to connote either a hero of pre-technological craftsmanship, or a change-resistant technophobe. It depends on your own view of technology, I guess. And as Richard Conniff points out in the 2011 article 'What the Luddites really fought against', while the Luddites of yesteryear could smash physical machines, modern Luddites find it more challenging to smash the nebulous cloud, hazy social media, intangible digital platforms and exponentially smarter artificial intelligence. The fact that some of this intelligence may soon be inhabiting actual self-driving cars might be some solace to those wishing to create a Luddite renaissance of machine smashing. For the more agile of us, we instead ask ourselves (in the spirit of Alvin Toffler) what we might need to learn, unlearn and relearn to ensure our continued relevance.

The world's oldest profession

While it is easy to be fearful of technological unemployment, history may be a useful guide to how productivity gains through machines actually affect us. When we were working with the Produce Marketing Association in North America in 2014–2015, helping their members with their future scenario planning, one of the aspects we diagnosed was the idea of 'man versus machine'. We explored the statistics that showed that US agricultural GDP, as a share of the total, had fallen from 6.8 per cent in 1945 to 0.7 per cent in 2002, and that according to the US Department of Agriculture in 1945 the agricultural industry's share of employment of total labour force was 16 per cent, while in 2002 it was only 1.9 per cent.

The agricultural modernisation that my Grandmother Ingrid experienced on that fateful day on the Swedish dairy farm in the early 1990s (refer to chapter 5) includes the invention of tractors, GMO crops, digital traceability, precision farming and the utilisation of drones. In 1931, the farming magazine *Country Gentleman,* in an advertisement for Timken Bearings, imagined what the farmer of 2031 might look like – and their imagination was particularly spot-on. In the advertisement, a farmer, in suit and tie, sits in front of what looks like a large LCD screen and remotely monitors his machines in the field. In his article '1931's remote-controlled farm of the future' (available at www.smithsonianmag.com), Matt Novak points out the ad was produced at a time when televisions were not a practical reality, and only 10.4 per cent of the six million farms in the United States had electricity. With the audacious headline '100 YEARS AHEAD', this advertisement was particularly futurephilic and visionary. And as Novak notes, if you compare this with John Deere's 'Farm Forward' campaign from 2012, you will see that this future may not be 100 years beyond 1931 but closer to the present day. In the John Deere campaign, Terry the farmer runs his whole operation remotely from his smart home – of course, with a freshly brewed coffee bespoke-synced to his waking time of 6 am. Thanks George Clooney. The modernisation of farming operations, whatever we might think of them, hasn't rendered all farm hands unemployed, but rather has produced greater yields, and enabled new skills, jobs and careers in waves of urbanisation. We should expect nothing less in our current era of technological innovation. It all comes down to our mindset, agility and our willingness to resist the temptation to smash machines. So try to control yourself, you neo-Luddite you!

Human muscular labour on the farm, to a significant degree, has been replaced by robotic and machine labour. But it is not just our brawn that has been challenged in the field. It is also our brains. At its core, agriculture is more science than art. And fields around the world are essentially large labs. As any farmer will tell you, yields per square inch, metre or acre will vary greatly. As French viticulture farmers might tell you (and as discussed in chapter 1), the unique 'terroir' – the complete natural environment in which a particular wine is produced, including factors such as the soil, topography and climate – greatly impacts their quality and the farmer's yields. And whether it is in France, Australia or in the United States, many of us imbue farmers with certain qualities, including a romanticised connection with the earth. We conjure up images of the rustic, flannel-clad cowboy in Montana sifting the dirt through his hands, or the goat herder in Greece guiding his flock up steep slopes against a Mediterranean backdrop. This romanticism feeds powerful messages and enduring traditionalism. It can also distort reality.

In a 2013 advertisement by Dodge Ram Trucks, released for the Super Bowl of that year, traditional notions of farming America were displayed against a backdrop of orthodox concepts of what an American farmer looks like. The religious imagery in the advertisement, which struck a chord with farming America, is set against a recording of a 1978 speech given by radio broadcaster Paul Harvey – 'So God Made a Farmer'. I recommend you check it out on YouTube (search for 'Ram Trucks farmer ad,). Depending on your disposition, it might pull on your heart strings.

The Dodge Ram ad was powerfully received. The problem, however, was that it misrepresented several aspects of modern farming. First of all, as Alexis C Madrigal points out in her article 'The whitewashing of the American farmer: Dodge Ram Super Bowl ad edition', published in *The Atlantic*, the ad whitewashed farming America. While the data shows that 96 per cent of farm *managers* in the United States are indeed white, the overwhelming majority of farm *workers* there were born in Mexico – 70 per cent to be precise. As Madrigal notes, fifteen of the people in the ad were white, one was black, and two (maybe three) were Latino – hardly demographically representative of present (or future) farming realities. As things go, advertisements do pull on heart strings and they are not often politically correct – and in this case, the ad makers knew the demographic that would be watching the Super Bowl and would be paying attention.

Beyond the demographic misrepresentation, another thing strikes me: the most modern piece of machinery shown in the ad is a Ram truck. This is also in stark contrast to modern realities in an age of precision farming techniques in these outdoor labs. Farming is science and, increasingly, precision farming techniques and intelligence are pairing up with machine labour to boost yield both in outdoor horizontal (or near-horizontal) fields and in vertical (urban farms). Farming might still be a lifestyle and a cross-generational business in some instances, but the world has moved on since Paul Harvey's conservative ode to farmers. Tomorrow, Farmer Joe or José might not need his son to 'do what Dad does'. A drone will do it instead. And, as a result, the world's oldest profession (not the profession you think of), might die out, or at least be further economised to Terry from John Deere's Farm Forward and the imagined farmer of the *Country Gentleman* magazine.

Precision farming and your white collar job

So, what is precision farming, and what can we learn from it? Precision farming, or precision agriculture, is important for several reasons. While I could wax lyrical about the fact that it is the point where science fiction meets reality, the bigger point is that the methodology is making a large impact on how the profession of farming is embracing the future. This is a farming management concept based on observing, measuring and responding to inter- and intra-field variability in crops (driven by GPS co-ordinates and automated machine-enabled monitoring). Remember the French 'terroir', and how every square inch has a unique composition? If you knew, based on data rather than on sifting soil through your hands, what that terroir would deliver, you're in front. As the font of all knowledge, Wikipedia, tells us working out crop rotation and variety works across time and space, making the technical calculations behind its formulation quite complicated. Of course, the aim is to increase outputs and returns while reducing inputs and resources used – with the ultimate aim of all this research being the development of a Decision Support System (DSS) for whole farm management.

In essence, precision agriculture helps farmers with field-level management with regards to crop science, environmental protection and economics. For example, precision agriculture can help advise a farmer on prescriptive planting, which Wikipedia describes as a type of farming system that delivers data-driven planting advice to help determine variable planting rates to accommodate different conditions across a single field, in order to maximise yield. Thus, precision agriculture has the ability to reduce the amount of nutrients and other crop inputs, while boosting yields. This goes to the core of what a majority of farmers seek, because it saves farmers on their investments, and optimises their yield at the farm gate. The methodology is also a core component of sustainable agriculture, because tailored, data-driven approaches to farming such as applying the right amount of inputs, in the right place, at the right time, benefits the environment through the whole cycle. And it means that not only is human brawn becoming less valued on the farm, but also the magic, romanticism and artsy decision-making that we credit farmers with can now be purely based on high-tech. Man versus machine? *It may just be that on the ninth day, 'God' made a machine that replaced the farmer.*

Now, you might be reading this and thinking that your white collar job is safe. And that the brains of farmers are somehow unique, and different from your urban sophistication. You could be right. And you could be wrong. Either way, you'd better start getting prepared for some alternative future scenarios, because a drastically shifted user experience of work is where you will spend the rest of your life. Why? Because something important has happened. Artificial intelligence is seeking to challenge your intelligence. And maybe coin a new retronym – 'human intelligence'. While consulting with Cushman and Wakefield in Asia – a global commercial real estate services company – on the future interface of work, one of the aspects we honed in on was what the future talent pool looks like. And that the future talent pool for knowledge work is not just human.

In their book *The Second Machine Age*, Andrew McAfee and Erik Brynjolfsson point to the crossing of the Rubicon by IBM's Watson in 2011, when Watson beat the two grand masters of *Jeopardy* – convincingly. Since IBM's Deep Blue beat Gary Kasparov at chess in 1997, IBM had been looking for a new challenge. The Watson computer system, named after IBM founder Thomas Watson, was specifically developed to compete at *Jeopardy*. Essentially, (as Jo Best describes in 'IBM Watson: The inside story of how the Jeopardy-winning supercomputer was born, and what it wants to do next') Watson downloaded all of Wikipedia into its 'brain' and had access to 200 million pages of structured and unstructured content consuming four terabytes of disk storage (but remained offline) while competing against Ken Jennings and Brad Rutter. Jennings had *Jeopardy*'s longest unbeaten run at 74 winning appearances, while Rutter had earned the biggest prize pot, with a total of $3.25 million. Two formidable *Jeopardy* machines, in other words. And *Jeopardy* was seen as a great test for this question-and-answer computer, because to be successful at *Jeopardy* you don't just need to possess a lot of knowledge, but you also need to be able to compute the questions, which are answers, into answers that are questions. This is a skill that some humans (like Jennings and Rutter) have been able to excel at, but artificial intelligence traditionally has not mastered because it involves complex natural language processing. Until now, with Watson defeating both Jennings and Rutter. Watson's victory happened three years prior to the computer Eugene passing the Turing test, and while Watson couldn't fool us that he/she/it was human, it sure could wallop human *Jeopardy* contestants.

The human reflections after the victory tell a provocative story. The final question/answer (which all three contestants answered correctly) was 'William Wilkinson's *An account of the principalities of Wallachia and Moldavia* inspired this author's most famous novel' with the answer being 'Who is Bram Stoker?' Ken Jennings' response included the cheeky appendage, 'I for one welcome our new computer overlords'. In an IBM interview ('IBM Watson: Final Jeopardy! and the Future of Watson', available on YouTube), Jennings reflected that 'I think we saw something important today'. In the same interview, Rutter, on the other hand, said, 'I would have thought technology like this was years away. But it's here now. I have the bruised ego to prove it.' The IBM side, through one of the development team's spokespeople, said, 'This was a big accomplishment for people. We won *Jeopardy*'. Well, a human didn't win *Jeopardy* on this occasion, but the human team behind Watson certainly felt as if they and their new darling did.

But while beating human *Jeopardy* geeks is one thing, how does this impact on your life? In February 2013, IBM announced Watson software system's first commercial application at Memorial Sloan Kettering Cancer Center in conjunction with health insurer WellPoint, as an aid to utilisation management decisions in lung cancer treatment. According to *Forbes*, IBM Watson's former business chief highlighted that 90 per cent of nurses who use Watson at work follow its guidance. And Watson's applicability is far-reaching because (as noted in the article 'IBM's Jeopardy-playing machine can now beat human contestants', available on www.networkworld.com), according to IBM, 'The goal is to have computers start to interact in natural human terms across a range of applications and processes, understanding the questions that humans ask and providing answers that humans can understand and justify'. You or your employer might value that, mightn't you? Healthcare, legal research, pharmaceutical advice, financial advice, insurance, accounting – you name it. And if you are a CrossFit or other personal trainer, you might be interested in the following – just make sure you don't throw up your next paleo meal as you read on. Under Armour and IBM released a new partnership at CES2016 that takes wearable technology to the next level of 'cognitive coaching', with the initiative serving as a personal health consultant, fitness trainer and assistant by providing athletes with coaching around sleep, fitness, activity and nutrition.

But, among all this, surely some fundamentally human skills like storytelling are not at risk, Anders? Nope. Artificial intelligence can already perform even this essentially human skill. Narrative Science's Quill service delivers readable and engaging narratives for companies like CreditSuisse, Forbes, MasterCard and USAA that are both marketing and compliance approved. You give them the data, and Quill's artificial intelligence cranks out a story. And who better than artificial intelligence to be a futurist, and show us visions of tomorrow? *Touché, Anders.* All of this made my clients in the commercial real estate industry slightly nervous, because fewer people at work in buildings means reduced demand for commercial, physical space. We are all being impacted by the new, artificial knowledge worker.

Like Frodo, many business leaders (including my heroine) think that the human disruptors of the extraordinary world have been making too many inroads into the world they know. By ignoring these signals, not tuning into trends and delaying necessary investment decisions, they are left vulnerable and unguarded. When you don't have a strategy, well, you are part of someone else's. And if you as a business leader think that things have changed a lot in the last few years, exponential change – enabled by machine-to-machine learning, artificial intelligence and cloud computing – is about to really speed things up. We are at the knee of the curve of exponential change – so, hold on for dear life. Mum's human customers changed yesterday. It's now her time to change. Yet, she still calls humans doing their due diligence and acting like they are on procurement 'virtual shoplifters'. A world where talent, resources and customers are no longer human but cyborg, android or non-human is too far removed from the ordinary world of an analogue menswear seller in Sweden. But I hope that in her journey into the future she realises that her reverse mentoring son, the futurist, is not an enemy, but her friend and ally. Mum, I want to help you. But you have to want it.

CASE STUDY:
HOW TED REINVENTED THE CONFERENCE SCENE BY MERGING OFFLINE AND ONLINE

As my head of research at the think tank Thinque, Anton Järild is constantly searching for new insights into technology, design and business trends that might be relevant for our clients. The following provides his insights into some of these trends.

A few of my personal favourite inspirations are techcrunch.com, wired.com, fastcompany.com, forbes.com, economist.com, hbr.org (*Harvard Business Review*'s website) and businessinsider.com. However, one source of content appeals to me more than all the ones I've previously mentioned, and that's ted.com.

TED stands for technology, entertainment and design, and is a platform and a community where people from a vast range of different disciplines and areas of expertise meet and share their thought-provoking, alluring and innovative ideas about the world. It all started back in 1984 as an analogue conference, where prominent researchers and business men and women met and discussed ideas around technology, entertainment and design. Some of the technology innovations that were displayed during that first conference were the compact disc and the e-book. The event was not a financial success, despite having some of the most prominent thought leaders around the world speaking and attending the conference. So the second conference wasn't organised for another six years, but after that the TED conference became an annual event with a growing number of influential followers from different disciplines. What probably increased the exclusiveness of the event was that back then it was an invitation-only event.

In 2006, TED redefined its business model and decided to launch a website. At the time of the launch, the brains behind TED initially offered around a hundred TED talks and, as they moved the renowned TED experience online, they made exclusive content available to anyone with an internet connection. As Bob Tedeschi notes in the *New York Times* article 'Giving away information, but increasing revenue', this was a way for them to embrace the future and break the traditional business logic. Chris Andersson, curator of TED, commented on this in 2006 in a blog post:

> ...Until now, the TED experience has been limited to 1000 people each year. But we believe passionately that these talks deserve a much wider audience. Now – thanks to the maturation of online video and podcasting, ... we can share them for the first time... They're ideas worth spreading.

Another effect of the launch of ted.com was that the keynotes lived on, past the live presentation, which in turn increased the expectations and thus many people's view of how a great talk should be structured.

Since 2006, ted.com has grown from a website to a digital community where knowledge, insights and ideas from around the world are seamlessly distributed and shared. The launch of TEDx boosted the brand's awareness and recognition even further. The 'x' in TEDx means that it's an independently organised event, and its launch and growth can be described as a grassroots phenomenon that enables anyone to run a TEDx conference. This way of opening up the brand and making it accessible to anyone proved to be a huge democratisation success. As TEDx has expanded into more than 133 countries, however, some critics argue TED risks losing control of the brand. However, Karl Ronn, in his 2014 *Entrepreneur* article 'Why TED gave up control of its brand and why you should, too', argues that this is precisely what enabled TED to scale its business globally. Gaining control, by giving it up. Furthermore Ronn asserts that TED still manages the main conference, held every year in Vancouver. I think it's admirable that they have managed to open up the brand while maintaining brand consistency seamlessly across the brand's analogue and digital touch points.

We can conclude that one of the keys behind TED's success is their combination of live events and digital media that creates an immersive experience regardless of whether you are interacting with the brand via a local TEDx conference, or via ted.com or via their main event. In other words, TED is seamlessly weaving together the offline and online experience and removing any potential friction points. One potential friction point that you might experience when watching a presentation online is that it's hard to hear what the person is saying, meaning you have to pause and rewind all the time. TED solved this problem by launching the interactive transcript feature, which allows you to more easily follow the talk. Moreover, it enables you to select any sentence in the transcript and then go directly to that moment in the video. Another benefit of the transcript functionality is that transcripts are fully indexable by search engines, thus making it easier for anyone online to find the right TED talk through not only the title of the talk but also the actual content and quotes.

With the launch of ted.com and TEDx, TED reinvented its business model and blurred the lines between the producer and the consumer of content. In turn, TED made their fans feel like they are not just passive viewers, but instead also active co-creators of the brand. In 2015, over 18 000 speakers presented at TEDx events and, as I'm writing this in July 2016, around 70 000 TEDx videos are available online. As we enter the extraordinary world of the future, TED is our ally in helping us meet tests and enemies, and enabling us to better imagine extraordinary worlds through the dissemination of ideas worth spreading.

Ask yourself ...

Think about the following with regard to your business:

1. What can you do to open up your brand and turn your customers into active co-creators and allies?

2. Which digital technologies are you underutilising and how can those tech allies help you amplify (or even reinvent) your business?

3. How can you differentiate your brand by creating a unique combination of digital and analogue touch points?

STEP 7

HERO'S JOURNEY WHEEL FOR MAMMA SÖRMAN-NILSSON

The landlord actively halts financing of the strategy, and the landlord at the main haberdasher announces that they will disrupt the haberdasher for up to 6 months with repairs to their inner plaza, which is contemporaneously Birgitta's shop's ceiling. Birgitta, Lars-Olof and Anders join FBN to learn the family business force of collaboration, succession and family values. Birgitta and Co. decide on a brand concept that is to be rolled out over 12 months.

EXTRA-ORDINARY WORLD

Approch the inmost cave

Preparing for a big change

7

Approaching the inmost cave

For this stage, the 'inmost cave' could be an analogue location but it may also be represented by a deep conflict, or even a depression, in which lies a terrible danger or internal dilemma that the heroine has not yet had to face. As the heroine moves toward the cave, she must make careful and final preparations before taking the ultimate leap into the great unknown. As the heroine crosses the Rubicon into the inmost cave, she may once again face the same doubts and fears she first encountered upon her call to adventure. At this juncture she may need to stop and reflect upon her journey thus far and the potentially treacherous landscape ahead of her to rediscover the courage required to continue into the future. This brief point of reflection and respite empowers us to empathise with what is at stake and the magnitude of the challenge or ordeal that is waiting around the corner for the heroine. This also exacerbates the tension and anticipation of the ultimate test.

Here's how Luke's inmost cave looked:

- *Inner journey:* Preparing for a big change – on the Millennium Falcon, Obi-Wan teaches Luke about the Force.

- *Outer journey:* Approach the inmost cave – the ship is captured by the Death Star, and the group finds itself inside the enemy's stronghold.

And here's how it looked for Birgitta:

- *Inner journey:* Approach the inmost cave – digital disruption keeps eating away at Georg Sörman's margins, the Old Town landlord actively halts financing of the revitalisation strategy, and the landlord at the main menswear store announces that they will forcibly disrupt the store for up to six months with repairs to their inner plaza, which is also Birgitta's shop's ceiling.

- *Outer journey:* Preparing for a big change – Birgitta, Lars-Olof and Anders have joined the Family Business Network to learn the family business force of collaboration and succession and, in its second module, learn and agree on family values. Together, Birgitta and Co. decide on a final brand concept that is to be rolled out to clients over twelve months, and that is to become the symbol of the renaissance of the brand. The new brand is launched in an initial phase for the April VIP Day in 2015, and is recommitted to at the second module of FBN in September 2015.

7: Approaching the inmost cave

The future is a scary place for futurephobes.

Preparing for all challenges

We were all in agreement – or, at least it felt like it. We had participated in the first round of the Family Business Network Owners Program in April 2015, and it had gone very well. This took place just before the internal launch of Georg Sörman 100, and timing was perfect for the VIP Day in late April 2015, where we set a new sales record for the shop. The second module of the course was set for early September 2015, just a few weeks after my brother's wedding in Watsons Bay, Sydney. The dust had settled on our agreement to disagree and not proceed with the creative solution for the smaller Old Town shop (refer to chapter 6), and we felt like Gustaf's wedding had re-united the family spirit a bit. And so with four other families we entered the halls of Säby Säteri (an old converted horse-breeding estate) curious, yet a little bruised, and enthused, but a little scarred from recent events. Here was our last chance to make things right. We entered the reflective cave of Säby to gain strength, and our heroine retreated to make final preparations for the next phase of the implementation of Georg Sörman 100.

The last few weeks had been challenging. Along with our problems with the acting landlord for the Old Town store, the landlord at Kungsholmen had also thrown up some challenges. About eighteen months earlier, he had announced that, at an undisclosed time in the future, the strata would repair its inner plaza, which is Mum's shop's ceiling. The dark cloud of uncertainty surrounding the timing of this suspected collateral damage weighed on our heroine until finally, in July 2015, the landlord suddenly announced that renovations would commence sooner rather than later. Much sooner. And that we had a choice – we could either accept slow, grinding noise for six months, and a lot of dust, while the shop (600 square metres) was still running, or close the shop, give them full access and have the job completed in two weeks. Mum hated the idea of an extended disruption to normal trade, as well as the thought of dust-induced clothing damage, so option b (that is, ripping off the bandaid in one movement) seemed like the lesser of two evils. Of course, if you've had a carpenter or builder work on your apartment or house, you know that project management and timelines are not always their strong suit. After almost four weeks of forced closures in the lead-up to my brother's 15 August wedding, 'carrying a lot of milk' – literally, as the whole inventory was moved from street level to the lower mezzanine – and a new layer of paint due to the dust, our heroine breathed a sigh of relief, thinking the worst disruption was behind her.

However, I remember entering FBN with a level of scepticism. Things had been tense. In the lead-up to Gustaf's wedding I had been away with consulting, elearning and speaking clients in Australia for nearly five weeks, followed by work with Bharti Airtel and IDG in Goa (India). I had been very busy. And, of course, as our heroine loves pointing out, this meant I had been 'not carrying the milk'. Janitor duties were nowhere in our formal contract of delivering management consulting, digital communications and branding advice and execution; however, as any person who has experienced a partner with a 'bee in their bonnet' will attest to, no matter what you do in these sorts of situations, you are wrong.

At this juncture (and in the interest of full disclosure) I should probably point out that the only reason I could take on Georg Sörman as a client was courtesy of our multinational conglomerate clients. In many ways this project worked in a philanthropic manner – I earned revenue from Fortune 500s by delivering extraordinary work, and then invested my time and money into a not-for-profit. No regrets, says the reverse mentor. Nonetheless, I could tell my parents were a bit angry that they again had done all the (physical) clean-up work caused by the landlord and his mates. At the same time, I was curious to see whether attending Gustaf's wedding and re-focusing on the importance of family had led to new reflections and insights for them. At the back of my mind, I have to admit I also kept thinking that this was their last chance. I really felt like I had given my all for three and a half years, without a single note of appreciation. Seemingly we were all in the inmost cave, and yes, as the hero's journey goes, maybe some of us were also a little depressed.

But, FBN delivered. Again. We spent a lot of time working on family values, and how to tune into family values as a guiding light not only for cultural, leadership and family business collaboration purposes, but also branding and communications purposes. What if the same values we had as a family could also be lived in the business? Mightn't this actually strengthen not only how we showed up as leaders and family members, but also what we communicated to our customers and media curious about our story? Could this be the glue that would keep us together? As we spent time in that inmost cave, making preparations – together – it seemed like it might. As a family and as a brand, we developed, agreed on and signed up for the following:

- *Empathy:* To be empathetically inclusive and welcoming to our clients and staff.

- *Family traditions:* To steward family traditions, both our customers' and our own, on to the next generation.

- *Fingerspitzengefühl:* To always have *Fingerspitzengefühl* in our collection and curation.

- *International:* To be both Swedish and contemporaneously international in our perspective and to source the best that the world's artisanal craftsmen and women have to offer.

- *Harmony:* To be harmonious through balancing personal warmth, colour and style for our clients and our mutual wellbeing.

As any friend of my brother's or mine will attest to when they step into the Sörman-Nilsson home, these values and the living of those values is evident. To me, it felt like codifying these values, which we have always lived socially as a family, in our struggling commercial project might make a big difference. I feel like we were all empowered in articulating what had been a guiding social and cultural lighthouse. During the final reflection in front of everybody at FBN my mum, our heroine, stood up and shared how resistant she had been to joining FBN. She shared her mental association of FBN and how she had originally equated it with a gynaecologist chair, but that she had cherished the opportunity of working with other family business owners, and 'Next Gens'. She also shared what she had learnt, and what it done to empower and embolden our family. Dad chimed in to say that he really wished my brother, Gustaf, could have joined in and shared the experience. Multiple times. I could sense something good was happening, that something at our cores had shifted. That an annoyance had shifted and a blocked energetic pipe had been flushed out. That our common chakras had aligned. We left FBN emboldened to steward Georg Sörman towards its second century, beyond its centenary in January 2016.

Then the roof caved in. Literally. The landlord and his mates hadn't properly done their piping above Mum's shop and when the first autumn rains descended on Stockholm, their culpability led to water damage, forced repairs and the partial closure of the shop – and, importantly, a big mental setback for the joint owners, senior management team and board members of Georg Sörman, Lars-Olof and our heroine, Birgitta. Sometimes you have to wonder whether someone is sending a signal that it is time to quit.

Fighting futurephobes in my mental cave

Have you ever had your heart broken so miserably that your formerly fantastic vision for your future was shattered beyond recognition? Let me start us off in this magical place. I promise, I will be gentle...

Your sense of meaning is obliterated. All the hopes you had pinned on your mental Pinterest board are destroyed by the emotional infection seeping through your system. Your identity is compromised. You listen to Bon Iver's 'Skinny Love' on repeat. You wonder whether you will ever be able to trust again. Your friends covertly create a Tinder account for you. You pour your every thought and impulse into a Moleskine notebook. You circle-breathe the printed words back into your lungs to add fuel to your fire of internal anguish. Your verbal vomit transforms into nonsensical haikus. They are no good. Because nothing makes sense you consider joining a cult. Because a cult doesn't make sense, you see a psychic instead. She speaks in tongues. Your yoga teacher instructs you to open your hip flexors as pain is stored in the sacral chakra. You cry uncontrollably while doing the pigeon pose. You buy Joni Mitchell. On vinyl. And listen to it while reading *Eat, Pray, Love*. Even if you are not of the female sex. Your sibling makes you watch *Forgetting Sarah Marshall*, and tells you to restore your sanity by forgetting about Elizabeth Gilbert. Instead you fall in love with Zooey Deschanel's character – Summer Finn – in *(500) Days of Summer*.

Your cognitive behavioural therapist, recommended to you by your flatmate who is sick of pro bono counselling, tells you to mindfully meditate. You go on a sex binge. Internationally. You live in the present. Occasionally mindful. Or at least a related cousin of it. And the lofty emotional and spiritual standard you set for yourself with that special someone keeps being compromised. Nostalgia kicks in – often while drinking single malts. You try to maturely dismiss your psychotic episode with reference to mature-sounding words like 'everyone has one that got away'. You're unconvincing. And your friends call you on it, and tell you to keep swiping right, because the metaphor reminds you there's plenty more fish in the digital sea. Incidentally, you're Piscean. Your well-meaning friends tell you to maybe modify your expectations and take a rational, 'tick the box' approach to irrational matters of the heart. You can feel the damp, plastic tarpaulin of futurephobia being slowly dragged across your field of dreams, blocking any hope of photosynthesis and pre-emptively destroying your rare green shoots from ever blossoming. This thwarted outlook on life is unusual for you. You used to love the future. And now the future, represented by a figment of your imagination, has sent a heat-seeking cluster bomb straight into your vulnerable heart. Your context, values, identity, taste in music, flirtation with spirituality, wellbeing and discourse are all collateral damage.

You might be guilty of some of the same gut-wrenching, self-despising and sabotaging coping mechanisms outlined here. You may not. You may be a stronger, more evolved human than me. I for one am guilty of all of them. They may well be based on a true story. (You could check my Moleskine entries.) My cool, rational mind wishes this wasn't so. But what doesn't kill you makes you stronger, right? Time heals all wounds. And slowly I am starting to forget about Zooey Deschanel and Elizabeth Gilbert's books have been turned into pulp. All those highlighted sections have been repurposed as environmentally friendly espresso cups. Aren't you happy you bought an inspirational book about the future? And what does this confession have to do with you? Why does futurephilia, in the ways it's been described so far in this chapter, sound suspiciously like an Adele song? Why would a futurist paint such a gloomy picture of the future? Where is the promised antidote to futurephobia?

I have asked you to reflect upon heartbreak. Why? Because to me it illustrates wonderfully the friction, the struggle and the conflict that exists between people in intimate relationships with each other. People who may even care for each other. Such as families in business. People who either define the future together or separately. They may be lovers with different time horizons. Or one may be monogamous, the other polyamorous. One heterosexual, the other bisexual. One fertile, the other infertile. One clean-freak, the other 'creative'. One futurephile, the other futurephobe. And we have all been there. The friction and conflict that results may well be the thing that grants you access to adulthood.

But this friction between futurephilia and futurephobia exists not just in romantic relationships. These differences, which make the world so complex and intellectually stimulating, also create grating seams in families between the generations, inter-and intra-generationally, and even with the dear departed. They mess with teams. They can destroy cultures. They stuff up global negotiations between developed nations and emerging economies. Our outlook on life and, by extension, the future, is determined by a smorgasbord of values, resources, neurological processes, contexts, influencers, the commodities markets, the fuel pump, our wearable technology, our moods, the abrupt miscalculation by our scales this morning, and our favourite team's performance on the weekend. What I am curious about here is the clash of the titans – that epic battle between futurephiles and futurephobes. Because when futurephiles and futurephobes engage intimately, romantically, familially, commercially, environmentally, socially, politically... holy shit, sparks can and will fly. And if their visions for the future don't align, heartbreak, separation, trauma, friction, and counselling ensue. Trust me. I have studied these patterns. Subjectively and objectively.

These sparks kept flying after that weekend at FBN, and after the ensuing, partial caving in of Mum's shop's roof. I can respect that stress scientifically makes us dumber, and leads to stupid decisions. But as a futurist and strategist, my job is to elevate my client's and my partners' perspectives. Would these family values now fly out the window because of rain? Seemingly yes. A few weeks after the roof collapse, Mum sent one of our graphic designers an image from a competitor's ad in the Swedish newspaper *Göteborgsposten*. It was neither a particularly good ad nor very enticing or cleverly executed. It did point out that this particular competitor had a generous selection of sizes. Mum demanded that we collaborate with one of her vendors, who wanted to sponsor a once-off, small, reactive ad in a paper newspaper, while articulating our core values. In the process, Mum claimed that one of those core values was 'big sizes'. And my heart sunk as I realised that three and a half years of coaching, consulting, facilitation, listening, and common deep reflections at FBN didn't compete with the lizard brain that gets awoken by an immediate physical threat of an event in-store.

This type of family friction is painful when you should have noticed the signals, particularly because those signals are cross-contextually relevant. We can learn from romantic relationships, friendships and bloodlines. We may apply the lessons in business, entrepreneurship, leadership, change management and negotiations. Personally, as a futurist, whose job it is to be 'positive about the future', I can learn to curb my enthusiasm by paying closer attention to the facts on the table. Hope, I have learnt, is not a strategy. That doesn't preclude me from being a perpetual futurephile who is hell-bent on defeating the world's futurephobes, and helping to create transformational futures that leave the status quo in the dust. And while I will transparently share both failures and successes from my own life to help illustrate impactful lessons, I want the remaining chapters to equip you with the strategies and tactics for designing superior outcomes for you, your loved ones, and the planet.

CASE STUDY:
HUBSPOT — ENABLER OF SEAMLESS MARKETING IN THE TWENTY-FIRST CENTURY

As digital devices and screens become ubiquitous in modern life, we can see that marketing is changing. Today's consumer has an ever-growing number of media choices and is met with a huge number of marketing messages across different platforms every day, both in the online and offline world. Today's brands are not limited by the size of the physical advertising space in a magazine or the length of a television commercial. The digital revolution has removed that limitation and enabled brands to reach consumers almost anytime and anywhere. Meanwhile, consumers have become very good at blocking out interruptive marketing tactics such as direct mail, email and cold calls. Traditional online marketing tactics like online ads are having a declining effect – according to www.statista.com, for example, in June 2015 worldwide 198 million users actively used adblock plugins when going online (a big increase from January 2013 with 54 million adblock users).

It was this realisation that sparked the idea behind the inbound marketing and sales platform HubSpot. The company was founded back in 2006 by MIT graduates Brian Halligan, CEO at the time of writing, and Dharmesh Shah, CTO, and they soon came to the understanding that the old tactics and best practices simply weren't effective anymore.

Digitalisation has changed, and is still changing, the way people shop, putting pressure on brands to innovate and get a deeper understanding about their customers in order to truly reach out to digital minds and analogue hearts. However, getting to know your customers is easier said than done in today's digital landscape with so many sources to retrieve information from. HubSpot's platform helps businesses and entrepreneurs tackle this problem by giving its users a holistic picture of how their customers have interacted with the business via social media, email, phone and much more.

Furthermore, HubSpot offers tools for social media marketing, content management, web analytics, landing pages and search optimisation. The combination of all of these aspects on one single platform enables businesses around the world to seamlessly connect with their customers by earning their interest.

The founders of HubSpot travel the world advocating not only for HubSpot as a platform and service, but also for spreading the concept of 'inbound marketing'. In their 2014 book *Inbound Marketing: Attract, Engage and Delight Customers Online*, Halligan and Shah define inbound marketing as follows:

> We started talking about this transformation in how people shop and buy. We called the traditional, interruptive methods 'outbound marketing', because they were fundamentally about pushing a message out, and started calling the new way 'inbound marketing'. Inbound was about pulling people in by sharing relevant information, creating useful content, and generally being helpful.

Furthermore, Halligan and Shah write that inbound marketing means 'we are liberated from the tyranny of having to interrupt people's daily lives'. The concept of inbound marketing is clearly aligned with the idea of seamless. No interruptions. No friction. The inbound methodology is all about empathically designing a customer journey that is personal, relevant and context-based, with the ultimate aim of helping customers to achieve their goals. In order to succeed with this methodology, of course, you need to gain a deep understanding of your customer. What are his or her needs? What is the problem that he or she is actually trying to solve? What are their main obstacles? How can you remove them and guide customers closer to a solution? These are the sorts of questions you need to address if you want to earn your customers' interest and be successful at the inbound methodology.

Needless to say that at Thinque we are big fans of this platform, and the main reason we like it so much is because it's the perfect enabler of seamless communication. HubSpot helps us reach out with thought-leading content on the latest disruptive business trends, while also empowering us to improve customer intimacy and digitally connect with people who are genuinely interested in the content and the stories we are sharing. Furthermore, HubSpot encourages us to learn more through their educational platform, HubSpot Academy, and by connecting us with over 150 000 other likeminded marketers via the marketing community inbound.org.

Ask yourself ...

Think about the following with regard to your business:

1. How can you become better at helping your customers overcome their challenges? What valuable tools can you provide for your customers?

2. How can you move from interruptive marketing tactics to an inbound marketing strategy where you focus on earning your customers' interest? And what kind of content would move your customers further into the buyer's journey?

3. How can you turn your customers into fans and brand advocates by creating a digital community? Come up with a few creative ideas on how you can enable your customers to share insights and help each other.

STEP 8
HERO'S JOURNEY WHEEL FOR MAMMA SÖRMAN-NILSSON

The alliance between Georg Sörman, Anders and Thinque is tested as they engage with lawyers in negotiations with landlords of the two retail properties, and Thinque proposes to take over the management and launch of Georg Sörman & Sons. Birgitta travels together with Thinque to Pitti Uomo in January 2015 to collaborate on the launch of the two brother brands. Thinque puts in place a project plan for the phased transition of management, which is accepted by Georg Sörman.

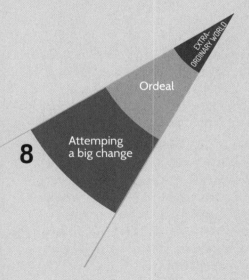

EXTRA-ORDINARY WORLD

Ordeal

8 Attemping a big change

Ordeal

The ordeal in stage 8 could be a deep test of physical agility or mental fortitude, or even a deep inner crisis that the heroine must face for her world, family, community and loved ones to continue to exist. This may take the form of the heroine facing her greatest fear or most dreaded enemy, requiring the heroine to pull on every bit of external and internal resource gathered at every junction of the journey to the inmost cave so that she grows into a David who slays her Goliath. Only through some form of 'death' can the heroine be re-born, rejuvenated or enter a renaissance, undergoing a metaphorical resurrection that grants her great powers, foresight or insight to fulfil her destiny, or reach her journey's end. This is the great challenge of the heroine's journey and where everything she values is at stake. If she fails, she will either die or life as she knows it will never be the same again.

For Luke in *Star Wars*, this stage looked as follows:

- *Inner journey:* Ordeal – on the Death Star, Luke and Han dress as Stormtroopers, discover the princess and attempt to rescue her, but they are discovered.

- *Outer journey:* Attempting a big change – the alliance is tested as they engage with enemy troops.

For Birgitta, it looked like this:

- *Inner journey:* Ordeal – the alliance between Georg Sörman, Anders and Thinque is tested after the positive reflections and agreement on the family values (the 'force') at FBN. The collapse of the roof in the main shop at Kungsholmen disrupts revenue, and momentarily shifts focus, and leads to injections of further 'artificial breathing' funds.

- *Outer journey:* Attempting a big change – according to the Georg Sörman 100 strategy plan and brand rollout, and in line with the impending 100th birthday celebration in January 2016 (only three months away at this stage of the journey), Thinque Digital has been working closely with several printing partners to help in the final execution of the brand rollout, and makes a final recommendation on the preferred supplier (not surprisingly, not the more expensive, and simultaneously less qualitative incumbent).

8: Ordeal

Some animals adapt when their external environment changes.
Others lose their natural habitat, go into decline and die.

Moods had waxed and waned. At times, for example, Mum would vehemently oppose the idea of a new brand as the symbol of the Georg Sörman 100 strategy. She would say that Georg Sörman's neon sign and neon logo of the man with the walking stick was iconic (see figure 8.1). Indeed, it had been voted the inaugural 'sign of the year' in 1998 when Stockholm was the EU's culture capital, and a replica had been turned into the Oscar of Swedish design awards by becoming the actual prize for subsequent winners for a decade (which had ended in 2008, mind you). The neon sign even had its own Wikipedia listing (see sv.wikipedia.org/wiki/Sörman-skylten; use Google if you'd like to translate the page into English). I would counter that the brand was known as a shop for geriatrics, and that today's sixty year olds are more like forty year olds. I would also point out that the universal iconography of a geriatric (used on buses and trains, for example) is a man with a walking stick, not dissimilar to our logo, and that if we were to use a man with a walking stick, the man should at least have a spring in his step, like the one used in the Johnnie Walker logo (see figure 8.1, overleaf).

Figure 8.1: the old logo and the former brand perception

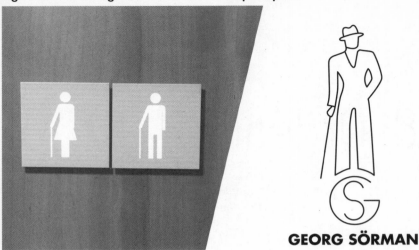

GEORG SÖRMAN

The business was in deep need of a re-brand that connected us historically to our roots, and that tuned us back into the values that had been evident when my grandfather's father started it in 1916. I offered to invest in a Georg Sörman private brand to vertically integrate the brand – to which Mum asked why anyone would want to buy something with our logo on it. This left me curious. If the old brand was so amazing, and as holy a cow that it couldn't be touched, wouldn't it be great to amplify that supposed brand recognition through your collection of clothing? Unfortunately, this was the kind mental seesawing and illogic that I had to get used to. And incidentally, if you search on Sweden's equivalent of eBay for vintage clothes, lots of Georg Sörman produced garments from yesteryear turn up, including hats, jackets, blazers and beanies. In these listings, the Georg Sörman name is always highlighted as a sign of quality. Whoever said that being the mentor, trying to be Yoda, would be easy. I wonder if Yoda ever got upset with Luke.

One of Mum's mental ordeals has been that she feels like a few 'pipsqueaks' are telling her how to run her business. And that maybe the brand that got the business to where it was is not the brand that will ensure succession or success. This makes her defensive. And while our heroine desperately needs help, she is unwilling to accept it. Meanwhile, one physical or attitudinal obstacle after another has blocked her energy from focusing on the things she can control – these things being attitude, mindset, strategy and execution. Firefighting is something she is pretty good at, but if you are always running around fighting fires, you never have time to build a fireproof home. And with the latest instalment of CO_2 leaking into her shop from above, Mum's energy waned (understandably) dealing with contractors, strata and lawyers, instead of the new brand rollout. And her 'Robin', my dad, loyally followed her on this path. Nothing is like disruption and financial fears to strangle the oxygen out of a project that is about to take off and lead to us overcoming obstacles we could control – enticing more customers to buy from us, more often, while spreading the word about our little shop and the renaissance of Georg Sörman to their friends and loved ones. Everyone loves a good comeback story. And while the owners of Georg Sörman like to cry poor, I remind them that it is not the size of the dog in the fight, but the size of the fight in the dog that matters. With a newly released *Välsytt Herrnytt* broadsheet (see figure 8.2) and upcoming VIP night in 2015, a smart campaign, and an open letter built on the hero's journey to mobilise our customers, we were about to show some serious size of the fight in the dog. Or so I thought.

Figure 8.2: front cover of the *Välsytt Herrnytt* broadsheet

The obstacle is the way — turning 'in the way' into 'the way'

In *The Republic*, Plato (the philosopher and not my first dog, who went by the same name) argued that if the utopian city state of Kallipolis was to ever emerge, 'philosophers (must) become kings, or those now called kings (must)…genuinely and adequately philosophise'. Plato defined a 'philosopher' by its eponymous occupation: 'lover of wisdom'. He made the important distinction between one who loves true knowledge (as opposed to mere experience or education) by arguing that the philosopher is the only person who has access to ideas, which are the archetypal entities that exist behind all representations of the form – for example, the idea of 'beauty', as opposed to a concrete manifestation of beauty such as a flower. Thus, in *The Republic* Plato fashions his Ship of State metaphor, which holds that a 'true pilot must of necessity pay attention to the seasons, the heavens, the stars, the winds, and everything proper to the craft if he is really to rule the ship'. To this effect, in 170 AD, Marcus Aurelius – arguably the first example of a philosopher king – ahead of an epic battle in Germania, sat down to write the following reflective lines:

> Our actions may be impeded, but there can be no impeding our intentions or dispositions. Because we can accommodate and adapt. The mind adapts and converts to its own purposes the obstacle to our acting.

He then concluded with two further sentences: 'The impediment to action advances action. What stands in the way becomes the way'.

This idea became central to the philosophy of Stoicism, a school of thought that focuses on free will and living in accord with nature. It argues that errors in judgement are what cause destructive emotions, and that the best way to see a person's philosophy is by looking not at what they say but at how they act. In a modern form, this means that we don't control what happens to us, but we do control how we respond to what happens to us. Difficulty can make heroes and heroines great.

Stoics also have a saying that encourages *amor fati* – which roughly means 'love of fate'. With this mindset, we can deconstruct problems as an indication that we are on path. Consequently, optimistic stoics break problem-tackling into three (simplified) parts:

1. perception (the way we see the problem and the story we tell ourselves)
2. action (the problem is what it is, but we can creatively solve it)
3. will (looking at what we don't control, and what we can do about this).

In Ryan Holiday's awesome book *The Obstacle is the Way*, he tells the story of Thomas Edison, who experienced a setback when his factory and a large part of his stock in trade suffered a destructive fire. Partly unfazed by the event, Edison told his family to go quickly and view the fire in amazement, because they would never see a fire like this again. In his book, Holiday, a modern-day stoic, argues that obstacles don't inhibit success but instead create success, and that as humans we must see 'through the negative, past its underside, and into its corollary: the positive'.

Marcus Aurelius also said of obstacles, or problems:

> Objective judgement, now at this very moment. Unselfish action, now at this very moment. Willing acceptance – now at this very moment – of all external events. That's all you need.

I have often reflected on this idea that 'the obstacle is the way', because the heroine's journey in the renaissance of Georg Sörman has certainly been marred with challenges and setbacks – be it landlords, Cinderella's sisters, digital disruption, frequently forgetful general managers and financial accomplices covering up the traces of dementia. It is a wonder that the business is still alive – all things considered. And while the heroine and her partner have certainly been persistent (you have to acknowledge that my parents have grind and grit), my question is whether they have been bold enough to truly take a leap of faith and 100 per cent commit to an uncertain, yet highly believable, future journey – to the adventure and vision that we once collaborated and agreed on. At times, for Mum, mere survival and 'hanging in there' seems enough, but I wish for her a better fate, a fate of transformation and fruits for all her hard work, grit and grind. But it seems like we are living in a world that has moved on from the Lutheran work ethic of 'hard work pays off'. Hard must be married with smart. Brawn and brains must collaborate, if Providence is to move.

CASE STUDY:
OSCAR JACOBSON – A SEAMLESS REJUVENATION JOURNEY

An ongoing renaissance is taking place within the menswear industry. With the success of television series such as *Mad Men*, *Boardwalk Empire*, *Peaky Blinders* and *Downton Abbey*, we are seeing more and more men develop a genuine interest in classic styles that last beyond one season. This trend is not just a result of style-conscious consumers being inspired by popular costume dramas, however. The renewed appetite for classics and wardrobe essentials is, according to the marketing intelligence company Mintel, also driven by the uncertain economy. This means more men are thinking that investing in quality garments over fast fashion is worthwhile.

One among a rising number of renowned Swedish menswear brands that are successfully capitalising on this trend is Oscar Jacobson. However, this has not always been the case for the business founded in 1903 – just eight years ago the brand was not considered to be relevant at all for the urban and style-conscious man. At that time, it was seen as a brand for the older gentlemen. The big challenge for Oscar Jacobson was that they had an ageing customer base – around sixty to sixty-five year olds – who lived in rural areas in Sweden and didn't buy many new garments each year. In other words, their main customer base was becoming less profitable.

The owners of the heritage brand quickly understood that the brand and the business as a whole had to be rejuvenated in order to appeal to a younger and more profitable clientele. At the same time, they didn't want the evolved brand to alienate the old customer base. This was, of course, a difficult task, so the owners recruited Roger Tjernberg and Mats Pettersson, who had successfully helped Tiger, another Swedish brand, transform itself from a tailoring brand for gentlemen to a contemporary and edgy designer brand.

At its inception in 1903, Oscar Jacobson specialised in work wear such as overalls, work trousers and basic shirts. After a generational shift in the company, they decided to launch the (at the time) novel concept of ready-to-wear men's clothing in set sizes. (Prior to this, all clothes had been made according to the individual customer's measurements.) The shift to ready-to-wear enabled Oscar Jacobson to lower production costs while still delivering a high-quality product to the end customer. During the 1950s the business refined their expertise and craftsmanship within tailoring, sewing and fashion, and the founder's son convinced the business that the brand should let foreign influences and exclusive materials such as cashmere and lamb's wool lead the design process.

Fast-forward to the twenty-first century and as Tjernberg and Pettersson initiated the repositioning of the brand they came to the conclusion that the change process had to permeate all parts of the business. This meant they started to look at everything from distribution and marketing to the design process and manufacturing. The brand didn't transform overnight, but changes happened incrementally and after a couple of years they started to see their hard work was paying off. Since the repositioning began they have had a yearly growth of around 8 per cent. Oscar Jacobson's turnover grew from the equivalent of around US$14.5 million in 2009 to US$28 million in 2015.

In an interview in *Dagens Industri*, the most influential business paper in the Nordic countries, Roger Tjernberg argued that the clear focus on what he calls the 'Scandinavian Sartorialist' – that is, the tailored Italian look with a Scandinavian touch – has been key to their success. During the change process, their collection has evolved from a very traditional silhouette to a slimmer and more modern one, characterised by tapered suit pants and a shorter jacket, often unconstructed with soft shoulders and wider lapels and inspired by the Neapolitan tailoring tradition. Looking at Oscar Jacobson's growth we can clearly conclude that this look appeals to the younger clientele, and by offering three different kinds of fits, thirty-five sizes and the best pieces from their previous collections, they have also managed to keep their old customer base.

Some of many milestones during recent years for the brand have been their participation in Stockholm Fashion Week and Pitti Uomo in Florence. Their collaboration collections with key Swedish retailers have also been important building blocks in the repositioning journey. Meanwhile, they've also expanded their retail operations by launching a web shop for the end customer. Moreover, Oscar Jacobson have opened up retail concept stores in Gothenburg and Stockholm (the two biggest cities in Sweden), where style-conscious gentlemen can meet and relax – and, of course, experience the feeling of wearing a jacket made out of cashmere from the renowned Italian textile supplier and high-end luxury brand Loro Piana. Just as with many other brands, they've realised that bricks-and-mortar stores are a valuable asset that can seamlessly weave together the online and offline brand experience.

Oscar Jacobson (a Georg Sörman partner and inspiration) is still evolving and searching for new and creative ways to reach out to style-conscious gentlemen. Its successful repositioning proves that heritage brands have an opportunity to use their unique history and identity as a means to seamlessly bridge the age gap and cross-generationally reach out to men of all ages, just like we are focussed on doing with Georg Sörman 100.

Attempting a big change for your brand demands that you go beyond updating your logo. Yes, symbolism is important but a transformation is only possible when you question the status quo and back up the visual renaissance with real change in strategy, thinking and culture.

Ask yourself...

Think about the following with regard to your business:

1. What emerging trends has your business failed to capitalise on? What can you do in order to win the digital minds and analogue hearts of today's and tomorrow's customer?

2. How can the unique heritage and traditions of your business be used as a means to bridge perceived age gaps and expand your brand's reach?

3. What can you do to ensure that change permeates all parts of your business? Do you have the technology and staff that can help you successfully drive change internally?

STEP 9
HERO'S JOURNEY WHEEL FOR MAMMA SÖRMAN-NILSSON

Thinque sources a new supplier of brand touch points. Despite months of illustrating the benefits of the new supplier, Georg Sörman decides to stay with its legacy provider, who goes behind Thinque's back to ultimately put the renaissance temporarily on ice. Georg Sörman delays the implementation of the brand rollout because of poor cash flow, but several milestones are achieved, despite forced renovations and the temporary closure of the shop for three weeks.

Consequences of the attempt
(improvements and setbacks)

Reward
(seizing the sword)

EXTRA-ORDINARY WORLD

Reward (seizing the sword)

The heroine is transformed into a new state after triumphing over her worst enemy, surviving death and finally overcoming her greatest personal obstacle. She emerges from the battle a stronger person but often this has come at some kind of price. Her reward could, however, come in a multitude of forms – it could be in the form of greater knowledge or insights, a reconciliation with a loved one or an ally, or a secret revealed or some kind of object of gargantuan importance. This treasure will help the heroine return to the ordinary world again, but the heroine cannot begin celebrations yet as she must prepare for the last leg of the odyssey.

Here is how Luke's reward looked:

- *Inner journey:* Reward (seizing the sword) – in the trash compactor, Luke is pulled underwater by a creature but is rescued by his friends.

- *Outer journey:* Consequences of the attempt (improvements and setbacks) – the alliance begins to work together as a team to escape the Death Star.

And here's how Birgitta was travelling on her journey:

- *Inner journey:* Reward (seizing the sword) – the Georg Sörman and Thinque alliance begins to work as a team as they formalise a twelve-month rollout of the 'Georg Sörman 100' brand strategy and execution, spanning from March 2015 to March 2016, and the family engages deeply with the Family Business Network's Owner Program. But internal challenges still remain.

- *Outer journey:* Consequences of the attempt (improvement and setbacks) – cash flow is tough for the business and so Georg Sörman consistently delays the implementation of the Georg Sörman brand rollout. Several positive and profitable milestones are still achieved, despite external challenges like forced renovations and the resultant involuntary, temporary closure of the shop for almost four weeks (and subsequent repairs of the renovation). In the meantime, friction and broken promises in the negotiation phases regarding the management transition of the Old Town shop leads to Thinque withdrawing from the negotiations. Georg Sörman maintains the status quo in its positioning, despite the availability of a full business plan for Georg Sörman & Sons.

9: Reward (seizing the sword)

Disruption is only disruptive if you are not adaptive.

Blood is thicker than water

Family relationships and loyalties are the strongest and most important ones. Or so the theory goes. And all of this can be challenged and confused in family business contexts. *Bloodline*, one of my favourite Netflix original series, begins with a thrilling narrative by John Rayburn, the second eldest of four siblings in a family business:

> Sometimes – you know something's coming. You can feel it. In the air. In your gut. You don't sleep at night. A voice in your head's telling you that something is going to go terribly wrong and there's nothing you can do to stop it. That's how I felt when my brother came home.

The Rayburn family operates a seaside hotel in Monroe County, Florida, and are somewhat of an institution down in the Floridian keys. (A word of warning: the following contains a few spoilers, so maybe skip the next few paragraphs if you're planning a *Bloodline* binge.) They are part of the 'establishment' and their name is imbued with respect. John is a successful detective, Kevin runs a local marina and Meg is a lawyer with a local firm. The black sheep of the family is Danny, the eldest son, who returns home for the forty-fifth anniversary of the resort owned by the family matriarch and patriarch – Sally and Robert. Danny has a chequered history of criminality and drug use, and we learn that the origins of his troubled life come down to the untimely death of their younger sister, Sarah, when he was a teenager. As Danny settles back into the resort and family affairs, we start learning the family's secrets, and that his father, Robert, badly beat Danny after Sarah's death, with Sally requesting that the siblings cover up the beating by lying to the police. While Danny initially seems to have turned over a new leaf, after staying – against the will of his siblings, who asked him to leave the family alone, pretending that this request is an expression of the patriarch Robert's desire – he eventually turns the family business into a gateway for drug smuggling, jeopardising the whole family and their business. After threatening John's daughter, surviving a drug cartel hit man's attempt on his life by killing the hit man, and acting increasingly erratically, Danny is slain in rage by John (the detective), who recruits his siblings, Kevin and Meg, in covering up the murder. Season one ends with some kind of calm before the storm, with a well-thought-through carpet to conceal what happened to Danny, and the return to some kind of normalcy. The storm clouds start gathering, however, with the arrival of Danny's unknown son, Nolan, who is coming home to uncover what is under that concealing carpet.

Of course, not all family business contexts are this troubling. But certain themes feel eerily familiar – particularly the family dynamics, tensions, secrets and cover-ups, and the way these eventually surface. On the other hand, reflecting on my own journey with Georg Sörman, researching family business as a business model and learning from other family businesses, I am grateful that the situation in our case is not as bad as in this American TV drama.

In the following sections, I reflect on some of the dynamics within family businesses.

Business is personal

As it turns out, business is deeply personal. This is perhaps one of the reasons that suicide rates among farmers are elevated across a variety of nations. Bob Katter, Australian MP, claims that one farmer dies from suicide every four days in Australia and, while the data he refers to when making this claim come from the 1980s and 1990s (as pointed out by the ABC's Fact Check), the latest statistics show that suicide rates for agricultural workers are elevated compared to other professions, with variations in that elevation across Australian states. Katter's claim originated in a famous statement by former Victorian Premier Jeff Kennett, current chairman of Beyond Blue, an Australian charity focused on men's health. Kennett was quoted in 2006 at the time of 'The Big Dry' (a prolonged drought) in London's Telegraph newspaper as saying, 'My fear is that when under prolonged stress, and when they see their assets totally denuded of value, that we will see an increase [in suicides]'.

Globally, a 2013 analysis by Melbourne University researchers (included in the article 'Suicide by occupation: systematic review and meta-analysis', published in the *British Medical Journal*), found that the suicide rate for agriculture workers was 1.6 times higher than the average for all employed people. Farmer suicides are the highest of any profession globally, including in the United States, where farmers are twice as likely as the general population to commit suicide. According to the 2014 *Newsweek* article 'Death on the farm',

> In the UK one farmer a week commits suicide. In China, farmers are killing themselves daily to protest the government taking over their prime agricultural lands for urbanization. In France, a farmer dies by suicide every two days ... India yearly reports more than 17 627 farmer suicides.

The *Newsweek* article also notes it is likely that the real numbers are even higher, because suicides by farmers are underreported, as they may be mislabelled as hunting or tractor mishaps. Arguably, many farmers who commit suicide 'stoically' make it look like an accident to ensure their families will be paid the life insurance, which would be otherwise invalidated. Wow. This is depressing, yet fascinating, and deserves enquiry. In the United States, for example, farmers have flipped from the bottom of the suicide list to the top since 1890. In that year, researchers for the US Census Bureau ranked professions that had the highest rate of suicide. Tailors, accountants, bookkeepers, clerks and copyists were those who were most prolifically impacted. At the extreme bottom of the list was a career least likely to lead to self-harm: farming. Things have changed. Why?

According to research and interviews with American farmers on the reasons for the elevated incidence of farm suicide, a confluence of factors has emerged. Some point toward the sense of loss of community due to urbanisation, and others to lost income; some hint at automation and the depersonalisation of agriculture, while others believe it has to do with the loss of independence. The idea of 'betting the farm' holds true for some with increasing financial leverage and exposure due to higher loans for fertilisers, seeds, equipment and pesticides. And some feel ashamed that they are not able to be self-sustaining like previous generations of family farmers. In his 'Death on the farm' article, *Newsweek*'s Max Kutner quoted one of the two suicide notes found in dairy farmer Dean Pierson's barn in upstate New York: 'Lonely. Discouraged. Overwhelmed. No hope. Can't go on. Danger to my family. Worn out. The kids are so talented. Gwynne you are a good person.' The other simply said: 'So sorry'.

Michael Rosmann, PhD, was described in the *New York Times* article 'As agriculture struggles, Iowa psychologist helps his fellow farmers cope' as 'a fourth generation farmer as well as a clinical psychologist, [who] speaks the language of men and women on the verge of losing their place on the land'. Rosmann has been specialising in mental health among farmers since 1979, when he left the psychology department at the University of Virginia to dedicate himself whole-heartedly to farming mental health. He analyses the situation with reference to what he calls the 'agrarian imperative', which is the idea that humans have an innate drive to work the land and produce food for their loved ones and their communities. Rosmann argues that farmers take significant risks to satisfy that drive, and if they are unsuccessful, they develop a deep sense of failure. 'Farmers are motivated to hang on to land at almost all cost,' he says. Business is personal. And it is perhaps even more so in one of the oldest professions on earth. When an industry is exposed to substantial structural change, and when the profession in the United States has seen an almost 90 per cent employment drop since World War II levels because of automation and productivity gains, we start to see a modern situation where some of the people who feed the world are struggling to get by, both economically and mentally. As a result, for some, suicide seems the only way out. Which is the reason that Rosmann, the United Kingdom's Farming Community Network, Beyond Blue and others are investing in providing preventative measures to boost mental health prior to a 'loaded gun' emergency phone call. As in health, as in business, prevention is better than cure.

I know how much business and her brand matters to my mum, our heroine. And I know they matter just as much to other family business owners and entrepreneurs around the world. Their businesses are an extension of themselves – their hopes, aspirations and family legacies. A lot is wrapped into a sign bearing your name on the door. Pride. The judgment of your siblings. The expectations of your (dead) forebears. The nagging of your partners. And the fearful thought of succession and letting go of control. And these feelings are all at play while having to learn an entirely new language – digital – that is now an essential tool for business survival.

As I've mentioned, Dad has often in exasperation thrown out the idea of 'shut the shop down and throw away the key', but I fundamentally have never believed this to be the right strategy for Mum's mental stability in the future. Underlying issues continued to bubble beneath the surface throughout my mum's heroine's journey, and many of the issues could not be resolved. These issues came to a head, for example, when Thinque sourced a new, competitive supplier of printing and analogue brand touch points. Despite months of illustrating the service and cost benefits of the new supplier, my mum and Georg Sörman decided to embrace the status quo and stay with its legacy provider, who then went behind Thinque's back to ultimately put the renaissance on ice.

But my mum has spent forty years working this business, and conceding defeat is not in her mental range. She will continue to the bitter end, whatever that means. In my efforts to help, the thought of the cautionary tale of those farmers has been in the back of my mind. And touch wood it never comes to such a mental breakdown for Mum. This caution has been another reason that strategic mentoring and the brand renaissance have been so important. Yet, despite this, I have still struggled to win her old-school heart and mind, and she is still a long way from truly seizing the sword.

We can be heroes

Ideas and texts can inspire huge change. David Bowie's 'Heroes' is the tale of two lovers, one from East Berlin and one from West Berlin, during the Cold War. The song was inspired by David Bowie seeing his manager, Tony Visconti, embracing his girlfriend by the Berlin Wall. In 1987, David Bowie performed the song at the German Reichstag building in Berlin, and together with Bruce Springsteen's performance at Radrennbahn Weissensee (a large cycling track in Berlin) a year later, the song is credited with 'helping bring down the wall' by the German government. In his book *David Bowie: The music and the changes*, Bowie scholar David Buckley has written that 'Heroes' is 'perhaps pop's definitive statement of the potential triumph of the human spirit over adversity.'

I wished that *Digilogue: How to win the digital minds and analogue hearts of tomorrow's customers* would equally bring down Mum's mental wall, and get her to embrace change as the strategy forward. I wished FBN, the publicity we secured, the new customers we created, the brand we launched and the content we created would ensure the brand's survival in one form or another. I wished that Mum would gain control, by giving some up. I had hoped to be the fourth-generation owner of Georg Sörman, and that we would successfully cross the abyss that seems so hard – from third to fourth generation, when a family business turns into a crown jewel (see chapter 4). I wished our heroine had realised that control is an illusion, and only by giving other people what they want do you achieve what you want. But Mum can still be a hero. And if she won't listen to her reverse mentor, maybe she might lend an ear to the dearly departed David Bowie…

Where one story ends, another begins

I thought the help I provided to Mum and 'her' business was a narrative of transformation, but I have started to accept that it may instead be about endings and letting go. In fact, after writing my love letters, my EMBA thesis and *Digilogue* to my mum and seeing them go unrequited, and after Thinque needing to walk away (or be ejected) from a key part of the brand's renaissance strategy, I sat down for an attempt at a reconciliatory dialogue with my parents on 13 March 2016. During this conversation, part of Mum's world view came alive. (Remember the idea that it only takes one psychologist to change a light bulb, but the light bulb has got to want to change?) During our March 2016 conversation, we talked about the fact that under her (sometimes mis?)management of the business, it had consistently lost money for most of the thirteen years (this is public information in Sweden, courtesy of allabolag.se) and I argued that I was home to help her turn things around, and ensure she could one day relax in the knowledge that the business would live on and that she had done a good job of being a responsible steward of it, and had managed to perhaps also proactively plan for its succession to my brother's and my generation, the fourth generation of menswear-selling Sörmans.

The conversation then became far from constructive. I had had a sneaky suspicion that Mum's pride prevented her from thinking of 'help' as something positive, but her tirade that evening about how 'help' is 'offensive and invasive', was the final straw for me. How can you help someone who neither wants help, nor considers it a kind act? The closest I had come to this kind of reaction to my intended help were the outbursts of threats, physical and verbal abuse from a friend of mine who is a diagnosed alcoholic. Pulling away the bottle(s) from him has never been met with much approval. Since May 2012, Mum has managed to facilitate similar levels in me of feeling unappreciated. Yes, I know, I choose my own response. You might empathise or not. Either way, there you go; apologies if I have gone too Dr Brené Brown 'vulnerable' on you in this chapter. Transformation in our family's case has frequently been a case of friction.

So what is invasive and offensive about help from a futurist son? I have thought deeply and vulnerably about this, and my therapist, my EMBA cohort and the Headspace meditation app have all been valuable contributions in this self-reflection. Feel free to add to this list or contact me or my mum if you think I have missed something – and, importantly, have a think if you can identify any analogues in your own business or organisation. I also remind you that Mum and Dad's perspectives on the odyssey are also contained within this book and I encourage you to read them for a balanced view. The following sections show my take on what caused most of the problems.

Getting advice from your son

Mum carried me for nine months, gave birth to me (incidentally, under hypnosis and with no drugs), changed my nappies and nurtured me as an infant and beyond. All of a sudden, the 'child prodigy' (I am thirty-five and an adult but, in the eyes of parents, you are always a child) returns home to fix something that she doesn't think needs fixing. Combine this with the fact that in her case and in her father's case, the norm was that you studied under the previous generation with quiet awe and respect for several decades. Instead, the successful management consultant/strategist/futurist comes home, with 'no dirt under his nails', and upsets the apple cart. This changes the dynamics between mother and son. I can empathise with the fact that it takes a lot of agility and open-mindedness to take advice from the next generation (while, of course, a lot can be said for its merits).

Exposed by the futurist

Courtesy of my own business, Thinque, which I founded in 2005, I have a global audience and clientele, and associated media and PR channels. According to my therapist's analysis, Mum may have started feeling exposed when I shined a public light on her management of the business. Mum, as a very private person, was brought up with the idea that politics, money and sex would never be discussed around the family dinner table, and that no family skeletons would ever come out of the wardrobe. So I can empathise with the fact that Mum found it difficult that I share a (carefully curated and partly censored) version of events with tens of thousands of people globally each year. As she said when she resisted the idea of joining the Family Business Network, this support organisation would make her feel like she was in a 'gynaecologist chair' exposing our private bits. Meanwhile, her son travels the world and utilises this family story as a cautionary tale of what happens when you resist change, with my mum as exhibit #1 (with her permission, mind you). That's tough, and I applaud her for viewing it in the distance. Hearing it in the physical context of her own store is a bit close to home.

Feeling like a failure

I can imagine that Mum feels like she has failed her father and her grandfather. Again, I am projecting and hypothesising here, yet it seems reasonable that such feelings might occur. Georg Sörman was built over nearly ninety years into a cultural and sartorial institution in Stockholm, and became a centenarian in 2016. Grandpa, on his deathbed, expressed his wish (or *curse*, depending on how you look at it) that my mother and my father would help continue the legacy. Now, Mum continues to heed the wishes of a person who has been dead for more than thirteen years. At the same time, her sense of duty is neither rewarded by the marketplace, nor reflected in the financial statements (which continue to show red figures).

As a custodian, and despite the fact my mum is quite creative, she has failed to leave a real impression or personal touch on the business in terms of branding and positioning, which I truly believe she is deserving of. Despite her father's flawed, short-term, pre-internet thinking, and her grandfather's sartorial and quality bent, Mum has continued to echo her father's positioning for Georg Sörman, rather than really leaving her own unique mark on the business's brand, which I understand can be disappointing.

Jealousy

Dad would be the first to say that Mum's staff like me, confide in me and are inspired by me (the ones who are left who I have worked with, anyway). Again, I can imagine that this is annoying for my mum. It's like the flighty uncle who comes in a couple of times a year, is admired by the kids, amps them up, and then leaves the hyperactive nieces and nephews with the parents – who have to deal with the quotidian responsibilities of parenthood, while hearing the kids speak highly of their convivial uncle. I get it. It would probably piss me off as well.

Additionally, the staff have a much clearer sense of the future direction of the business and the strategy when I communicate it than when Mum micro-manages them in the store every day. Mum and I have different skills in this regard. And while the strategy and vision is a co-creation, when Mum tries to articulate it, she often weaves in nostalgia and management lessons from her father, Per, as opposed to amplifying what she, Dad and I have co-created together. When she witnesses the way her staff lend me their ears, I can sense that she finds this challenging, or even demeaning. Again, you would have to ask her.

I can do it myself

While Mum, Dad and I did the Family Business Network's Owner's Program together in 2015, Mum came back to the word 'pride' to openly describe what drives her. Pride in being a business woman, pride in the family heritage, pride in being the one (and youngest) daughter out of her sisters who wanted to take the baton from her father. She also feels immense pride in the idea of 'going it alone', being fiercely independent, and showing her sisters (Drizella and Anastasia) that she can do it and that they were wrong in questioning her ability.

Mum is up at 5 am every morning and in the office no later than 8 am, until 6.30 or 7 pm, seven days a week. She is stoic in the modern sense of the word (as opposed to the philosophical), and has a firm belief that she can move through her challenges on her own. She gladly receives help, but only the kind of help she ordains. In other words, if she wants inventory received to be carried from street level to the storage beyond her tailor's desk, she will gladly ask for 'help'. But on a more philosophical level, it's her against the world (with Dad as the overqualified cook, emotional support, driver and househusband). During Mum's outburst in March 2016, which then turned into my plate-smashing and chair-destruction outburst, Mum said that she would gladly accept assistance, contributions and task completions. This is qualitatively different from making any real difference, but they are acts of service that would momentarily make her life easier – on her terms. I would argue that nothing significant has ever been achieved by going it alone (and this comes from a person who likes to describe himself as an occasional 'lone wolf').

Different generational values

While I have been brought up by my parents to respect my elders, including them, Mum's and Dad's Swedish style is quite diplomatic and courteous. It respects boundaries, and believes it is rude to get involved in people's private affairs. They are also quite old-school in their empathy and respect for their own elders. Historically, a great trust has been put in a carpet's ability to magically solve issues by having them brushed in underneath it. Sound familiar of people in past generations in your family?

My style is a bit more open, transparent and, from their perspective, confrontational – very uncomfortable in a Swedish setting where the veneer is very important. My belief that issues and problems should be discussed and then resolved through mutual agreement and consultation doesn't come organically to them and, as such, I have had to play the constant facilitator and initiator of all difficult conversations. While I certainly don't mind this role, my impression is that my mum has found these heart-to-heart and tete-a-tete dialogues about vision, purpose, values, strategy and tension exhausting (and often refers to them as *mycket snack, lite verkstad'*, meaning 'lots of talk, no action'). Or as she likes to say, 'You're very wordy,

Anders'. I, meanwhile, prefer a few more minutes of courageous conversation to a lifetime of unresolved passive aggressiveness.

Female versus male

In media interviews and family discussions, Mum reiterates her pride in being a business woman, running a gentlemen's clothes store. She succeeded two patriarchs and alpha males, and now she gets to be the matriarch and alpha female. Given that she also portrays a certain sense of righteousness in the way she chooses to run the business according to her own whims, and inject it with her life savings in times of need, she also creates a sense of an expressive finger to the world – that she will do exactly as she pleases as a 'strong' woman. Admirable perhaps.

While I am for gender equality, I am also very much for diversity, tolerance and consultation. And I don't believe that there is strength in doing exactly what you want because you momentarily can. Just like grandpa Per, the patriarch among four women, Mum, the matriarch amongst three men, likes to show who is boss, and who is wearing the pants. Compared to my brother and my father, I am more in her face about this decision-making and communication style – something which is not appreciated.

Not 'carrying the milk'

My parents often use this expression which showcases the admirable virtue of working hard. 'We are the ones carrying the milk' is a common refrain – which means they are convinced that they are the ones doing the hard work. Meanwhile, their arrogant son is the one who makes a strategic plan for how the milk should best be carried. Suffice to say, a difference in respect for thinking versus doing exists between the two generations. In some ways this is ironic, because I, like so many generation Yers, was told by my parents that getting a job where you used your intellect was the best investment you could make. My dad always said, 'Son, become a lawyer or a doctor, because they make the most money'. He also added that doctors also did some good. He did not say this for lawyers.

While my dad certainly used both brains and brawn, Mum's side of the family has been obsessed with the virtue of manual and menial labour. Blood, sweat and tears have an inordinate amount of kudos and respect on this side of the family. My brother and I have been sitting through family dinners for three and half decades (and my dad for even longer), listening to tales of the heroism of guest workers and handymen with pearls of sweat dripping down their faces as they 'work like horses' and drag firewood, tree trunks and gardening equipment in mystical wheelbarrows. My mum is famous among my friends for frequently asking them to 'hugg i', literally 'chop in', and give her a hand carrying stuff. My Australian friend Mark visited our house one summer, and for two of the three days he stayed with us we were given the task of clearing the forest and chainsawing the pine trees between Per's and my parents' house. This gift of dangerous work, ideally carried out by a professional arborist or lumberjack, was instead bestowed upon the family, until both Mark and I, seriously uncoordinated and as untrained as our over-cognitive minds were in the art of physical labour, both nearly lost limbs on day one. As such, we kindly refused the non-OHS-compliant work.

So, yes, I admit, menial or manual labour is not my favourite pastime. Having read the Strengthsfinder tool and believing in the merits of the 4-Hour Workweek, I also know where my mind can make the biggest contribution to a business, and that is in the strategy. My worldview is that if you 'fail to plan, you plan to fail' and as such, continues to differ greatly from my mum's. While my mum thinks that I deliberately avoid carrying the milk, my counterarguments that 'thinking is the hardest labour there is' and 'work smarter, not harder' don't go down too well. Okay, I get it, and it's another reason for Mum to resist my contributions.

Anders complicates things

As I have described, Georg Sörman in 2012 was suffering from an image crisis, which had been affecting the bottom line for nearly a decade or more. Together with my parents (also owners and board members), and their team, we developed 'Georg Sörman 100' – the name of the strategy that would take us into the next century of business for this now centenarian business. This strategy was born out of strategy days with the whole Georg Sörman team, discussions with accountants, family dialogue, occasional inputs from Grant Thornton and PwC consultants, my EMBA project at the University of Sydney Business School, Family Business Network courses, dialogue with vendors, and long-standing conversations with an international peer network of owners of other sartorial menswear stores and family businesses, like Henry Bucks in Australia.

The next step was to marry the strategy, which ultimately came down to an 'old meets new', 'tradition & technology', 'timelessness & timeliness', 'baby boomer & gen y', 'father to son' transition/ampersand vibe – or not throwing the analogue baby away with the digital bathwater. (And if you want to find out more about these ideas, pick up a copy of the love letter *Digilogue*.) We needed a visual identity renaissance (see figure 9.1). The logo of an elderly gentleman with a cane – or, according to our focus group, 'the geezer with the walking stick' – while a Stockholm neon-classic, was very similar to some of the iconography on the first few seats on Stockholm buses. In the case of the buses, the iconography was used internationally – to remind users to save the seats for geriatrics and people with special needs.

Figure 9.1: brand perception map

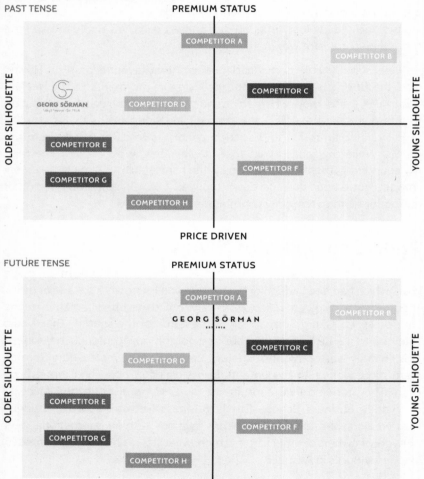

While this communicates empathy with the Georg Sörman cane geezer icon, we know that many men in Stockholm take a 'Simon says' approach to their shopping, and sartorial young professionals often want to shop where other young professionals shop. We needed to shake up the perception about Georg Sörman among customers and non-customers alike and so, as mentioned, my firm, Thinque, contracted in two-time Cannes Lion–winning designer and brand strategist Hema Patel to conceive of the renaissance and revitalisation of the visual identity of the brand, which was to become a central pillar in the strategy. Normally, we would never have been able to afford her, but because of her ties with my family – she has known us as a friend, girlfriend and consultant for nearly twenty years – we were given a great 'mate's rates' discount. Hema did a stellar job and, after narrowing down the diverse options from seven to one final brand chosen by the business owners, the various touch points were to be updated with the new design (see figure 9.2).

Figure 9.2: narrowing down the new brand design options from Hema

While highly strategic and conceptually brilliant, Hema was too expensive for the ongoing, daily brand execution. Life and business at the time (2014–2015) had evolved and changed for me personally as well, and after trying to protect her from my somewhat crazy family for a long time, I decided to introduce my French graphic designer and then-girlfriend, Clementine D'arco, to the strategy execution. Clementine, together with

Thinque's Stockholm-based content marketer and head of research, Anton Järild, was tasked with updating the visual identity and project managing the implementation of brand Georg Sörman 100, as part of the consulting agreement we signed. Anton and Clem were involved from the beginning in Stockholm, and constructed the proposal and eventual agreement of the delivery of services to Georg Sörman, which the three of us co-delivered to Georg Sörman for approval. Neither of my parents know, or have really asked, what a graphic designer, brand strategist or content marketer does, so this set up was highly confusing for them. My mum, in particular, struggled with the idea that her finance assistant (skilled in Excel, but not really in Adobe InDesign or Photoshop) couldn't apply her economics brain to visualising brand Georg Sörman 100, co-developed by two great graphic artists, Clementine and Hema. And this idea still hasn't sunk in.

Again, Mum also found it offensive and invasive that two of my staff members would get an insight into family affairs and how we ran the business. For me, on the other hand, having people working with me who I know deeply respect and care for me and my family is an asset, *not a liability*. Mum viewed both with extreme distrust and scepticism, and has had more than heated dialogues/monologues with both. Again, you would have to get Clem's, Anton's and Birgitta's version of events here to know the full story (and to read my mother's version of events, please see appendix 1 in this book).

The other upside for me in working with people who have a deep sense of purpose and love for this transformational project is that they are likely to work harder and more productively. Ultimately, I feel they are likely to be a better return on investment than a disengaged staff member, who only views a project with cold professionalism. This small team made great economic and output sense for Georg Sörman. However, from my mum's perspective, this set up was an example of 'Anders complicating things', despite the fact that we had a formal agreement in place that concretised the services, who would deliver them, and the outcomes sought and needed by Georg Sörman.

An eye for detail

Mum has an eye for detail, and a perfectionist streak, but also a sense of Fingerspitzengefühl (fingertip feeling), if you'd like. As far back as I can remember, she has also had an occasional inability to see the forest for the trees – which, as you can imagine, can be annoying for her son, seeing I prefer to see the whole picture, as opposed to the micro detail (while I have also been known to have an eye for detail). In this regard, we are quite different. Again. I remember doing homework with Mum as a child when I was studying at the German School in Stockholm. Neither my handwriting nor my German grammar was especially stellar at the time, and I valued speed over accuracy, and as such I remember preferring to do homework with Dad – not because he was more lenient, but rather more pedagogical. Mum would frequently forget to look at the whole assignment and context, and would instead focus in on minute details, sometimes to the detriment of other, more 'big picture' ideas, and my assignments used to come back bleeding with red ink as a result. This should literally have been a red flag for me, shouldn't it?

So, fast-forward twenty-five years, and Thinque's PR efforts have paid off – business, fashion, men's magazines, blogs, industry papers, radio and television are seeking interviews and want to feature the story of 'mum collaborating with son to turn around faltering family business'. After securing and collaborating with a glossy Stockholm magazine on a six-page editorial story about the business, Mum comes up to me with the magazine (to congratulate me on work well done, I thought), and instead is upset that her great-grandfather's job title on a canal boat is incorrect. When Sweden's most respectable business daily did a two-page article about us, Mum criticised me for the title chosen by the journalist (of course, I didn't write the article, but that was a minor detail).

Georg Sörman received more publicity in two years than in its 100-plus history as a result of our work. All in all, Thinque secured PR to the value of over SEK1 million (more than €100 000) for Georg Sörman, and on all occasions, red ink has been metaphorically applied to each assignment. Now I should add that, again, I understand that Mum can get upset with details and facts – I agree these can be critical components of media stories. Based on our use of Herrmann Brain Dominance Instruments (used for mapping the whole Georg Sörman team, including consultants), I understand that our thinking and communication styles are very different, and that this would be upsetting for her. While my thinking and communication is more innovative, creative and strategic, Mum's thinking and communication is more grounded and practical. Again, this diversity can create a grating seam – or the potential for a golden collaboration.

Scrapheap fears?

In May 2013, three of my EMBA colleagues (all highly successful in their own right), Mum and I sat down for a lunch at Restaurant Brillo at Stureplan in Stockholm to brainstorm the future of the business. While courteous at first, Mum quickly took on a defensive stand (which happens consistently when she speaks with people who offer their help and insights). When one of my colleagues asked her a very pertinent question regarding her objective in running the business, the best response Mum could offer up was, 'It would be nice to meet payroll without stressing each month'. When asked about her plan for the future, it was very difficult to get an affirmative response about what she proactively seeks. So we got answers like, 'Well, I am not going to work there until I die', or 'I don't want to sell the business while it is losing money'.

I hazard a guess, and Mum wouldn't speak these words herself, that the business provides her with immense meaning, identity and a sense of purpose – maybe even doing something she believes contributes positively to the urban pulse and cityscape in Stockholm. All of this I admire in my mother, of course. At the same time, I also understand that my interest in her business, my digging, exploration, examination and proposals of strategic direction, might make her feel like she is ready for the scrapheap. She has consistently maintained that she feels 'too energetic and young to retire', and that she doesn't have anything in particular to retire 'to'. And I can understand that the business is what provides her with a sense of identity and purpose. Succession planning and even collaboration with the fourth generation could be seen as the beginning of the end, or at least the beginning of the end of her business/professional relevance. Again, I fully empathise with the fact that this could be a scary proposition. Mum has often told me and my brother that once she 'loses her wits' we should organize an *ättestupa* (Swedish for kin/clan precipice) senicide for her. In other words, she prefers the idea of being euthanised to being a vegetable. I don't know whether my strategic contributions and constructive criticism have been viewed as the onset of an involuntary metaphorical senicide (I deeply hope not) but, then again, who knows in a family business context? Especially as these things and feelings are left untouched, safely stored under the carpet for future reference and consumption.

Waste of time

Pre-dating the internet, but gaining notoriety because of it, Nigeria letters were supposedly a highly effective scheme to con the recipients out of money. Often, post-digital disruption, the victims are gullible, elderly and unaccustomed with the ins and outs of 'being on the line' (as my girlfriend's mother calls being on the internet). The psychology of Nigeria letters is also one of gradually staggering the losses for the victims. For example, in the first instance, the victim may help a Nigerian prince retrieve an inheritance of several million pounds by making a significant but smaller investment or transfer. When the victim realises that they have probably been conned, they may feel both embarrassed and unintelligent and, as a result, rather than telling friends, family or the authorities about the con suffered, when approached by the con artist again, are more likely to agree to paying a smaller sum of money to get the initial 'investment' back. And so the evil cycle begins. In 2008, an Oregon woman lost US$400 000 trying to recoup her promised inheritance, despite her family, bank and law enforcement officers telling her to stop. According to the ABC News 2012 report 'Protect elderly relatives from credit card fraud', the elderly seem particularly vulnerable to these scams because they arguably are more trusting and too proud to report falling prey to the scams. Or they might be concerned that relatives would see their participation in the con as a sign of declining mental capacity, and they may be worried about losing their independence. Similar psychological reasoning can apply in the refusal to 'cut your losses' – through obeying a stop-loss in trading, for example – or doubling your bets at the casino to recoup the original 'investment' you have lost. None of these economic behaviours tend to be particularly well rewarded.

For my mum, she went against the advice of her sisters, friends, brothers-in-law, husband and her children when she took over Georg Sörman in 2007. Since then she has been propping up the failing business with her life savings. And while I cannot claim to diagnose this economically (ir?)rational behaviour, I can imagine that every time she artificially keeps the business alive, she hopes that this time, this gamble will turn things around, and she will recoup her original investment. The more she distances herself from the advice of loved ones and professional accountants and management consultants, the more exposed she becomes, and while most of the other people offering advice haven't quite been as prepared as I have been to strongly speak up and shine a light on affairs, I hypothesise that my doing so is highly annoying for my mum. So, she continues in the belief that the good old days are just around the corner.

CASE STUDY:
HOW ZADY'S BRAND EXPERIENCE DRIVES SUSTAINABLE BEHAVIOUR CHANGE

In today's hyper-connected consumer society we have been educated to prefer quantity over quality. We have been trained to constantly renew our wardrobes and never be completely satisfied with what we have. Over the last twenty years, the clothing industry has been increasingly successful with manufacturing low-quality goods at low prices, while at the same time hiding the big social and environmental costs of its production. According to figures available via truecostmovie .com, globally, we consume about eighty million pieces of clothing each year, which is 400 per cent more than the quantity we bought only twenty years ago, and Americans alone generate more than eleven million tonnes of textile waste each year.

However, during recent years we have seen the rise of the conscious consumer, and more businesses have joined the slow fashion movement – which can be described as a reaction to the industry's seeming incapability to produce and source clothing in socially and environmentally sound ways.

Previous generations such as our parents, and maybe even more so our grandparents, had a great insight into how their clothing was produced and where it came from, but as the industry became globalised and the value chain more complex, we lost our connection to the people who actually make our garments. This is something that the New York–based online retailer Zady aims to change – they want to reconnect consumers with the people and businesses that make their clothing, while at the same time inspire them to choose quality over quantity.

Research highlighted in Aarthi Rayapura's article 'Millennials most sustainability-conscious generation yet, but don't call them "environmentalists"' (available at www.sustainablebrand.com) indicates that the young generation of consumers, generation Y (those born between 1980 and the early 2000s), are less likely to define themselves as environmentalists; despite this, however, a global study by Nielsen found that they are the generational cohort that is the most willing to pay extra for sustainable offerings. In the 2015 study (*Green generation: Millennials say sustainability is a shopping priority*), 66 per cent of the global generation Y respondents stated that they were willing to pay more for products and services from organisations that were focused on making a positive social and environmental impact on society. In 2014, the same number was 55 per cent and in 2013 it was 50 per cent. This means that companies like Zady with a sustainability marketing strategy have a growing number of consumers who are prioritising social and environmental claims on products and services.

Zady, which today is seen as a pioneer within the slow fashion movement, was founded back in 2013 by Maxine Bedát and Soraya Darabi. Since the start, they have been working hard on building a platform for companies and brands that care about sustainability, timeless style and quality. The online retailer represents around fifty different brands and also produces their own line of clothing, consisting of wardrobe essentials like simple t-shirts, sweaters and cardigans. One of the pieces in the collection is a wool sweater that's completely created in the United States, and because it's a garment produced with an all-American supply chain, they had to partner with ranchers, washers, dyers, millers, knitters and sewers across the country. And as a customer you can get an insight into every single step in the manufacturing process via the mini documentaries that are available at zady.com. The private label collection has been a huge success, and according to *Epoch Times* (in its article 'Feeling the magic behind sustainable fashion') in 2016 accounted for 75 per cent of the overall sales (the remaining part comes from third-party company products).

Since its start Zady has expanded their operations and increased their sales significantly. Another sign of success is that the entrepreneurs behind the brand have drawn venture capital from a range of important investors like Google Executive Chairman Eric Schmidt's Innovation Endeavors, which backed Uber. And in 2014 Zady was chosen by the renowned magazine *Fast Company* as one of the top 10 most innovative companies in retail. Zady has also been nicknamed 'the Whole Foods of fashion' because of their genuine focus on sustainably produced products made from high-quality fabrics and raw materials. Co-founder Bedát was interviewed for the *Epoch Times* 2016 article, and is quoted as saying that, 'Whole Foods did a beautiful job of making organic foods and telling the stories behind them. We thought we could do the same with clothing and tell the story behind it.'

The key behind the brand's success is, unsurprisingly, their digital presence – and, more specifically, the memorable, distinctive and seamless user experience that's delivered via their social channels and website. The website is regularly updated with inspiring content (video, images and text) that is focused on educating their customers about how the brands that Zady represents source and produce their products. It's all about getting the customer to connect with the people behind the brand and making them realise the value of purchasing something that lasts. Even the product descriptions have a narrative that gives you a short story behind each product, regardless of whether it's a t-shirt or an expensive jacket. This ability to tell the fascinating and inspiring stories behind each garment is one of their big strengths.

Zady.com also has a blog where they post stories about topics related to sustainable living, such as food, interior design and travel. They have realised that it's valuable content, not just sales-focused promotions, that will get people to come back to the site and engage with their brand.

To reach new audiences, the entrepreneurs behind the brand decided to open up pop-up stores in New York. This proved to be an efficient way to expose the brand to people who weren't actively seeking sustainable clothes and accessories. Zady is one of a few online retailers that manages to create a seamless customer journey where content, storytelling and rich media (and physical pop-up stores) are truly helping, educating and inspiring customers to make conscious purchase decisions.

Ask yourself ...

Get yourself thinking with the following questions:

1. How can you use digital storytelling to communicate transparency and build trust?

2. How could an inspiring narrative elevate the value of your products and services?

3. What topics related to your business might be of interest to your customers? And how can you create content around those subjects that is helpful, educational and inspiring?

4. How are you distributing content throughout the customer journey? Which questions and thoughts are you not responding to or can you be better at addressing?

STEP 10
HERO'S JOURNEY WHEEL FOR MAMMA SÖRMAN-NILSSON

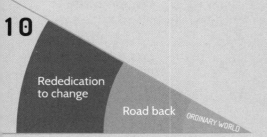

10

Rededication to change

Road back

ORDINARY WORLD

Georg Sörman together with Anders write an open and vulnerable letter to clients in September 2015 about the brand's values and ways of meeting the external digital threat with a renewed heartfelt focus and a renaissance of the personal touch. The letter combined with the launch of Georg Sörman's second broadsheet *Välsytt Herrnytt* leads to a record sales result at the autumn VIP day in 2015, and clients join the collaborative call to arms.

Road back

This stage represents the antonym or antithesis to the initial call to adventure, when the heroine had to first cross the threshold. This is the time she must return home with her reward, and on this journey fears are replaced with potential vindication and acclaim, or even absolution or exoneration. At this juncture, the odyssey is not complete and the heroine may need one last push back into the ordinary world. The moment before the heroine finally re-commits to the final stage of the odyssey may be a moment in which she has to decide between her own personal goals and that of an even higher cause.

Here's what the road back looked like for Luke in *Star Wars*:

- *Inner journey:* Rededication to change – Obi-Wan sacrifices himself to help the team escape. The Death Star follows them to the Rebels, determined to destroy their base.

- *Outer journey:* Road back – Luke joins the Rebel's attack on the Death Star.

And here's where Birgitta was up to:

- *Inner journey:* Rededication to change – after completing the FBN Owner's Program Module 2, Georg Sörman together with Anders write an open and vulnerable letter to clients in September 2015 (incidentally, inspired by a version of the hero's journey) about the brand's codified values and ways of meeting the external digital threat with a renewed heartfelt focus and a renaissance of the 'personal touch'.

- *Outer journey:* Road back – the letter, combined with the launch of Georg Sörman's second broadsheet *Välsytt Herrnytt*, leads to a record sales result at the autumn VIP day in 2015, with clients joining the collaborative call to arms to bring the personal touch back to retail.

10: Road back

The good old days are not just around the corner.
Hoping they are is not a strategy.

A call to adventure for our clients

Thinque had had to walk away from the management transition of the Old Town shop in autumn 2015 but, even so, hope for Georg Sörman still glimmered. Maybe the final FBN module had helped us re-focus and gel again. And perhaps the family *coeur d'esprit* has been re-ignited by my brother's wedding. Whatever it was, we had an important (semi-annual) autumn VIP event coming up in October 2015, our last one before the centenary celebrations. We wanted (and needed) to make it count. Together with Georg Sörman, Thinque Digital had constructed a staggered omnichannel campaign, beginning with the segmented snail-mail arrival of *Välsytt Herrnytt* (our broadsheet) into our clients' mailboxes, which garnered immediate interest and sales. The timing was great as people were coming back to work after long summer breaks and the quicksilver had dropped. Sales of autumnal brands like Alan Paine, Inis Meain, Barbour and Andersen-Andersen took off. Next, we alerted the client base to the upcoming VIP night. Previous themes for these nights had included the 'family tree', 'jazz duos', and 'Italian ice-cream' and we built on these themes to evolve into the more seasonally adjusted focus on artisanal beers (from countries that our brands hailed from, including Denmark, Germany, England, Ireland, Italy... you get the idea) and premium handmade hot dogs – a much appreciated innovation in the Swedish fall. We then continued to very deliberately stagger and intermingle the digital and analogue communications and attraction strategies – MailChimp emails and content marketing, video invites, Instagram collages and Facebook events management, and texts all sowed the seeds of interest among our clientele. But the clincher? The beautiful, analogue touch point of the broadsheet was followed up by a physical invite on thick, textured stock paper, which encouraged clients to pre-register for the event on a tailored landing page. (This, of course, meant we got an idea for the pre-interest as well as captured email addresses for our HubSpot CRM.) Included in the same invite envelope was a handwritten letter from the owners of Georg Sörman – Birgitta and Lars-Olof – encouraging people to mobilise in our quest of 'restoring the personal touch to retail' (more on this soon).

While Mum and Dad prefer the words 'encourage' to begging or asking, suffice to say that the letter was an FBN-inspired way of communicating our timeless values in a timely fashion. The store needed the income and we wanted to make this VIP night the best one ever. Our Stockholm team worked closely with Georg Sörman in coordinating the event. Unfortunately for me clients in Malta, Mexico City, Heidelberg (Germany), Gothenburg (Sweden), Karlstad (Sweden) and Queenstown (New Zealand) needed my attention and had booked me in (in the physical world) way before Mum decided on a date for the VIP night, which meant that I couldn't physically be there on the night. We have a policy of first in, best dressed, which our clients usually respect. (Mum, however, as mums do, wants to always come first.) So, even though Gothenburg and Karlstad (both kind of on the west coast) are only a short distance apart, after finishing up with my Gothenburg client in the early afternoon of the Wednesday, I flew back to east coast Stockholm to run the pre-VIP briefing and Georg Sörman 100 strategy update with the whole team, before getting my Stockholm driver to take me four and a half hours west again to Karlstad in western Sweden.

We had also agreed internally that Mum would do a heartfelt speech, to help rally the troops in preparation for the important event on 29 October. We had just hit the countdown to 100 days until the centenary birthday, and the clock was ticking. We still had a lot to complete in the renaissance rollout, both on the digital and analogue sides. New business cards were now in-store, visual merchandising in-store signage was now on-brand with Georg Sörman 100, the broadsheet was a massive success (self-funded because of advertisements from vendors like Eton, Alan Paine, Resteröds, and St James), as were digital touch points like the newsletter, Instagram and Facebook. But the website was still in development and, crucially, our printer and manufacturer of bags, boxes and wrapping paper was continually causing delivery delays. These were a crucial addition to the store and brand in the lead-up to Christmas, the busiest season of the retail calendar. Tick-tock the Time-Crocodile was coming after us.

The results of the VIP night promotions 'came like a letter on the post'. Sorry for throwing out Swedish sayings again. But if you invest in something or take a positive action and the result '*kom som ett brev på posten*' it means the causality is proven and the positive results didn't take long to materialise. The VIP day in October 2015 was our best ever, and a real hit with this invited inner circle. Many clients also commented on the finely crafted, handwritten letter, and said they hadn't received a handwritten letter in years. When everybody else zigs, make sure you zag! In a 2012 study by the Swedish Post, Swedes (who as I have told you before love Christmas cards) were asked how they prefer their Christmas greetings from loved ones. Almost 80 per cent said they preferred a Christmas card, and 3 per cent said they'd prefer no greeting at all over receiving a text or a Facebook wall message (see figure 10.1). In other words, we mustn't throw away the analogue baby with the digital bathwater. The personal touch that we spoke of in the open letter was accompanied by real, genuine efforts – or, in other words, we put our money where our mouth was. The staff were rejuvenated – to the extent that one of our staff members, seeing we were €100 short of the total (sizeable) target for the night, bought a nice jumper to get the team effort across the line. We hit the goal!

Figure 10.1: Swedish Post study showing preferences for physical Christmas cards

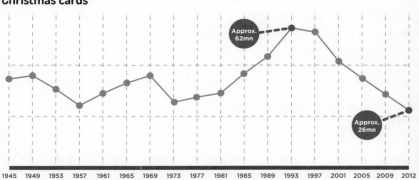

Source: Postens Julundersökning 2013, Sweden by TNS SIFO

The letter was in many ways inspired by the hero's journey, or at least a version of it. At Pixar studios they use a template when they pitch stories – essentially, the story line structure stays the same, but they tweak the details, context and characters. With six steps instead of twelve, it's a short-form version of the hero's journey:

1. Once upon a time there was...

2. Every day...

3. One day...

4. Because of that...

5. Because of that...

6. Until finally...

The curious thing about the Pixar pitch is that it has become the secret weapon of marketers, technology start-ups and entrepreneurs pitching their ideas and products. And if it is good enough for Pixar and *Finding Nemo*, it must be good enough for Georg Sörman, we figured. But it did take some convincing. My dad was slightly sceptical at first, but enjoys writing, so he soon came on board willing to test the idea. Mum was adamant (from her pride perspective) that we mustn't seem desperate, or appear as if we're begging for the business. (Ahhh, Swedish pride...) The outcome was that Anton, Lars-Olof and I co-wrote the letter (with some edits from Mum's new CFO, Linda, and Birgitta). I think when you read this letter, not only will you be able to see how it follows the structure of the Pixar pitch, but you will also find that is an empowering call to action, and has both drama and strength to it. Heck, you might even want to use this structure yourself in a campaign, pitch or writing project. Embrace the hero's journey. In this simple, but powerful letter, we invited our allies and friends to join Mum's hero's journey into the future. And it was a call that was answered by many.

Figure 10.2 shows an image of the letter in Swedish.

Figure 10.2: a copy of the handwritten VIP day letter

GEORG SÖRMAN

EST 1916

Stockholm den 9 okt 2015

Bästa kunder och vänner!

I början av förra seklet hade en ambitiös
man vid namn Georg Sörman sökt sig till
Stockholm från Sörgärde vid Tåtorp i Västergötland
för att ekipera dåtidens gentleman och skapa en
framtid för sin blivande familj. Han slog upp
portarna i sin första butik på Stora Nyggatan i
Gamla Stan den 29 januari 1916.

Varje dag tog Georg och medarbetarna emot
sina kunder på ett familjärt och varmt sätt.
Med en bakgrund i Tåtorp vid Göta Kanals mynning
i sjön Viken och med en far som var kapten på
Kanalbåtarna föddes tidigt en nyfikenhet på
omvärlden. Denna nyfikenhet förde han vidare
till sin familj och vidare till framtida generationer
Sörman. Familjen har sedan dess haft en
genuin stolthet i att expediera gentleman i
livets alla skeden.

Sveriges textilbransch och handel har förändrats
märkbart och i viss mån utarmats. Högkvalitativa
svenska fabriker har flyttats utomlands.
Kunskapen och hantverket förs inte längre
vidare från generation till generation. Den
småskaliga butiken fick ge vika för varuhus och
"kedjor." Stadsbilden förändrades som en effekt
av framväxten av gallerior och "outlets". Via
e-handeln har det personliga bemötandet
nedprioriterats.

På grund av denna utveckling så har
många affärer av olika slag, bland annat
herrekiperingar, skivaffärer och bokhandlare
tvingats stänga, och med dessa har en del
av Stockholms hjärta slutat att slå. Även vi på
Georg Sörman har starkt upplevt förändringens
vindar.

Vi vänder inte "kappan efter vinden"
utan möter hotet med ett förnyat
renässans focus på det personliga.
Därför har vi beslutat att bemöta hotet
frontalt – med hjärtat.
Vi är en vital 99-åring som fortsätter
att anta utmaningarna och att personligen
ekipera Dig och Dina vänner. Men vi
behöver er hjälp vid vårt vägskäl –
detta stundande sekelskifte – att anta
denna utmaning tillsammans.
Som ägarfamilj gör vi en kraftsamling
för att föra det goda, traditionella och
ibland något gammelmodiga arvet
vidare till nästa generation.
Vi vårdar det goda arvet från Georg Sörman
med ett tidlöst och tidsenligt focus på att:
- föra familjetraditioner, både våra och era,
  vidare till nästa generation
- Möta och ta hand om våra kunder med värme
- Ha fingertoppskänsla i vår kollektion och
  vårt urval.
- Balansera personlig värme, färg och stil för
  vårt gemensamma välbefinnande.
Ge oss en möjlighet att fira vårt
sekelskifte på ett mänskligt och framåt-
blickande sätt tillsammans, genom att
stödja vår gemensamma kulturinstitution
som är Georg Sörman.
För bevarandet av anrika och värdefulla
traditioner och skapandet av berikande
nya traditioner.
Väl mött!

O. Sörman Wiman med familj

And here is the letter translated into English.

Open letter for VIP day 2015

Stockholm, 9 October 2015

Dear customers and friends!

At the beginning of the last century, a man named Georg Sörman travelled to Stockholm from his farm Sörgärde in Västergötland to outfit gentlemen of all ages with timeless garments and to create a prosperous future for him and his future family. He opened up the doors to his first store on 29 January 1916.

Every day Georg and his co-workers took care of their customers in a familiar and warm fashion. As a result of being brought up close to the mouth of Göta Kanal (the biggest canal and the biggest building project in Sweden) next to Lake Viken with a father as a sea captain on the canal boats, Georg developed a genuine curiosity for the surrounding world. This curiosity was later passed on to his family and future generations of the Sörman family. The family has ever since taken pride in outfitting gentlemen through all stages of their lives.

Sweden's textile and retail industry has clearly changed and in some aspects been impoverished. The knowledge and craft are no longer being passed on from generation to generation. The independent retail store has been outcompeted by shopping malls, chain stores and outlets. The cityscape has changed as a result of this development. And the growth of e-commerce has led to a lower prioritisation of the personal face-to-face meeting.

A lot of family-owned and independent stores like classic menswear stores, record stores and bookshops have been forced to close as a result of this. Stockholm has therefore lost a bit of its soul. These winds of change have not passed unnoticed at Georg Sörman.

But we don't change our ideals. Instead we will face up to these threats warm-heartedly and with a renewed focus on the personal. We are a vital ninety-nine year old who continues to meet today's modern challenges and keeps on outfitting you and your friends. But we are at a crossroads and we need your help at this approaching centenary to overcome these challenges together.

As family owners we are making a concentrated effort to pass on the traditional and the slightly old-fashioned heritage to the next generation. We are looking after the unique heritage from Georg Sörman with a timeless and timely focus on:

- passing family traditions, both ours and yours, on to the next generation

- greeting and taking care of our customers warm-heartedly

- offering a carefully curated selection of menswear

- balancing personal warmth, colour and style for our common wellbeing.

Give us the opportunity to celebrate our centenary together in a genuine and forward-thinking manner by supporting our mutual cultural institution that is Georg Sörman. Come together for the preservation of unique and valuable traditions and the creation and enrichment of new ones.

Looking forward to seeing you!

On the surface we seemed to be making progress again. But, behind the scenes, frictions were still bubbling. We were doing a lot of things right, but it always felt like we were paddling upstream with broken oars. Every little decision, every sign-off involved huge efforts. Facts, case studies and figures were ignored, and emotional pleas to trust in the competence of Thinque were often met with a lack of interest. When I reflect on it now, I think that the mental commitment from the leadership at Georg Sörman was never really there. At times, they were happy to say yes, but often still did no. Often, they were scared to put their money where their mouth was, and agreements, both oral and in writing, would be forgotten in the implementation stages.

And in some ways, maybe because I often had to drag my unwilling heroine across the thresholds of the different stages (kicking and screaming), this was a journey of transformation that she actually never wanted to undertake (despite thirteen years of poor results and the danger to the business). This meant, while we were technically getting to the later stages of the outer journey of putting in place the strategy and the plan, culture started eating that strategy for breakfast. And, yes, maybe Mum, our heroine, had never truly completed her inner journey of believing we could be, and deserved to be, successful. Or maybe she couldn't understand the difference between working harder, and working smarter. I will leave you to be the judge.

The curious case of Georg Sörman

Nothing about this transformation process has been without friction. And maybe this is what you'd expect, given what might happen when a futurist and a traditionalist meet in business. The future and the past clashing in the present moment. As a futurist, this failure to reinvent feels like a blemish, and it is something I have thought long, hard and deep about. It is also something I have shared in private with the other protagonists/ antagonists in this journey, and I continue to work regularly with my therapist to gain further insights and the resources to ensure a successful resolution. Whatever happens with the business, the family relationship will endure and must be rebuilt with time, and hopefully with greater levels of awareness and emotional resources for each person involved in the tempest.

So, how did it come to this? As the aphorism goes, 'the road to hell is paved with good intentions'. And Georg Sörman's intentions when he started his store back in 1916 were very good indeed. Figure 10.3 (overleaf) shows the reference Georg received from his previous employer before starting out in business by himself.

Figure 10.3: reference for Georg Sörman from his previous employer, dated 16 August 1915

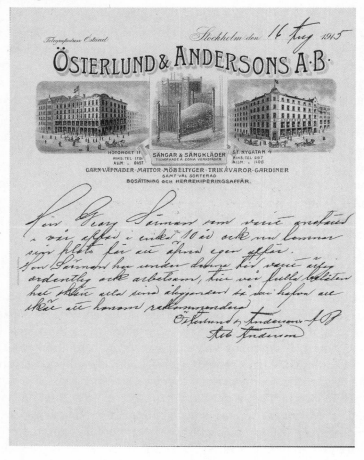

And here is the English translation of that reference.

Mr Georg Sörman has been an employee in our shop for around ten years and will now leave his position to open up his own shop. During his tenure, Mr Sörman has proven himself to be honest, proper and hardworking, to our complete satisfaction. As he has performed all of his duties to a high standard, we can recommend him.

Österlund & Andersson

Nils Andersson

And the business started very well, as shown by the first-year financials in figure 10.4 (at a time when average yearly earnings were between 800 and 2000 Swedish Kronor).

Figure 10.4: first-year financials for Georg Sörman

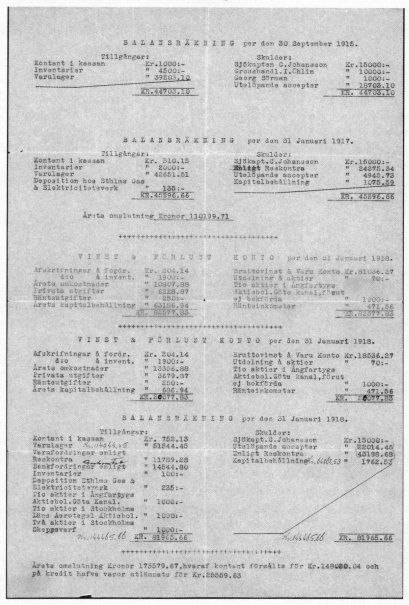

But something else is relevant here too. Both my grandfather Per and his father, Georg, were savvy share investors. And while many small business owners will re-invest potential profits in the operations, Georg and Per re-invested profits in the share market. This meant that Georg Sörman's core competence, albeit never discussed in the family or publicly, was as a finance and holding company (and this information, courtesy of Swedish company law, was always publicly disclosed and searchable). However, it was not until Per and Ingrid passed away that the daughters, including my mum, knew that Per had been using the offices of the retail shop as his trading office. While of course compliant and legal, this set-up does remind my imaginative mind of a speakeasy or Capone-esque operation where the front business, often a restaurant or other retail establishment, is used as a cover for the real trade. In Georg Sörman's case, beyond being Stockholm's longest running traditional menswear store, the retail operations made up only a quarter of total operations. The profits from these total operations, however, made the company, on the surface at least, look like a sizeable retail company by Swedish standards.

It seems both Georg and Per were quite mysterious and secretive men. While I never met Georg, my grandfather Per was a man of few words, and when I discuss his personality with my cousins, not one describes a particularly warm relationship with our grandfather. Instead, hard work at his hobby farm at Färingsö outside of Stockholm comes to mind. I remember him as being quite intimidating, and that he focused his life on his hobbies, which included largely solo activities like jogging, pistol shooting, rifle shooting, kayaking, cross-country skiing (occasionally with his brother Sven once they reconciled after several decades of estrangement), and weeding the garden (which he frequently outsourced to his grandchildren during our school holidays). And while never attending one of my brother's or my soccer games through our childhood, he did take me to my first ever adult soccer game at the old Olympic stadium in 1992 when my favourite team, Djurgårdens IF, played GIF Sundsvall. This was a big event for me, and one of my fondest memories of my maternal grandfather (morfar in Swedish). The other thing we had in common was an interest in the share market. Mum encouraged this, and morfar Per used to send company reports home with Mum so that I could read them and get an understanding of the share market, aged nine. Mum always told me she was totally uninterested in this depersonalised business. So what she didn't know was that her work in the retail business as an underpaid sales and office associate (isn't that always the case in family businesses?) was buoying the core business at Georg Sörman – Per's active share investing. Meanwhile, Mum, like her sisters, unaware of the extent of the company's investment portfolio, studied the supposed retail expertise of her father, seeking to mirror how he ran the retail operations on the surface. All she saw was the overall profit that she and her father built collaboratively, year after year, so the retail positioning, branding, inventory management and marketing must have been done intelligently, right?

Well, in reality Mum and Grandpa were building a decent, but not an extraordinary, menswear store. What my mother saw as profits, were instead profits created by *morfar* Per's share investments. This led to the company being highly solid, with great cash flow, and great liquidity. This in turn meant that suppliers could always be paid on time, and the business could even receive a discount for early payment, meaning the retail operation's margins were improved. The size of the finance side of the business also meant, however, that when my mum was in her thirties and forties, and between her sub-market pay and my father's public service salary, there was no way, despite her intention, that she could buy out her two share-holding but non-operational sisters, who always had equal shares in the business to my mum (which, of course, from my mum's perspective was unfair, given her operational contributions).

As I've covered earlier in the book, the retail operations also include a small shop in Old Town Stockholm. When I got involved with the strategic turnaround in 2012, I interviewed my grandfather's accountant, who mentioned that this shop was largely a hobby project that had given my grandmother her own business to run. Given shifts in accountants and lack of documentation, I cannot say for sure whether this is the case, but this is what was related to me by my grandfather's financial confidant. Either way, the long and the short of it is that the company Georg Sörman was acquired by my mother (and father) with parts of the proceeds from the divestment of the share portfolio and the splitting of assets between the three sisters. Since the retail operations had not been turning a profit for several years, and had either just broken even or lost money, the final purchase price was ultimately achievable for mum, who re-invested parts of her life savings along with the inheritance to get rid of the influence of her two operationally non-contributing sisters.

Only at this stage did it become evident to Mum and her sisters that Georg Sörman at its core was a finance and holding company. This is highly relevant because identity-wise my mum has always held on to the belief that she and her father built up a great retail operation, and she hadn't truly investigated whether those retail operations actually were as optimal as they could, or can, be. I questioned those processes, habits and holy cows as part of our strategic examination of the management of the retail business, but was often met with the Swedish expression 'you mustn't urinate in the well that quenches your thirst'. The problem is that the well, which mum assumed had quenched her family's thirst, was not menswear retail, but the share markets. Imagine finding this secret out after clocking into a shop day in and day out for thirty-one years. I cannot even begin to imagine the wool that Mum had had pulled over her eyes, and this is something I need to empathise with.

Mum, however, didn't seem dismayed by this. My dad became a minority owner, and a non-executive member of the board, and in one fell swoop, Mum became CEO, majority owner and chairman of the board – and 'judge, jury and executioner', as I like to call it. In other words, Mum has since been able to make all decisions without transparency or checks and balances. The structure and dynamics are such that whatever Mum's whims are, she will execute on them, and as such this retail operation has become a small 'dictatorship', which I am sure a lot of people who are involved in small business, or family business at that, have seen before. Stalin is known to have once said 'trust is good, but control is better'. With all due respect to my beloved mother, who is a wonderful person socially, this is a business archetype which is not entirely ill-fitting. She is someone who loves the illusion of control, and treasures the idea of independence in decision-making. Unfortunately, this also means a management and leadership style that is heavily resistant to outside influences, or even the contributions from her closest family members, including my brother, Gustaf, our father (aka her husband), and myself. Meanwhile, my mum stoically embodies her version of feminist pride, which seems to be to go Teflon on new ideas.

Mum's apprenticeship with her father, Per, focused solely on the retail operations. Per's management style was an impersonal one of 'sticky note delegation'. Upon clocking in, the staff would collect their 'to-do' tasks from their pigeon hole, without any personal or human interaction with Per. Instead, the information they needed was on the sticky note. So, when I started working in the business as a child (family businesses still support child labour), this would be the extent of my interaction with my grandfather. Even back in the 1980s and 1990s this was a pretty old-school version of management, but the ageing staff members, who were of the builder/ veteran generation, accepted this leadership style of 'Director Sörman'. Because Per wasn't a 'people person' all, HR matters and conversations involving potential controversy would be delegated to my mum. The extent of reflection on HR matters would be limited to Sunday dinners when Mum and grandpa might whinge about *facket*, the Swedish trade unions, who still had some relevance and influence back in the 1980s and 1990s. (Ah, the things you soak up at the family dinner table.) Every day, Mum observed her father and his leadership style, and continues to try to emulate it. In subsequent interviews with media and in family business contexts, she always highlights how great their cross-generational collaboration was. Meanwhile, Dad's memories of those days is of a wife who was deeply underpaid, who was forced to deal with conflicts Per didn't want, who was frequently disrespected by older co-workers, and who was the target of scorn because she was perceived by some as having her general manager role only as a result of family bonds. Meanwhile, her reverence for the family patriarch – the business oracle, Per – remains strong to this day.

As I have already touched on in this book, I get the sense from Mum that she believes that being nostalgic is the same as being strategic – which is, of course, ludicrous. One example of Mum's nostalgia is that she believed it was a genius move by her father to position Georg Sörman as the empathetic menswear store that catered for the 'big and tall' segment. With monikers like 'King Size', 'Also for Big Boys' and with sizes up to 8XL, Georg Sörman niched themselves according to long tail economics. This was a departure from the original positioning of 'Välsytt Herrnytt' or 'well-tailored sartorial fashion'. ('Välsytt Herrnytt' rhymes better in Swedish than in English, clearly.) The upside of this positioning, beyond many happy customers who had unique clothing needs, was that the brand became known as the exclusive outfitter for 'big and tall' executives, ice hockey players and the like. The downside was that visual merchandising became difficult and, to this day, the store organises clothing based on size rather than style or colour. This gives a visually confused impression, and means that clients have to ask a staff member for help to find the right brand, colour, or fit among a sea of sizes. Additionally, the strategy is problematic because the data shows that these unique sizes are both more expensive to procure and sell less frequently than mainstream sizes. In line with Mum's empathy with this client group, she refused to charge more for the additional materials and cost of holding this inventory. On top of this, the data showed us that the 'big and tall' segment were doing more of their shopping online, as the process of shopping face-to-face could be confrontational for them.

And while I mentioned that the brand became associated with an empathy with this clientele, it disenfranchised the mainstream and the increasingly style-conscious young professionals who started inhabiting the island of Kungsholmen, an emerging epicentre of business in the early 2000s. Georg Sörman was seen as a brand for 'old geezers' and 'big boys'. At the same time, these core client segments were abandoning the store as a result of life events, or the ability to shop from the comfort of one's home. Something had to be done. Despite the facts, the data and visualisations, however, Mum still partly insists that the niche of 'big boys' is the future. I am not saying that she should abandon this clientele, but I do believe she can serve them gently with the same level of empathy (and sustainably so) by focusing more on on-demand offers, such as tailoring, online retail and special orders, instead of carrying a mammoth inventory on behalf of an increasingly irregular customer. I am asking her for 'reflective nostalgia', yet all I seem to get is 'restorative nostalgia'. I am sure you have probably come across similar mindsets in business, but in this case what is truly tragic is that what Mum believes was the good old days of 'loyal retail clients' was actually a mirage. The moderate profits that the store did generate were consistently invested in the share market rather than re-invested in the retail operations, which over time exposed the retail brand's lesser relevance in a modern day of changing consumer habits.

Did it have to get this far, or be this way? No. Contemporaneously with her buy-out of her sisters, my father, who had worked in the public sector in defence his whole career, took an early retirement at fifty-five (or semi-retirement, as he has stayed active on not-for-profit boards since then). At the time, Dad was hoping his retirement plans would coincide with Mum's retirement plans. I vividly remember sitting down with both my parents, individually and together, in the summer of 2006 and recommending that before they decided to take over full ownership and management of Georg Sörman, they go and see a business coach or therapist to ensure that they were fully aligned as a couple – with regards to time frames, vision, beliefs, risk appetite and work–life balance. I even connected my parents with one of Sweden's foremost coaches. Suffice to say, he never received a call from either of my parents. So my advice to consult, reflect and align fell on deaf ears. Instead, Mum promised Dad that she would run the business for between three and five years – in other words, until between 2010 and 2012. During a family holiday in 2012, we sat down again as a family and reflected on this broken promise, with Mum deflecting the broken promise and saying that she would run the business for another three to five years, meaning an expiry date of 2015 to 2017. At the time of writing, it's now mid-2016. If you asked anyone within the close family unit if the longest extreme of the 2017 deadline is likely to be adhered to, I think their responses would not indicate any confidence in such adherence.

So, in many ways Mum and her beliefs in Georg Sörman and what made it successful are a case of mistaken identity. Her father pulled the wool over her and his family's eyes, and what she identified as success factors were more of a liability than an asset by the time she took over the business. Combined with a management style that echoed her father's, and with a serious distrust for anyone wanting to help her revitalise the business, Mum is now finding herself to be an isolate. The last whisperer of a language and business culture that actually doesn't make sense, and maybe never existed in the first place.

CASE STUDY:
HOW SEAMLESS DESIGN CAN REMOVE FRICTION

What many successful brands and start-ups have in common is that their product, services and/or ideas were developed to solve real human problems. In order to do this, you have to put yourself in the other person's shoes and think about what he or she is motivated by – what makes them tick, what drives their behaviour in a certain direction and what mental, digital or physical barriers keep them from making a purchase, using a service or taking a specific action?

It's essential to ask yourself these questions if you want to create a product or a service that truly addresses and solves human problems. One of the key aspects here is to remove the friction and pain points that lower the quality of the brand experience or, even worse, entirely halt the customer from achieving their goal.

The Swedish fashion brand Uniforms For The Dedicated, which creates contemporary and sustainable garments for the modern gentleman, most likely asked themselves these questions when they developed the 'Rag Bag'. Most of us can probably identify with the problem of having a wardrobe full of garments that rarely get used. While you might be okay at occasionally cleaning out your closet and donating your unwanted garments to charity, it's often a time-consuming process that you probably don't look forward to. You might well remember your last 'op-shop day', as we call it in Australia. The packed-up bags of clothes likely sat in your garage for months before you eventually returned them for recycling.

Uniforms For The Dedicated realised that one of the key pain points here is actually the extended process – you need to pack a bag of the garments you don't want to keep, find the closest charity shop or collection bin, and then lug everything there. It's a multi-step process that demands you invest a lot of time and effort. This is why Uniforms For The Dedicated launched the Rag Bag, which is a biodegradable shopping bag that can be used to easily send your surplus garments to a charity. And you can get the bag when you shop from one of Uniforms For The Dedicated's retailers.

The bag is reversible, and on the inside it is pre-addressed and postmarked, so the only steps the customer has to take are to remove the new garment, turn the bag inside out, replace it with some unwanted piece of clothing, seal the bag and mail the package. Seamless, right? On one side of the bag the text says, 'Buy something new: Turn me inside out and donate something old' and when you reverse the bag, it becomes black with white text saying, 'Donate something old'. (Perhaps this also provides some design inspiration for how I could have thought about designing the transformation journey more 'seamlessly' for our heroine!)

The Rag Bag is more than just a bag; it's actually helping customers to clean out their wardrobes while also encouraging them to recycle textiles. This clever and streamlined concept is designed and manufactured by the renowned communications agency DDB Stockholm, and has since its launch received a lot of positive PR nationally in Sweden and internationally as well, and also won design and advertising awards such as the Cannes Lion in 2014. In the *Sustainable Brands* article "'Rag Bag'" makes it easy for shoppers to donate unwanted clothes', the team at DDB Stockholm (who developed the concept together with Uniforms For The Dedicated) explained the thinking behind it in this way:

> We consume too much. With this in mind, we wanted to find a way to convert every purchase into something that would do good in the world. We wanted to influence brands and consumers, and help them take a practical stand for sustainable fashion, recycling and social responsibility.

The Rag Bag shows that insightful and clever design can reduce and even remove the friction and help customers overcome the barriers that sometimes can stop them in their tracks.

Ask yourself ...

We have a lot to gain if we begin to think differently about the customer journey and start focusing on what happens after the decision and usage phase, and how those touch points can drive positive behaviour change. When designing a customer experience related to a new product or a service, ask yourself the following questions:

1. Where are the friction points in your business? What can you do to better understand the friction points that might frustrate your customers?

2. How can you turn friction points into creative brand touch points that truly help your customers?

3. What happens after the decision and purchase phase? What can you do after and during those phases to reinforce customer loyalty and brand engagement?

STEP 11
HERO'S JOURNEY WHEEL FOR MAMMA SÖRMAN-NILSSON

11

Final attempt at a big change

Resurrection

ORDINARY WORLD

Georg Sörman begins to communicate along a specific, agreed brand line, and effectively mobilise its staff in getting behind the brand strategy. Georg Sörman pulls back from the execution of the brand, and starts doubting its merits and places the brand rollout on ice. In combination with new partnerships for our broadsheet, events, and positive PR, Georg Sörman achieves an increase in sales. But no event is held to mark the 100th centenary on 29 January, 2016.

Resurrection

At this climactic stage, the heroine must have her final and most dangerous meeting with death. This final encounter symbolises something that is even bigger than the heroine's own existence, with consequences that are grander than her own existence. The consequences will have long-term and massive impacts on her ordinary world and on the lives of those left behind in the ordinary world. Unless the heroine succeeds, people around her will suffer and this places even greater weight upon her shoulders and conscience. These consequences reach out to us so we feel like we share the heroine's hopes, aspirations, fears and doubts. In the end, the heroine will triumph, destroy the enemy and emerge from battle cleansed and reborn.

For Luke in *Star Wars*, this stage played out as follows:

- *Inner journey:* Resurrection – Luke uses the Force to make an impossible shot that destroys the Death Star.

- *Outer journey:* Final attempt at a big change – in the final battle, Luke hears Obi-Wan's voice and uses the Force.

And for Birgitta:

- *Inner journey:* Resurrection – buoyed by the mental clarity and agreement on our inner force, our family values, Georg Sörman begins to consistently communicate along a specific, agreed brand line, and effectively mobilise its staff in getting behind brand Georg Sörman 100. A new sense of vision and clarity vibrates in the team, and Birgitta makes a heartfelt plea in the pre-VIP Day dinner for her staff members based on her seeming belief in Georg Sörman 100. Meanwhile, though, Georg Sörman pulls back from the execution of Georg Sörman 100, and starts doubting its merits. Ultimately, it places the rollout of the renaissance brand on ice, including avoiding having sponsored landmark events to mark the centenary in 2016, and continuing with the old and new brands sitting side by side, communicating confusion.

- *Outer journey:* Final attempt at a big change – in combination with new vendor partnerships from partners like Eton, Barbour and Mackmyra, and sponsorship from vendors for our broadsheet, as well as in-store events, Christmas cards, digital and analogue communication campaigns and positive PR from major news media outlets, Georg Sörman achieves progress and improvements on year-on-year sales (which were necessary after the forced closure for three weeks in summer 2015). But a lot of latent potential stays latent, however. No event is held to mark the centenary on 29 January 2016, and a local newspaper depressingly publishes an article on Georg Sörman with the headline 'Celebrates 100 – by staying open, as usual.'

11: Resurrection

The fact is that many brands today are perfectly prepared for a world that no longer exists.

Can old dogs learn new tricks?

It seems who we were, or believe we are, can be a true inhibitor to who we can be. And despite the findings of neuroscientists that neuroplasticity provides hope of old dogs learning new tricks, we often find that they keep repeating their old ones, even when the world has moved on. We cloak this inertia in words like 'heritage' and 'tradition', but perhaps at times these are in reality just remnants and leftovers, causing us to remain in the status quo, or worse, go backwards. When is it time to shed the old skin, and grow into a new one? Has the expiration date passed? Disruption is a signal from the future that it was time to change – yesterday, ideally. What if we designed our lives to be a constant quest for new learnings, new insights, novel skills, quantum leaps of understanding, and curiosity for the uncharted with a thirst for wisdom, knowledge and exploration? If we set up a life for ourselves that requested our omnipresent curiosity, might disruption not seem too disruptive? Isn't it perhaps the case that disruption is only disruptive if you are not adaptive?

While hope is not a strategy, I hope that hope remains for my mum and my dad. A part of me wishes that they will extend a welcoming hand and fully invite me to collaborate with them on transforming the business into its full potential. This may never happen. And I am slowly learning to let go of that idea. Maybe some things have served their time. Perhaps consumers have voted too loudly with their digits, and moved on, and no place remains for a sartorial menswear store that runs like it was 1956. And then, whose fault is this? Would anyone miss the brand, the empathy with its customers it stands for, the neon elegance of the Georg Sörman man at St Eriksgatan 41?

Was this always meant to be a cautionary tale of what happens if you don't evolve with the times (which doesn't mean throwing the analogue baby away with the bathwater), and in its exasperated last breaths, a signal to other business owners, whether moms and pops, shareholders or boards, that dismissing change, learning and agility will ring the death knell for your brands? Or could it be that from the ashes of Blockbuster, Kodak and potentially my family's business, new Phoenix-birds will emerge that serve the world even better, provide more jobs, contribute more to the local community, and help move the world forward, rather than just be a looking-glass into a bygone era? Maybe sometimes, something has to die for something new to be spawned. Creative destruction. If the world votes on our perceived utility and the value we contribute, and consequently either gives us the Hollywood gladiatorial thumbs up or thumbs down, this should turn the mirror on ourselves and force us to ask whether what we are doing is the right thing or if we need to change. Perhaps it is time to throw in the towel, wind down, or let someone else take over. Yes, I am a little scarred as you can likely hear.

Finding hope in Languedoc-Roussillon

It's May 2016 and nearly three years since I walked the vineyards of Languedoc-Roussillon with my EMBA peers. I find myself on a flight on Cathay 239 from Hong Kong to London in seat 23A. This flight is part of a quest from Elvina Bay on Pittwater in Sydney, via advisory work in Melbourne with two different clients, to a keynote speaking gig in Luton Hoo for an investment firm. Earlier in the week, my Facebook newsfeed, perhaps in its predictive analytics, had presented me with articles on the prevention of jetlag, and curious as I was on how to best handle my itinerary, followed by a subsequent forty-two effective hours in the United Kingdom before returning to a client in Brisbane, while contemporaneously managing this book's manuscript deadline, I learnt (again) that staying away from alcohol is good advice to minimise the effects of jetlag. Note to my neuroplastic brainy self. I normally heed this advice, and with my 240 international travel days a year, that is probably a sage move. On this occasion, however, someone from the Cathay staff had slipped a special promotional wine menu in the middle of the culinary delights we were about to enjoy during this daytime flight.

As I run the thick (and seemingly expensive) paper of the menu between my thumb and index finger, to my surprise my brain's reticular activating system zooms in on the region, the specialties of which Cathay's residential sommelier has curated for us to enjoy – Languedoc-Roussillon! Shock and awe. Yuko Sakashita, Inflight Service Manager and Senior Sommelier, with her Fingerspitzengefühl had cherry-picked bottles from Chateau des Crès Richards, Chateau L'Hospitalet, Domaine de Bila-Haut and a Chateau Rombeau, and noted in her description of the Oenothera 2013 that 'Domaines Paul Mas have been leaders in the renaissance in the Languedoc-Roussillon region'. She goes on to illustrate the history of the region saying 'Today, there is a new emphasis on quality, whereas in the past, it was quantity … investment in the wineries has also played a part in the production of many worthwhile wines'. Vive la renaissance! Revival and rebirth is possible, but it does require that you unshackle yourself from remnants that no longer serve your future. We all love a comeback story, but you have to believe in, act on and grow into a new tailored suit that helps you show off your best bits, just like the futuristic vignerons of Languedoc-Roussillon are doing to earn their place in Cathay business class. This is what I hope for my mum and Georg Sörman.

A platform for the future

I am proud of a lot of the progress with Georg Sörman's space odyssey into the future. Together with our heroine, Birgitta, and my hero Lars-Olof, who we must highlight as another change agent in this saga, we have made several inroads into the future. Our digital agency, Thinque Digital, has acted as the inbound marketing agency for Georg Sörman in a formal capacity since March 2015, and an informal capacity since November 2013. From a branding perspective, we have made huge strides in the professionalisation and communication aspects of the renaissance brand – Georg Sörman 100 – that we launched in April 2015.

Let me showcase some of the highlights of the inbound content marketing and branding successes so far. We hope that there will be many more to come.

The brand renaissance

The brand renaissance for Georg Sörman was rolled out in four distinct phases – yes, transformation doesn't happen overnight. In true *Digilogue* spirit, we divided this omnichannel approach into an analogue and a digital renaissance (see figure 11.1, overleaf).

Figure 11.1: the Georg Sörman renaissance strategy across analogue and digital

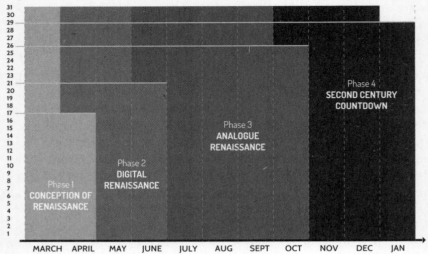

In the Georg Sörman 100 brand renaissance we sought to go back to the sartorial origins of the brand and the classic Grace period of Swedish design of around 1910 to the 1930s, during the latter part of which the original Georg Sörman neon sign was erected (see figure 11.2). You will notice that the typeface used in the brand renaissance has shifted towards a more classic style, and in its modern simplicity the cross-bars in the 'E' and 'A' have been lowered to reflect the original neon-sign (designed by the Graham Brothers for its 1937 inauguration at Kungsholmen). The collar cut-out in the 'M' used in the brand renaissance is an iconic illustration of menswear and shirts, and also indicates negative space – which we subconsciously associate with the timeless and timely idea of classic, yet modern, menswear.

By going back to many of the original design elements of this classic and award-winning neon sign, we believe the renaissance brand shows a futuristic outlook with confidence in its provenance and origins.

Figure 11.2: the Georg Sörman storefront and original neon sign

The following sections provide some highlights of the things we are most proud of and which continue to live on in Georg Sörman's second century. The great thing about the digital world is that we are always searchable, and everything can live on actively or in archival form forever. And I hope that Georg Sörman chooses to invest in a transformational future for itself, in a way that continues to serve its customers – old and new – seamlessly (see figure 11.3).

Figure 11.3: the new Georg Sörman brand identity

GEORG SÖRMAN

EST 1916

New Georg Sörman website

Since 1916, we have had a passion for style and quality. The relaunched website (see figure 11.4) and inbound strategy for Georg Sörman marked a clear delineation with its past, and showcases its relevance for both baby boomers, generation X, generation Y and tomorrow's gentlemen. Have a play on georgsorman.se, where you will also find the whole history, timeline, and relevant players in both Swedish and English. Together with in-store efforts, this has led to a 205 per cent increase in the digital database since our efforts began, which is promising for the future.

Figure 11.4: the new Georg Sörman website and inbound strategy

Välsytt Herrnytt — the Georg Sörman broadsheet

Currently in its third edition (see figure 11.5), this broadsheet was inspired by the age-old expression 'Välsytt Herrnytt', which has been the brand's tagline since time immemorial. 'Nytt' can also mean news in Sweden, so we wanted to make this broadsheet as newsworthy as a high-quality magazine, including content that ranges from clothing care, styling tips, men's health, Anglophilia, war history and its impact on clothing, and interviews with notables. Coinciding with the postal arrival of the second edition in 2015, sales jumped 47 per cent year on year, on a weekly basis.

Figure 11.5: the *Välsytt Herrnytt* Georg Sörman broadsheet

From father to son — the cross-generational appeal

The storytelling and authentic communication of the brand and values is clear in the cross-generational, ampersand (&) focus of the website (see figure 11.6). The imagery communicates timelessness and the passing of the baton between wise gentlemen and ambitious next gens, which is deliberate as the brand represents cross-generational values and succession, and aims to curate the same intra-familial bonds among its customers.

Figure 11.6: the cross-generational focus of the Georg Sörman website

Inbound marketing blog

Prepare once, use often. As we started producing written and video content for the broadsheet, events and newsletter, we knew these could also be repurposed for blogs to provide the content to new audiences and help with our search engine optimisation efforts (see figure 11.7). Investments in videographers and fashion photographers could be amplified via subscribable blogs, all built on the HubSpot platform for optimisation and segmentation, to ensure that the right customers receive the right information, and that their customer journeys are as seamless as possible.

Figure 11.7: reusing content and increasing optimisation via the Georg Sörman blog

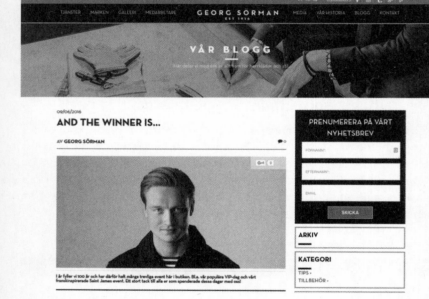

Social media amplification — Facebook

Social media and opening up our brand via channels like Facebook (see figure 11.8) has massively improved the reach. The digital version of the broadsheet and brand videos about Georg Sörman, with focused targeting on psychographics similar to our existing clientele, and representing the new type of clientele we also want in-store, were amplified in their reach, representing a great spend per dollar (or, in this case, krona) invested. Facebook has also been a huge asset in terms of event hosting, and scaling our family and social networks for organic growth.

Figure 11.8: the Georg Sörman Facebook page

Social media amplification — Instagram

Instagram is a channel where we began at zero and started building a solid following for the new brand, along the new brand guidelines (see figure 11.9). For a formerly old-school brand, Georg Sörman has built a decent following that is now engaging with a #virile #centenarian.

Figure 11.9: the Georg Sörman Instagram page

Partnerships

In combination with our elevated branding position, we have been able to secure new partnerships with brands that are closely aligned with Georg Sörman's renaissance of its historical origins and modern future. Brands we've formed these partnerships with include the following:

- Barbour
- Eton
- Filson
- Saint James
- Derek Rose
- SNS Herning

- Andersen & Andersen
- Tretorn
- Woolrich
- Johnstons of Elgin
- Farfalla
- Begg & Co

These partnerships don't just mean that Georg Sörman has become a licensed reseller of these brands; often the partnerships run even deeper. For example, *Välsytt Herrnytt* became a partner (advertiser) within the funded model, whereby brands like Saint James, Eton, Oscar Jacobson, Resteröds and Alan Paine contributed both editorial, historical and brand content. Because of the brand alignment with Georg Sörman 100, this content felt very contextual and was often met with great approval from customers. One customer, for example, walked into the shop with the broadsheet, pointed to a picture in it of Pablo Picasso (who used to wear Saint James) and said, 'I want to look like Pablo Picasso'. That customer walked out with a Saint James jersey.

With Eton, we hosted a collaboration with the Swedish whisky manufacturer Mackmyra, whereby we had a whisky tasting and Eton brought their engraving machine so our customers could get a monogram sewn into their Eton shirts. The NPS (net promoter score) from this event was the highest we ever had, and 93 per cent of the registered customers turned up for the event. As the Eton representative, Martin Narvelo, said at Pitti Uomo in January 2016, 'When Georg Sörman calls its customers, they come'. This was a nice compliment and testament to this partnership.

A third example was when Barbour, who are very selective in their partnerships and brand alignment projects, brought in their re-waxing machine for a full day co-hosted with the old fire station microbrewery of my cousin Stefan Funke – Bergslagens Brygghus – for beer tasting and refurbishing of vintage Barbour waxed jackets. Partnership and brand alignment is key to any brand's future, but these seamless partnerships have been a true pillar in the transformational journey for Georg Sörman so far.

In essence, we have provided Georg Sörman – including the leadership, board and investors – with a professionalised platform for the future. We sincerely hope that they will use this platform. The keys to that transformational future now lie in their hands.

CASE STUDY:
LEDBURY — ANALOGUE TOUCH POINTS IN AN ONLINE BUSINESS

As an Accenture article ('Customer 2020: Are you future-ready or reliving the past?') recently highlighted, as more and more consumer brands and retailers increase their digital investments, we as consumers are starting to expect more from the digital customer experience we have with businesses. This means it's also becoming increasingly difficult to create a unique, memorable and lasting experience for the customer. One way to create a distinctive experience is to use the power of surprise, and this is just what the Richmond-based luxury shirtmaker Ledbury has done.

Ledbury was founded in 2009 by Oxford University classmates Paul Trible and Paul Watson, and since then the company has experienced double-digit growth each year. The two entrepreneurs have seen their brand grow from a tiny shop to a global brand in just a few years. Companies like Ledbury that grow and scale up fast often have trouble with maintaining customer intimacy, but the two former classmates decided from the start to prioritise this aspect. An essential part of their strategy has been (and still is) to infuse their own personalities in the branding process, focus on spoiling their customers and telling stories and offering content that is hyper-localised and personal.

One thing Ledbury has got a lot of press for is the fact that the founders called the first 1000 customers who ordered via their website. And as noted in *Inc* article '4 ways this booming menswear brand gets intimate with its customers', in 2015 they were still sending personal, handwritten notes to their top 100 customers every month. Ledbury even then gets handwritten notes back from their customers, which has generated a genuine dialogue with their most loyal customers. This proves that these kinds of analogue touch points – like a simple phone call and a handwritten note – can make the difference between a good customer experience and a memorable and distinctive one. Analogue touch points can cut through the digital noise and boost relationship building.

Robert Cialdini, Professor Emeritus of Psychology and Marketing at Arizona State University, writes in his book *Influence: The psychology of persuasion* about six principles of influence. The first principle, reciprocation, recognises that people feel in debt to those who give them a gift or do something for them. So when businesses like Ledbury spoil their customers with great content, rich media or plain and simple handwritten notes, they are playing on this principle of influence.

Consumers are not as rational as we have previously thought, and we constantly let our emotions influence our decisions – whether it's while shopping for groceries in the local food store or buying a new laptop. The brand, its stories and the experience you get from interacting with a brand all play a part in the purchase decision.

Ask yourself...

Have a think about how you can spoil your customers during the different phases in the customer journey (awareness, engagement, evaluation, decision and usage). Just like Ledbury, you should strive to focus on the overall experience and not the different channels – it all comes down to how you weave together the analogue and digital touch points.

Think about the following with regard to your business:

1. How could you digitise your analogue stories and infuse your own personality in your brand? Think about stories that encapsulate your entrepreneurial spirit, local background and visionary thinking.

2. What analogue touch points could you elevate and adjust so that they feel differentiated and personal?

3. Where in the customer journey can you add extra value for your customers? Can you think of any touch points where you feel like an opportunity exists to spoil your customers and do something different?

STEP 12

HERO'S JOURNEY WHEEL FOR MAMMA SÖRMAN-NILSSON

12

Final mastery of the problem

Return with the elixir

ORDINARY WORLD

It remains to be seen whether this time around, this book might be the co-created elixir needed for Mum to finally solve her business problems. She has not yet been able to gain final mastery of the problem, and has not yet been able to get the results we all want for Mum (and Dad of course).

Return with the elixir

This is the final stage and it's the ultimate step in the heroine's journey, where she returns back to her ordinary world a changed wo/man. She will have grown as a person, learned many things, faced incredible danger, and potentially even had a close encounter with death, but at this juncture she looks forward to the start of a new life – a renaissance. Her return to the ordinary world may bring hope to those in similar circumstances or to those left behind, or she may return with a direct solution to their problems and even a fresh perspective for everyone to consider. The reward she obtains may be both literal and metaphoric – and potentially a cause for celebration, self-realisation or a peaceful end to strife.

Whatever is on the heroine's life menu, it symbolises three things: change, success and proof of her journey. Her return home also signals the need for resolution for the story's other key players. Her doubters will be ostracised, her enemies will be punished and allies rewarded. Ultimately, the heroine returns to where she started, but things will never be the same again, as she is fundamentally transformed as a character.

Here's how Luke's return looked in *Star Wars*:

- *Inner journey:* Return with the elixir – the main weapon of the Evil Empire is destroyed.

- *Outer journey:* Final mastery of the problem – the team members are honoured as heroes and peace (temporarily) settles over the galaxy.

For Birgitta, the journey continues:

- *Inner journey:* Return with the elixir – it remains to be seen whether this book might be the elixir needed to progress Mum's hero's journey, with little evidence that she has fully accepted the elixir that could solve her business problems.

- *Outer journey:* Final mastery of the problem – because the internal journey has not progressed like we had hoped, the hero has not yet been able to gain final mastery of the problem, and as such has not been able to get the results we all so desperately want for Mum (and Dad, of course)

12: Return with the elixir

We're craving seamless transformation – so indulge our digital minds and analogue hearts.

Seamless design and customer odysseys

My colleague at Thinque, researcher for *Seamless*, and occasional dandy – Anton Järild – and I descended from our mountain retreat at the chalet at Le Jorat on a misty January morning. Our planned journey of seven and a half hours from the Alps via the Mediterranean would take us all the way from Sainte Foy-Tarentaise to Florence, Italy. We were leaving behind a month of wood-chopping, powder skiing, snow, hammams, and Jacuzzi-based strategy and writing sessions. I promise you, it wasn't quite as *Brokeback Mountain* as it sounds. There were also vegan dinners, discussions about the merits of quinoa versus bulghur, and whether gluten-free beers qualify as craft beers. Wait – this does sound kind of *Brokeback Mountain*-ish or at least very hipster metrosexual. This is what can happen when you grow up in a sartorial menswear context as the son of a sartorialist.

As it was, Anton and I were destined for the eighty-ninth Pitti Uomo in Florence on behalf of our client – Georg Sörman. Florence, the mecca of sartorialism, dandyism, and metrosexuality. In menswear terms, we were making the pilgrimage from rural wooden-cabin fever and brands like Woolrich, Filson, Livid Jeans and Barbour, and entering the sophisticated urban piazza of L.B.M. 1911, Crockett & Jones, Berwich, Thomas Mason,

Brunello Cucinelli, and Loro Piana. We were undertaking an odyssey from a world of rugged durability and patina to one of style, savoir faire, and *sprezzatura* (Italian for 'studied carelessness').

Like 35 000 other fashionistas, we were descending on the epicentre of the Renaissance to geek out and gawk out. Our Airbnb host in the Alps, architect Jean-Pierre, drove us down in his beaten-up Renault minibus from the Le Jorat chalet to the nearest town with any decent infrastructure, Bourg-Saint Maurice, where we piled my waxed Filson bags containing our digital nomadic belongings into the Tiguan that was going to take us from this last large town, along the Tarentaise Valley in the heart of the French Alps and over into Italian territory. This was the German automobile – *Vorsprung Durch Technik*, as a certain car manufacturer within the Volkswagen family might say – that was going to take us from 1171 metres elevation, through the Mont Blanc tunnel, via Portofino on the Mediterranean, and then, finally, help us settle on the Tuscan capital. Coming to Florence is the semi-annual pilgrimage that global fashion buyers, family business owners, bloggers, photographers, fashion students and the world's most important brands in menswear style make. Like anadromous and catadromous schools of fish, they make this migration to feed, capture design nutrients (and maybe mate). It's a week of flair, male peacocking, narcissism, and voyeurism. And an extreme nerding out about seams, cuts, lapels, Goodyear welting, silhouettes, finishes, provenance, thread counts and stitching techniques. Pitti Uomo is in many ways an inspirational Italian finishing-school version of *Queer Eye for the Straight Guy* – with the essential difference that the people who pilgrimage to the Padiglione Centrale at Fortezza da Basso, and 'circumstrut' its fashion equivalent to the Kaaba at Mecca (the central piazza outside) are already well versed in the intricate and nuanced language of sartorialism.

Our drive took us through the snow-covered valleys of the Rhône-Alpes, past castles and cows from Milka chocolate ads. We are reminded about regional honour products like the Opinel knife and AOC protected Beaufort cheeses as French signs rush past us and we swish through tunnels and over infrastructure feats. And while Anton and I usually have lots of things to discuss and debate, on this occasion my co-researcher acted co-pilot, while we both quietly enjoyed David Brooks' 2012 book *The Social Animal* on Audible's audiobook. The only disruptions emerged from the central navigational dashboard occasionally highlighting a turn-off or, more frequently, one of many toll roads. The first time we had to pay a toll, I was convinced that our Volkswagen would become the first of many vehicles in a line-up of honking cars cursing the Swedish 'Volvo'-driver who didn't bring cash and coins to enable seamless transitions between regions and nations.

But I was pleasantly surprised to learn that the normally largely cash-biased Franco–Italian border regions had evolved to accept both credit cards and Telepass, making the journey rather seamless from a payments perspective. An important detail, as my payment diet doesn't include carrying either cash or notes (curse these bacteria-covered remnants of ancient empires).

And so with David Brooks providing some insightful white noise, speaking softly to our subconscious minds about what drives individual behaviour and human decision-making – an apt topic given the peacocking at Pitti – both Anton and I dreamed our merry selves away to the world of exquisite textiles as we emerged out of the Mont Blanc tunnel into the Aosta Valley. We cruised on, reflecting on Brooks' depiction of human beings as driven by the universal feelings of loneliness and the need to belong – what he labels 'the urge to merge' – and how we shortly would bear witness to the social circus in Florence, and headed south to Portofino on the Ligurian coast.

By the time we arrived in Portofino, the temperature had ascended by 18°C, the elevation had dropped by more than 1167 metres, and a cosy Mediterranean breeze greeted us with the aquatic scent of salt. And I had managed to illegally park our Tiguan by mounting the pedestrian harbour walkway in fancy Portofino. Like a true local I took one insouciant look at the wheels and arrogantly made my way with Anton towards the restaurants. By the time we arrived at the Foursquare-recommended eateries at sequentially 2.57 pm, 2.59 pm, 3.01 pm and 3.03 pm, all the maître d's announced that their kitchens closed at 3 pm and that it was impossible to serve us. All were wearing analogue watches. Of course, the fact that the Serie A was playing surely had nothing to do with their lack of customer-service enthusiasm. Our stomachs, which had been longing for Mediterranean fare all day, felt the grating presence of a frictive seam emerging. We continued our desperate search for food through the alleys and along the Molo Umberto I, with the same nod of low-season inhospitality at each juncture. Our journey continued along the waterfront until luckily our 'urge to merge' was convivially returned by the owners of Capo Nord, who had set up a wooden pop-up stand serving local delights next to the port. They managed to move us from awareness, to engagement, to evaluation, to decision and loyalty on our customer journey (see figure 12.1, overleaf) from Sainte Foy-Tarentaise to Portofino in a millisecond. A simple minestrone soup served in a plastic bowl with a glass of Montepulciano had never tasted so sweet. Their pop-up brand was immediately imbued with a superior sense of human dignity and empathy, as we sat slowly digesting the food and gawking at the splendid multi-coloured buildings lining this millennia-old summer home to aristocrats and artists.

Figure 12.1: designing seamless customer experiences with digital and analogue touch points

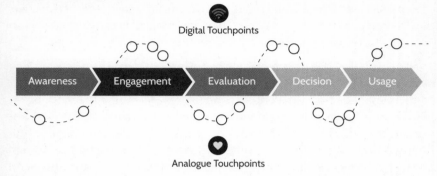

Digital Touchpoints

| Awareness | Engagement | Evaluation | Decision | Usage |

Analogue Touchpoints

A shot of espresso, or more accurately a ristretto, woke us up from our sense of timeless sophistication admiring the Tyrrhenian Sea, and alerted us to the sun's slumbering light. It was time to get back behind the steering wheel and emerge onto the final stretch of autostrada between Portofino and Florence. For the whole trip, covering 654 kilometres, I had felt vaguely in sync with the speeds on the motorway. Arriving in the Tuscan capital, we felt how the heartbeat of this medieval city rhythmically slowed us down. Soon, mopeds, models, tourists and streetcars were criss-crossing and messing up my seamless communications with the posh English female navigation voice (I like to imagine that it was Keira Knightley), and I even managed to feel like I didn't have any of Audi's 'Vorsprung durch Technik' on the few occasions when I stalled or mishandled the clutch on narrow cobblestone streets. We arrived on Via della Vigna Nuova 17 outside our regular Airbnb hostess Ilaria's palatial granny-flat and, treasuring my Florentine illegal parking skills, I was hoping Anton could briskly unload the car while I stayed in it in the one-way street adjacent to the bus station that was conveniently located outside this Medici-era building. Mea culpa. Within seconds my nightmares of being cursed had shifted from Francophobia to Italophobia. The blinding high-beam lights of the local bus quickly snuck up on my back, I waved Anton goodbye and emerged on a labyrinthine search for a way to asymmetrically 'go around the block' and return with our bags. This took fifteen minutes. Eventually, we managed to unload on the corner, and I gave up my search for street parking and amazingly found Garage Europa, courtesy of Ilaria who graciously had arranged an Airbnb discount for us. The journey from the chalet at Le Jorat in the Rhône-Alpes to the Renaissance building in old-town Florence was complete. This odyssey hadn't been entirely without seams, and while enjoying a dinner consisting of burrata, spaghetti, truffles, spinach and a nice bottle of Brunello red, I engaged in sleepy, philosophical discourse with Anton about how everything in life is either a physical or mental journey. Very deep and meaningful I know.

The journey is the destination

A magnificent saying holds that the journey is the destination; the point is not about arriving at your destination but rather about who you become – your transformation – as a result of undertaking the quest. We can all remember a personal growth journey we have undertaken, where the destination might have been rewarding, but we also knew that as a result of undertaking the journey we would never return to our previous life, or to the standards, values, income, shallow depth of relationships or fitness standards of the person we were before we set out on the path. Now I am not going to pretend that Anton or I changed paradigmatically during our little trip down from the mountain to fashionable Florence, but one of the things I did reflect upon is how an enjoyable journey can build glue, trust and mutual empathy. This is true not only of compatriot nomads on their way to Pitti Uomo (see figure 12.2, overleaf, for a photo of me at the end of the journey), but also of anyone in the business of curating or designing customer journeys.

Think about it: you as a business leader, as a visionary, a misfit or entrepreneur are in the business of helping mentally or physically move people toward your brand, your way of thinking, or a specialised line of products or services. But have you ever deliberately considered whether the transformational journey is enjoyable for your clients and prospects? Have you sat down and designed a journey that would help them grow into your brand's personality, and engage with you as a co-pilot, trusted advisor, squire or caddy? It is clear from our journey, which you have just followed vicariously, that while many aspects were seamless and well-designed (like the toll payment systems, border crossings and world-class infrastructure), others (like the closure of all bricks-and-mortar restaurants from 2.57 pm on a Sunday) were more frictive. Now, while no–one, other than ourselves, set out to design the specific journey for Anton and Anders from Le Jorat to Via della Vigna Nuova, we were able to enjoy a journey that was nonetheless fairly well designed by architects and thinkers who had empathy for travellers and had thought systematically about how to move people through various phases of that 654-kilometre quest. Are you doing the same when you reflect on how to attract people to mentally or physically travel to and with you into the future?

Figure 12.2: rubbing shoulders with the empire at Pitti Uomo

Seamless or frictive journeys?

During a recent cold winter's evening with my girlfriend Nicole, at our place in Elvina Bay, Sydney, I thought about the shifting sands when it comes to customer journeys and storytelling as customer service and marketing. Nicole was still soundly asleep and I had gotten up early to make some hot lemon and herbal tea, which is a bit of a morning tradition here. Particularly in winter. Having grown up in Sweden, I am quite used to it being cold outside, but even after spending nigh on twenty years in Australia, I still cannot get used to how cold it can be *inside* Australian houses. I am firmly of the view that no colder place exists on the planet than being indoors during Australian winters. Houses in Australia are simply not built for sub-10°C nights. In Sweden, we are spoilt by triple glassing and sustainable insulation. Each year, the Australian winter seems to surprise 23 million Australians, who during their ten months of summer forget that their cold snaps can last for a few weeks or even months south of the Queensland border.

So, on this particular morning, the cold got to me, and because we had gone to bed quite early the night before, the fire in the stove, the only source of heat in the house (in true Australian-winter-ignorance), had burnt out. We are in the habit of always getting the analogue weekend papers (just because the ink looks so great when left on your face because of blackened fingers), but because I had spent a lot of time at Elvina Bay on this book project during the preceding few days, last weekend's paper had already gone up the chimney. So I would have to use the current weekend's papers – presenting a big moral dilemma and a case for prioritisation and rational decision-making. Which pages to burn? Which pages would you choose? Advertisements, right? Advertisements were the first to go, and then the gambling odds, sporting tables and eventually the share-market data. I then carefully ripped out all advertisements from the other pages, because they have the very least editorial and cognitive value. And, of course, as humans we screen this stuff all the time. Why? Because advertisements are the opposite of great content and inbound marketing. They are rented attention, and while occasionally they can be useful for brand-building, when they are not in context or adding value on someone's customer journey, they go up the physical or mental chimney.

Text, textiles and the importance of seamlessness

So, let us take a look at how the brand of Pitti Uomo entices people from every corner of the world to make the pilgrimage to Florence. It being world-leading and the premiere menswear show globally helps. Getting the thought leaders and rock stars of sartorial flair like Lino Ielluzi, Luca Rubinacci and Nick Wooster to think of this as a must-attend event in their annual calendars is another way of ensuring that the event's brand becomes firmly burnt into the imaginations of every aspiring fashionista. Getting bloggers and photographers like Scott Schuman, aka The Sartorialist, and Instagram paragons like Karl-Edwin Guerre to the piazza ensures that peacocks and professional poseurs think it is worthwhile to be seen, to boost their social value and provide them with the social proof they desperately need (remember David Brooks' idea of the human cycle of loneliness and the need to belong?). Pitti also has a certain unspoken rule: being there, having travelled there and being accepted into this exclusive club of designers, cognoscenti, literati and buyers bestows upon you certain qualities. You are suddenly someone, and a certain air of respect and sophistication covers the attendees like fairy dust for four days. Similar to gatherings like TED, Aspen Institute, World Economic Forum, Burning Man and South by Southwest, the pilgrimage in and of itself removes certain social barriers, and people are left to their own devices to ascertain whether they want to continue the Medici merchant spirit of Florence with each other. It's good to be King, and Pitti Uomo has achieved indisputable alpha-male status among the world's dandies.

The result of this branding effort and design of client journeys was that in January 2016, 1219 companies attended the trade show and the total number of visitors was 36000. According to Pitti Immagine, the organisation behind the trade show, the success in terms of attendance was mainly driven in 2016 by the double-digit growth of almost all European markets. But, as figures available on the Pitti Immagine website show, even attendees from markets further afield grew in number compared to previous years, including those from the United States, Australia, Brazil, United Arab Emirates, Russia, China and Turkey. Pitti Uomo has become a true fashion pilgrimage and odyssey for sartorialists who have a passion for both the interweaving of ideas and physical form, and the seams between them.

Text, textiles and transformation

In Roxette's classic 1980s song 'Dressed for Success', we learn that clothing can be transformational. At least on the surface. The textile industry certainly are enablers of potential success and, as we have seen throughout *Seamless*, textiles play a huge role in every stage of Maslow's needs hierarchy including, of course, self-actualisation.

This contrasts to some degree, but also highlights the magic of clothing in our transformational journey, with the idea of *The Emperor's new clothes*, which is the fairy-tale by Hans Christian Andersen about an emperor who pays exorbitant prices for new magic clothes that can only be seen by the cognoscenti – in this case, wise men. The clothes don't, in fact, exist, but the Emperor, in his vanity, won't admit that he cannot see them out of fear of seeming stupid. Equally, the Emperor's ministers cannot see the clothes either, but pretend to out of fear of being unfit for their positions. Proudly, the Emperor wears his clothes in front of his subjects, all of whom pretend to see the clothes, until one child exposes him by calling out, 'But he isn't wearing anything at all!' Legend has it that Andersen was inspired to make the exposé the climax of his fairytale based on his experience of standing in a crowd with his mother to see King Frederick VI. When the king made his appearance, Andersen cried out, 'Oh, he is nothing more than a human being!' Among other themes, this satire illustrates the vanity and social status often imbued in clothes. Nonetheless, the fashion industry has played a crucial role in both embedding social strata and enabling personal transformation. And brands, whether in textiles or not, can learn from the emergence of a new type of economy – the economy of transformation, or the Transformation Economy.

For some time, brands have been focused on providing great experiences. Degustation menus, branded events, café milieus and tough mudders. Joseph Pine II and James Gilmore described this phenomenon in their 1999 publication *The Experience Economy*, where they argued that a progression of economic value occurs as products move from commodities to experiences. They hold up Starbucks as the old-school example of this progression. A coffee bean is a commodity; as it is roasted the 'Starbucks way', it becomes a product, while a barista making the coffee is a service, and providing a 'European café milieu' is an experience (which most Europeans would take offence at, given their general disapproval and independent fighting off of Starbucks' expansionism). Starbucks can charge a premium for the experience, and customers derive more value from it than just buying a coffee bean from Colombia. This is the basic idea (and builds on my futurist mentor Alvin Toffler's earlier work and prediction around the emergence of the 'experiential industry' in *Future Shock*).

In *The Experience Economy*, the authors foresaw the emergence of a new type of economy, which would morph the game even further: The Transformation Economy. In other words, in the future (which, as noted by William Gibson, is unevenly distributed and already here), brands need to curate, coach and nudge their clients along transformative odysseys. This is not just a marketing idea, but needs to be central to a company's brand, products and services. While an experience business, like Starbucks, charges customers for the feeling they get from engaging with it, hypothetically transformation businesses charge for the benefit clients or customers receive from spending time there (or with the transformation business). Of course, the business model for transformation businesses can vary. Examples of transformation businesses include yoga teachers, gyms, management consultants, psychologists, life coaches, business coaches, advertising agencies, branding experts, architects and designers – and, of course, Thinque/Thinque Digital.

Increasingly, though, product brands beyond these services, like Nike and Lululemon, are starting to metamorphose into transformation brands.

This phenomenon taps into the fact that we are now, more so than ever before, living in an abundant age. Consider this fact. In 2012, more people worldwide died as a result of obesity than because of malnutrition. Both are severe problems, but these rates mean more people are overeating themselves to death than undereating themselves to death, according to the WHO. In her *Business of Fashion* article ('Is the new luxury a better you?') author Lauren Sherman quotes Pine, who cites a 2014 Boston Consulting Group report that reveals that of the 1.8 trillion spend on 'luxuries' in 2013, nearly 1 trillion, or 55 per cent, was spent on luxury experiences, analysing this by claiming that a 'large part of that trillion is luxury transformations: people looking to recharge, revitalise, or to improve well-being in some way'. According to Sherman's insightful article, the market for wellness tourism – like yoga and meditation retreats – grew to US$493 million in 2013, a 13 per cent stretch from the previous year. Equally, transformational festivals like Burning Man, which I attended in 2012 and wrote about in *Digilogue*, and Further Future Festival, are mushrooming and expanding around the world. Again quoted in Sherman's article, Pine says that 'brands must remember that consumers are looking to become better people. If they're buying physical goods, it's to achieve aspirations, whatever they might be.'

District Vision, an eyewear brand specifically developed for runners, doesn't see its meditation and running programs as mere marketing exercises. The co-founder, Max Vallot, points out that events, improvement processes and congregations like Nike's running club, Lululemon's yoga classes, or our client insurance firm AIA's Vitality Health app, could eventually be packaged and productised too. B2B brands like HubSpot with their Inbound conference, Amex's Small Business Saturday, the financial professionals' Million Dollar Round Table (which I spoke at in 2013), and Salesforce with Dreamforce are other examples of brands that stage transformational events. These give a business angle to the hype of more traditional motivational or inspirational events from self-styled gurus like Tony Robbins, Deepak Chopra and Robert Kiyosaki. Self-improvement is big business, and while some might have been sceptical of the execution and style of big motivational conferences, more established brands are realising the value in the transformation economy, and my view is that being able to package and deliver on positive transformation is a huge opportunity for the future, and one that hopefully delivers good.

Thus it is perhaps no wonder that the founder of a 'religion' (a term you may or may not use, depending on your point of view) and science fiction author L. Ron Hubbard once said, 'You don't get rich writing science fiction. If you want to get rich, you start a religion.' According to a 1986 Forbes article ('The prophet and the profits of Scientology') the treasurer of ASI (Author Services, Inc), which existed to manage both Hubbard's financial affairs and those of the Church of Scientology, revealed that in 1982 Hubbard was pulling in US$1 million a week, and Hubbard's net worth had risen by US$30 million in a nine-month period in 1982. Clearly, Hubbard realised the money wasn't in the product – the book – but in the re-packaging of those ideas into services, experiences and 'transformation'. By no means am I encouraging you to go out and start a religion; I am just saying that religions, which sell the idea of personal transformation, riches and spiritual enlightenment, were probably early adopters and pioneers in the transformation economy (while also ensuring tax-exemptions). But let us go back to more evidence-based and scientific analyses of the transformation economy.

Take Nike as an example. They are now selling a way to be different. They think of themselves as a player in an economy that is about the exchange of value that could transform the quality of life of the consumer – for the long term. Advertisers would have you believe that we have always lived in this space, but often the Mad Men-esque misrepresentation of weight loss, whiter teeth, younger skin, longer life, happier children and so on is qualitatively different. I'm talking here about brands that are genuinely a transformation economy partner with you, for a particular phase in your hero's journey, and don't only push products, which you may or may not use correctly. They provide an ecosystem in which you can be a better version of yourself. This also means they are invested in your transformation, which forces brands to stick their necks out. And while consumers and clients cannot blame Nike for their being overweight or not having that sixpack after a certain duration of time (thanks to extraneous circumstances such as diet and genetics, for example), the transformation economy could be a scary place for brands with products that actually don't deliver value or results. Nike's belief for a long period of time has been that 'if you have a body, you are an athlete' and in its own transformational journey, Nike has stopped just peddling 'books', and is instead starting to focus on building a transformational 'religion'.

Nike's hero's journey has been about turning the tables, and moving the attention away from the egomaniacal swoosh logo and to enabling you as the hero. Undifferentiated shoes metamorphosed into a branded product with a futuristic waffle sole. Nike then peddled their products and apparel for many years, and I remember profoundly the status anxiety when my teammates could afford the more expensive Nike shoes (like the celebrity endorsed Airs) in the 1990s, while I was running around in inherited and oversized hand-me-downs from my cousins in England. It wasn't until the 2000s that Nike went through a paradigm shift, however, with the advent of mobile and contextual data. In *Digilogue* I tell the story of my digitised/quantified self running the New York Marathon courtesy of Nike+, the ecosystem and service launched by Nike in the mid-2000s. Nike believed in the philosophy of what can be measured can be monitored and managed, and applied this to its consumers as well.

Meanwhile, according to Pine (quoted in another *Business of Fashion* article by Lauren Sherman – 'Nike taps the transformation economy'), for the consumer, 'with every level, [they] gain new aspiration. Whether that means becoming more fit, from the physical, emotional, or spiritual (experience), increasingly it's about how everything we buy affects us in some way'. The Nike+ app straddled services and experiences, as all of a sudden athletes (human beings) could start not only improving themselves but also engaging with new friends and old friends via Nike curated events and experiences. Between the analogue and digital interfaces, and the increasingly intelligent apparel like the HyperAdapt (which enables hyper-personalised running experiences and tailored cushioning for users), the 2016 update for the Nike+ app provides a tailored online shopping experience, and nudges members to sign up for local running and training classes. A gamified interface also offers perks for healthy living and active lifestyles, rewarding positive behaviour and enabling transformation.

At the same time, Nike collects critical transformation pattern data, such as data showing that people who work out with a partner tend to stick with a workout program for longer. This then empowers Nike as a transformation brand to constantly iterate its offerings to clients. Combined with a future of artificial intelligence–powered personal trainers, you might soon find yourself doing CrossFit with a robot singing your favourite motivational classics ('Eye of the Tiger', perhaps?), and then telling you to drop and give it twenty. For Nike, the dollar transaction is still in the products, not in the religion, so it remains to be seen whether they will be able to shift into a space where consumers will want to pay for the end result – the outcome of the transformation. Would you rather pay for the shoes, or the sixpack?

These brands, in a non-paternalistic way, encourage positive change through nudging. AIA Australia, which we have advised over the last few years, licensed the Vitality app to deliver rewards and perks for its clients for living a healthier lifestyle, like giving up smoking and reducing other risk factors, and adopting fruitful habits like exercising regularly and eating more healthily. As a result of users of AIA's insurance products taking these steps, valuable points and rewards and other forms of currency ensue, but the risk to AIA is also reduced as they are less likely to pay out claims. Imagine the implications for insurance companies in the transformation economy driven by self-driving cars, cranes and trucks, or the human drivers still insisting on driving. A personalised defensive driving coach/Tamagotchi? Airlines have understood the engagement and adherence driven by gamification and our attraction to rewards for years (with frequent flyer points at one stage the second largest currency in the world behind the US dollar). And if you think that this transformation economy is only for people at the top of Maslow's needs hierarchy, think again. Nudging, designing for transformation and enabling transformation may have even greater impacts when enabled for consumers who are seeking to climb the societal ladder and reap the concomitant health and financial benefits.

Georg Sörman and transformation

Rather than being a mere purveyor of clothing, Georg Sörman is in the transformation industry. As we saw in chapter 1, Georg Sörman provides textiles for each level of Maslow's needs hierarchy, including for the top level of self-actualisation. This requires a total mindset shift in a brand's thinking about its role in the value chain – a similar mindset shift that occurred during one of my early summers at my grandparents' rented summerhouse at Färingsö outside of Stockholm, where my parents now reside. I remember vividly how each autumn we would be sent on a work mission by my grandfather to pick all the apples in the apple orchard and take them to market or sell them. These apples, in hindsight, were very 'organic' looking before that was a trend. Together with my mum, my brother and I would entrepreneurially take the apples up to the big road, and construct posters to entice passers-by to engage with us commercially. On this one occasion we didn't have much luck. And so Mum gave me an important lesson in marketing and communications, which continues to spur my interest in a transformational strategy career twenty-five years later.

I had created a poster that featured, in large red writing, 'billiga äpplen', Mum pedagogically told me that *billiga* (which translates as 'cheap' in English) is not a good word to use when marketing a brand or product. She advised me that we could instead package these fruits (which were *fall frukt*, meaning they had just fallen off the trees) as bio-apples and organic from the local island of Färingsö. All of a sudden, the branding penny dropped for me. We had transformed the value of what we were selling. Now, twenty-five years later, I dream that Mum will accept the transformational story I have been telling her – that if her mindset about what she sells transforms, she can transform her life and the lives of her customers – and, ultimately, she can find the elixir to her business woes. I would love to repay her for this lesson I learnt in the epicentre of the organic apple-farm district in Sweden. I imagine how transformational a brand Georg Sörman 100 could be for every generation of gentleman as they pass on traditions, wisdom and personal style, and how transformational the clothing, curation, education and services Georg Sörman can provide could be at each milestone in a gentleman's life. The future will tell us whether Mum is ready to transform, or if transformation seems like 'too much hard work'. And the future will tell us whether the brand will successfully cross the abyss and move from the troubles of the third generation to the success of the fourth (see figure 12.3), when a family business turns into a crown jewel. And who knows, maybe the only way for tradition to remain alive is for you to transform, adapt and evolve! Now is not too soon to embark on your hero's quest.

Figure 12.3: can this fourth generation turn Georg Sörman into a jewel?

Anders & Gustaf Sörman-Nilsson (4th Generation Georg Sörman in 1985)

The important question for now is, what is the transformational challenge for you? Is it in the 'too hard' basket or is it a call for you to fully immerse yourself in your hero's journey (see figure 12.4)?

Figure 12.4: start mapping your own transformational hero's journey

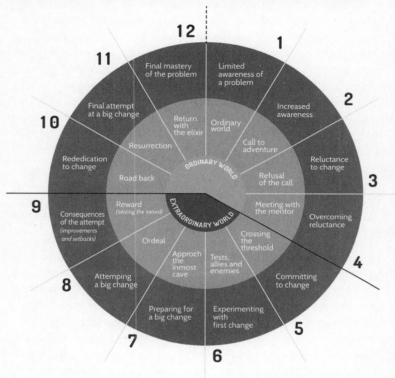

CASE STUDY:
ACORNS TURNS YOUR SPARE CHANGE INTO MICRO-INVESTMENTS

New consumer attitudes and behaviours driven by digitisation are upending the way the banking and finance industries are working. One of many consequences of the financial crisis in 2007 and 2008 has been the growing general and widespread suspicion of banks and other financial institutions. In its 2015 *Millennials and wealth management: Trends and challenges of the new clientele* report, Deloitte highlights that these kinds of attitudes are particularly common among generation Y (or Millennials, as they are also called). According to The Millennial Disruption Index, 53 per cent of Millennials in the United States don't believe their bank offers anything different from other banks, and one in three are open to switching banks within the next 90 days. With these insights in mind it's not surprising that digital start-ups like Swedish personal finance app Tink, peer-to-peer lending platform Lendico and micro-investing app Acorns have gained popularity among a young generation of digitally savvy customers and (potentially) ambitious savers.

As the PricewaterhouseCooper report *Millennials & financial literacy – the struggle with personal finance* highlights, one problem that many young people struggle with in their twenties is saving and investing their personal income. The reason behind this could be high student loans combined with low income and/or high costs of living. The founders behind the app Acorns aim to change this and make it easier to save and invest your personal income. As an Acorns user you first need to connect your accounts and cards to the app, and then for every purchase you make via these accounts, the app rounds up the purchase to the nearest dollar and takes the difference and invests it in an investment portfolio. For example, when you spend $3.60 on a coffee, the app rounds the purchase up to $4.00 and takes the difference, $0.40, and transfers it to your Acorns account. Your money in the account then gets spread across six basic index funds, with the amount distributed among those funds depending on the risk profile you choose. The investment process is automated and has been developed by a team of engineers and mathematicians – along with the Nobel Prize-winning economist Dr Harry Markowitz, who is often referred to as 'The Father of Modern Portfolio Theory'.

With 75 per cent of its users being aged between eighteen and thirty-four years old, we can conclude that they have managed to reach out to the digital natives who prefer to save in dribs (or see this as the only possible way they will save) and manage their banking on the go through their tablet or smart phone. A 2015 study released in the United Kingdom by the Savings and Investment Policy (TSIP) project supports this argument, revealing that 90 per cent of British people are comfortable with using technology to manage their personal finances. The app itself is free and fees are a dollar per month for accounts under $5000 and 0.25 per cent per year for accounts with more.

Acorns is not the only FinTech company that is trying to disrupt the financial industry and/or banking industry with a mobile-only approach. The British bank Atom has been internationally recognised for being the United Kingdom's first bank designed for digital and optimised for mobile. The bank owns no branches or call centres – every interaction takes place in its app.

Acorns is a great case study in permission-based content marketing (obsessed as we are at Thinque Digital with these sorts of examples, as a HubSpot Agency partner and inbound marketing aficionados). I found out about Acorns in 2014, signed up via Facebook pre-Australian launch, and have since raved about this brand to my loved ones and friends (and, as an added bonus, Acorns helps and nudges these referrals by incentivising them for the referrer, something which feels authentic for me – consult your financial advisor!). And, of course, Acorns also tunes into the friction we have all experienced with banks and financial advisors over the years, and solved this with a great mobile interface. Seamless!

The common thread among these financial start-ups is that they are user-centric – with the positive transformation of their clients' fortunes being their empathetic mission. Their business models are forward-thinking and focused on seamlessly bringing value to the client through a digital interface. Moreover, they tap into the underlying trends that shape young people's behaviours, views and opinions when it comes to banking, investing and saving.

A May 2016 press release from PR Newswire reveals that Acorns is the fastest growing micro-investing app in the United States. Their success can be explained by the fact that they've managed to simplify the investment process, thus making the experience of saving money and investing for the future frictionless, a lot less stressful and perhaps even joyful when you are able to track your weekly, monthly and annual savings. And as a user you get the freedom to choose your own risk profile and explore how much your savings can grow in the future. Additionally, Acorns' seamless digital interface and way of functioning generates a good habit among its users that is likely to last – transformational nudging at its best.

Another point that's worth mentioning here is that Acorns has a genuine mission of educating people and empowering them to make smart decisions about their personal finances. They are well aware that the only way of creating business success in the future is to create real long-term, transformational value for their clients and empower smarter decisions by their clients.

Ask yourself...

Think about the following with regards to your business:

1. Which underlying trends could help you attract new customers to your brand? List the top three trends that could help drive growth for your business.

2. How can you be more efficient at bringing value through your digital platforms?

3. What can you do to better help and educate your customers? What content, services and products will empower them in their decision-making process?

EPILOGUE

Imagine that it is now 020XX and on your watch, your company went belly up. What were the trends you missed, the signals you chose to ignore, and the investment decisions you delayed that led to this demise? What change will you make today to prevent this from happening?

When I reflect on my mentor's journey alongside the heroine of this story on her journey of transformation, certain questions appear. I ask myself what I could have done differently. What have I learnt from being a (reverse) mentor to my mum? How might I have approached this in a more psychologically astute fashion? Or was the transformational journey perhaps always destined to lead to this destination? Or was the journey, rather than the end result, the actual destination? At the end of the day, I sought to help with and solve several of my parents' issues, on both a personal and family business front (it's challenging to separate them cleanly). I wanted to help my mum be a hero, to go from being unsung to being truly sung, and to be a vanguard for the renaissance of 'mom and pop' shops prepared to embrace innovation. I wanted to assist her in understanding that disruption is only disruptive if you are not adaptive, and in developing a digital and analogue toolkit, so she could seamlessly build a brand that captured digital minds and analogue hearts, and which thrived in its second century of operations. A brand – Georg Sörman – which could get beyond the hump and the generational prophecy of 'three generations from shirtsleeves to shirtsleeves' and move into the golden era when the family business becomes the 'crown jewel' in family affairs. But until she decides what she really wants, I can only do so much.

But what I wanted wasn't just focused on the business. I wanted to help my dad enjoy his semi-retirement, and ensure he and Mum could live happily without the financial stress of worrying about payroll and evil landlords. I wanted their decision to work hard and take over the family business to pay off, and lead to some dividend for them. And I wanted to avoid the curse of the Sörman family, which is to never talk about issues until it's too late, not plan sufficiently for the future, and then leave the next generation to clean up the mess. I wanted to take proactive, futuristic steps, to ensure my brother and I (unlike previous generations of siblings in the family business) would remain close and brothers-in-arms on the fateful day when our parents are no longer around. To maybe fix what's broken, or make some kind of hay while the sun was shining. It remains to be seen what the future holds. But as I say to my clients around the world – the future is where you will spend the rest of your lives, so you better start preparing, today! We have certainly started preparing and I hope this preparation bears fruit for Georg Sörman and my parents.

At 100 years old, Georg Sörman could be just getting started. A few years ago I sat down to watch an epic Swedish movie that I can dearly recommend to you – *The Hundred-Year-Old Man Who Climbed Out of the Window and Disappeared*. The movie is about a centenarian who, just ahead of his 100th birthday party, jumps out the window of his retirement home and goes on an epic odyssey into the world. Allan Karlsson, the main character, is not interested in celebrating with the other geriatrics in the home, and escapes to the railway, where he accidentally comes into possession of a bag with lots of drug money. A chase and drama ensue and, as the journey unfolds, the story line is intercut with episodes from Karlsson's 100 years of life. We learn that he has led a rich life – helping to make the atom bomb, becoming good friends with Harry S Truman and General Franco, meeting Stalin, Kim Jong-il, Mao Tse-tung and Soong Mei-ling, foiling an assassination plot against Winston Churchill, and being a participant behind the scenes in many of the key events of the twentieth century. As I reflect on the juvenile, bon vivant, joie de vivre and energy of this 100 year old, I wish the same good fortune for Georg Sörman, and for all companies who embrace the idea of seamlessness and the combination of tradition and technology. And I certainly don't hope that the 100 year old at the centre of the heroine's journey of this book will disappear. I hope the elixir will finally be accepted and implemented fully.

I also hold dear hopes that this book will create a butterfly effect – in a smaller or bigger fashion, and in line with the *papillon* theme of the introduction and cover. The 'butterfly effect' is the sensitive dependence on initial conditions in which a small change in one system or state can result in large differences in another system or state. The name – important in chaos theory – was coined by Edward Lorenz for the effect which experts had known about for a while, and is derived from the metaphorical example of the specifics of a hurricane (exact time of formation, exact path taken) being influenced by such minor changes such as the flapping of the wings of a butterfly several weeks earlier in a distant part of the world. And I hope that in some small measure this book may be the transformational flapping of butterfly wings that creates a big, positive impact on our heroine, her business Georg Sörman, and your business, be it big or small, new or old.

Whatever happens, to some degree this book has also been transformational for me as a mentor. I have learnt to respect the old saying which holds that 'when the student is ready, the mentor appears'. The students, our clients, need to be fully ready for transformation, and from here on in I commit to only working with clients who are truly ready for transformation. My journey as mentor has also been transformational for me socially, as I realise that I want to spend the rest of my time with my ageing parents in a social rather than commercial setting. I want them to be 'Mum and Dad' again, rather than 'CEO and board member', and I am committed to making that happen. Blood is thicker than water, and while family business sometimes muddles that, I look forward to refocusing efforts on the social side of family.

And finally I ask myself the question I include at the start of this epilogue, just like I ask it of my clients, and our heroine in *Seamless*:

> Imagine that it is now 020XX and on your watch, your company went belly up. What were the trends you missed, the signals you chose to ignore, and the investment decisions you delayed that led to this demise? What change will you make today to prevent this from happening?

Start preparing for the future today, because it is where you will spend the rest of your life.

HERO'S JOURNEY WHEEL

FOR MAMMA SÖRMAN-NILSSON

It remains to be se
whether this time
this book might be
co-created Elixir n
for Mum to finally
business problem
She has not yet be
to gain final maste
problem, and has
been able to get th
we all want for Mu
Dad of course).

Georg Sörman begins to communicate along a specific, agreed brand line, and effectively mobilise its staff in getting behind the brand strategy. Georg Sörman pulls back from the execution of the brand, and starts doubting its merits and places its brand rollout on ice.
In combination with new partnerships for our broadsheet, events, and positive PR, Georg Sörman achieves an increase in sales. But no event is held to mark the 100th centenary on 29 January, 2016.

11

Final m
of the p

Georg Sörman together with Anders write an open and vulnerable letter to clients in September 2015 about the brand's values and ways of meeting the external digital threat with a renewed heartfelt focus and a renaissance of the personal touch.
The letter combined with the launch of Georg Sörman's second broadsheet *Välsytt Herrnytt* leads to a record sales result at the autumn VIP day in 2015, and clients join the collaborative call to arms.

10

Final attempt
at a big change

Resurrection

Rededication
to change

Road back

Thinque sources a new supplier of brand touch points. Despite months of illustrating the benefits of the new supplier, Georg Sörman decides to stay with its legacy provider, who goes behind Thinque's back to ultimately put the renaissance temporarily on ice.
Georg Sörman delays the implementation of the brand rollout because of poor cash flow, but several milestones are achieved, despite forced renovations and the temporary closure of the shop for three weeks.

9

Consequences
of the attempt
*(improvements
and setbacks)*

Reward
(seizing the sword)

Ordeal

The alliance between Georg Sörman, Anders and Thinque is tested as they engage with lawyers in negotiations with landlords of the two retail properties, and Thinque proposes to take over the management and launch of Georg Sörman & Sons.
Birgitta travels together with Thinque to Pitti Uomo in January 2015 to collaborate on the launch of the two brother brands. Thinque puts in place a project plan for the phased transition of management, which is accepted by Georg Sörman.

8

Attemping
a big change

Prepa
a big c

7

The landlord actively halts financing of the strategy, and the landlord at
haberdasher announces that they will disrupt the haberdasher for up to 6
with repairs to their inner plaza, which is contemporaneously Birgitta's shop
Birgitta, Lars-Olof and Anders join FBN to learn the family business
collaboration, succession and family values. Birgitta and Co. decide or
concept that is to be rolled out over 12

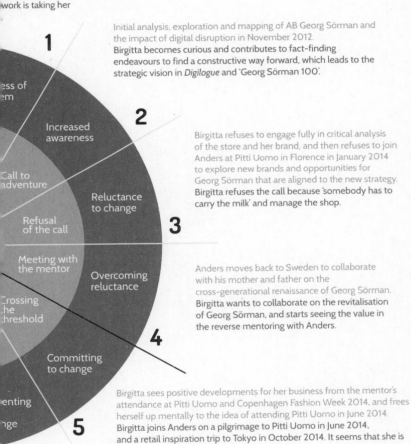

sruption sweeps
d of retail.
ine dreams of
er retail brand
örman) strong and
e again, but feels
work is taking her

1

Initial analysis, exploration and mapping of AB Georg Sörman and
the impact of digital disruption in November 2012.
Birgitta becomes curious and contributes to fact-finding
endeavours to find a constructive way forward, which leads to the
strategic vision in *Digilogue* and 'Georg Sörman 100'.

ess of
em

Increased
awareness

2

Birgitta refuses to engage fully in critical analysis
of the store and her brand, and then refuses to join
Anders at Pitti Uomo in Florence in January 2014
to explore new brands and opportunities for
Georg Sörman that are aligned to the new strategy.
Birgitta refuses the call because 'somebody has to
carry the milk' and manage the shop.

Call to
adventure

Reluctance
to change

Refusal
of the call

3

Meeting with
the mentor

Overcoming
reluctance

Anders moves back to Sweden to collaborate
with his mother and father on the
cross-generational renaissance of Georg Sörman.
Birgitta wants to collaborate on the revitalisation
of Georg Sörman, and starts seeing the value in
the reverse mentoring with Anders.

Crossing
the
threshold

4

Committing
to change

enting

Birgitta sees positive developments for her business from the mentor's
attendance at Pitti Uomo and Copenhagen Fashion Week 2014, and frees
herself up mentally to the idea of attending Pitti Uomo in June 2014.
Birgitta joins Anders on a pilgrimage to Pitti Uomo in June 2014,
and a retail inspiration trip to Tokyo in October 2014. It seems that she is
stepping up to the plate.

nge

5

and Anders hire brand strategist Hema Patel to visualise the
ated brand. Georg Sörman attempts to divest its second, smaller
tore in Old Town, Stockholm, but faces a greedy landlord.
resents the brand concepts, and after failing to reach an
ent with the landlord for the divestment, a brother brand, Georg
& Sons, is developed by the mentor for Old Town.

APPENDIX 1: A LETTER FROM BIRGITTA

Dear Anders,

I was so thrilled and happy when you asked me if I, your mother, as director and part owner of Georg Sörman, would be interested in being part of your Global Executive MBA!

We took long walks in the forest next to our home on Färingsö, the island we live on, twenty-five kilometres west of Stockholm, Sweden. We had long conversations, discussed and agreed. I remember how well prepared you were, as always, before our talks and was smitten by your convincing enthusiasm. You have always been a strong and shining leader; everyone in a room, friends or strangers, will look at you as you enter the premises. You love being in the limelight and thrive there, and you are the born leader and bright shining star! Other people like to be close to you. I was proud that you, at last at the age of 30-plus, wanted to take a real and professional interest in our business, Georg Sörman. (Georg Sörman being a menswear retail store with two shops: one in Kungsholmen, Stockholm, and one with knitwear in Old Town, Stockholm.)

During that first walk I told you that I, of course, was very happy supporting your decision to write your thesis about Georg Sörman, which my grandfather

Georg Sörman started in 1916. But I also raised my doubts, and talked about some of the problems and difficulties I thought could arise. I already worked more than full-time in the business and would soon be sixty years old, so I was very clear with you that I did *not* want *more* work. I was also clear that I did not want a new boss, and I especially did not want one of my sons stepping in as my boss! I thought my workload was heavy enough and also didn't want more stress, having felt the economic stress at times.

Anders, you and I were both aware that the two of us were more interested in the family business than your younger brother, Gustaf, and your father, Lars-Olof, my husband and part-owner of our company. Lars-Olof has always been very supportive and someone whom I always could count on and rely on to be 100 per cent loyal and who has worked thousands of hours for free in the business. We were both aware of the fact that Gustaf and Lars-Olof were not at all positive about you stepping in and taking on this project and that both your brother and Lars-Olof were afraid that this could cause future problems in our own family. You and I discussed the importance of agreeing! We agreed, all four, that our family always is and will be most important, whatever business project could develop or arise in the future. Our family is more important than any project, book or university paper. Gustaf only wants us all to live in peace and to have a nice family spirit and Father would like us two to work less and spend less time in the business. This is not an easy task to make this happen, but let me try!

Dear son, you pushed for Georg Sörman becoming a member of Family Business Network. We agreed, even though I had my doubts because I am not too keen on being too open with my feelings and problems. But we signed up as members of Family Business Network and the three of us have been to two weekends at Ingarö, an island east of Stockholm. These workshops have opened our eyes and helped us in many ways as we heard from other owner families of business, smaller and larger than our own, and they were very open with their difficulties with having family members in their business, some working in the business, some 'only' being shareholders or part-owners. You stressed the importance of making plans, keeping to these agreed plans and also finding other young, enthusiastic co-partners, and offered some very smart and well-educated and successful options.

We have had long, interesting talks and discussions also with our staff. These workshops have been interesting and very good for our Georg Sörman team spirit. We agreed and decided to make changes in our 'touch points' for bags, home page and advertisements, as well as in our window displays, flags on the façade of the building and also the music in the store. Before starting off with all this you consulted Hema Patel, well-known art director and good friend from Canberra, Australia, who now lives in the United States. She put a lot of effort and professionalism into making our 'Future Book' – the Georg Sörman 100 repositioning. This book has been of very good help and has provided lots of inspiration and a good guideline for us in our ongoing work as Georg Sörman moves into the future.

This year (2016) we turned 100 years old! This is, of course, something that we all are very proud of. We have a guestbook in the shop in Kungsholmen, Stockholm, where old and new customers write comments and we often hear from satisfied customers, and get positive feedback on our efforts to make our customers happy, content and wanting to come back to us. This we are proud of but we definitely need to work hard every day to become even better, more professional, more impressive, inspiring and interested in our customers' needs, and also open to new ideas and ways to work and to keep in touch with our devoted customers.

We need to work towards a mutual goal daily and every week with our staff who are in the shops. Our salespeople, who meet our customers and who are our ambassadors every day, are very important to us. We need to improve and to develop together and when we are working in peace together we can pull our company forward. It is easier for me to talk to our team in the shop in Stockholm, we can speak with each other daily and look one another in the eyes, and we can easily hear and feel if we are in agreement with each other, or not. If we are on the right track together, or not. We have been discussing, comparing and agreeing with the GS strategy paper in a lot of matters, but also disagreeing and we have had some difficulties in our work relations as a result.

In my opinion, some of our problems could have been avoided had you not chosen to include your graphic designer and then-girlfriend without discussing this decision with either me or your father. We were not included at all in that decision of yours. Many times you put yourself in the position where you had to choose between your ex and me, and this was very upsetting at times – you had to deal with two strong women and there were at times a lot of emotions involved! Some of these disagreements might not have occurred had you yourself been in Stockholm full-time. Being away from Stockholm was not a wise move. You also persuaded us to, in principle, leave our shop in Old Town, which was opened by my grandfather Georg Sörman in 1928, his second shop at that time in Old Town, in the hands of your company, Thinque, and your Thinque team. You wanted to have full control over changing things around; the logos and the clothing that you wanted to sell would all be a totally new concept, under the new shop name

'Georg Sörman and Sons'. I shall not go into details but let me just say it did cost us a lot of time and money before you and your team decided turn your backs on the idea and the shop! From my point of view, when running a smaller family business, you need to be here, on the floor; you cannot live on the other side of the globe.

I still think we could have been successful in moving Georg Sörman into the new digital era together! Father and I know you are very intelligent and successful in what you are doing and we are very proud of you. Anders, if you want to return to Georg Sörman in Stockholm, the doors are still open. I respect you, and many times it has been a lot of fun and inspiring to work with you and I have learned a lot from it. Now we have to do this without you but we have faith in our future and in our very devoted and skilled staff – so future here we come!

I love you!

Mother

APPENDIX 2: A LETTER FROM LARS-OLOF

Since Anders started his engagement in the family business, a lot of things have happened. His enthusiasm gave inspiration and hope to the company, including staff and owners. All staff took part in 'brainstorming' meetings and many good things came out of these strategy meetings. A strategy was created for the company and everyone was motivated and continued to come up with creative and useful ideas.

After this the 'hard work' started, some of it very challenging. The strategy needed quite a lot of investments and early on I understood that many of the objectives would never come to reality. I may have been a boring person in this stage of the change process for the old family business, but I think it was necessary to be the 'breaker of bad news'. One of the difficult things was that Anders wanted to work *on* the business, not *in* the business. He made this statement very early and clearly. I accepted it to start with and encouraged him to stay with his own successful business – Thinque. But sometimes I thought it would have been great if he had worked on the 'business floor' to understand the limitations and opportunities in our family business.

Over the years there have been a lot of frictions, mainly between Anders and his mother. Sometimes the emerging problems have been easy to solve and sometimes more difficult. I have had a role of being the negotiator and many times I had difficulties. There have been a lot of emotions, based on the fact that my wife is the third generation in the company and has inherited a lot of things from the previous owners and operational managers. Some of the things that were inherited have become the core problems for the company, in Anders' opinion, and I agree with many of his statements. But I also think that all the necessary experiences that Birgitta has gone through have also been like gemstones. Sometimes Anders and Birgitta have been open to their different positions, and I think they could have been better and serious listeners.

Working with Anders has, most of the time, been nice and beneficial. He has been brilliant, demanding and very stubborn. Stubbornness is something he inherited from both his parents. But as I have had another relationship to the family business (and one different from my wife's perception of it), I may have been more of a diplomat in many of the more difficult situations. Anders was professional and organised written agreements between his business and our family business. And sometimes we could, because of financial reasons, not fulfil parts of these agreements. We then thought that Anders was tough, and that he could have been more 'open-minded'. One of the reasons for his reaction may have been that he was disappointed with us, and I also think that he made a mistake by involving his ex-girlfriend and one of our former employees in his business to give us support and help. The problem was that they became dependent on our different opinions and we found it difficult to cooperate with them. Anders had to be dependent on his staff and his parents, and to balance and try to keep good relations with both sides. That must have been difficult for him. To satisfy all is always difficult, and choosing which side to support the most a hard process. But his intentions were always good and I think he had some angst in solving these problems.

Sometimes, and most times, people are enthusiastic about development, but when it comes to specific changes they are not interested in taking part in the developing work. This has maybe been the case but I think the financial costs created the main reason for not fully accepting all necessary steps to achieve every part of the basic strategy. Sometimes we felt as if we were trapped because of the strategy. We have always tried to do our best and my wife has been on the business floor every day during the time of the process. She has been the person with the 'sensor' to determine if the progress was going in the right direction, because she has been involved on a daily basis with the operational work. Sometimes it has been very difficult to accept steps that were expensive and seemed unnecessary. On our way to fulfil the strategy, however, a lot of very positive things have happened and I give Anders and all those involved full credit. I also know that, without Anders engagement, this process would never have started. Anders has also made us aware of the necessity of using social media and to think in new ways.

So what will happen in the future? I hope that the business will attract new and old customers and that it will grow. And, as a result, that someone else will take over the business and fulfil the journey we have started to walk.

As a conclusion I need to say that change must be started by someone, and without Anders it wouldn't have started at this time.

Another conclusion is that you have to formalise things even when the agreement is in the family, because many misunderstandings and misconceptions will occur on the way to achieving the strategy objectives, so it helps to be able to go back to written and agreed arrangements.

Another important thing is to be good and humble listeners and show full respect to the different acting partners.

We have achieved many things, but it has not always been easy. Today's competition is brutal – with internet shopping and business chains – but I hope that the strategy will lead the family business right. To those who have similar problems as we have had I must point out that changes take a longer time than you have expected, and the process is more difficult.

Anders has, by introducing a new way of thinking, created a good base for development and better results.

INDEX

THINQUE

Thinque Digital is a studio that combines the art of design with the science of marketing. We work with brands that are ready to scale and seek transformational results. We have designed an omnichannel methodology to branding and marketing which helps you connect with the digital minds and analogue hearts of tomorrow's customers.

Thinque Digital was founded in 2013 by futurist Anders Sörman-Nilsson, author of *Digilogue: how to win the digital minds and analogue hearts of tomorrow's customers* and *Seamless: a hero's journey of digital disruption, adaptation and human transformation*. It is the digital arm of Thinque – a strategic think tank which provides foresight, curates innovation, and facilitates digital adaptation and human transformation for organisations on a global and local level.

If you are seeking to scale up your brand, execute on the potential of the extraordinary digital world, stop singing in the analogue shower, and get transformational results in your business, contact Thinque Digital today.

www.thinque-digital.com